Community and Culture in Post-Soviet Cuba

Following the disintegration of the Soviet Union, the globalization of Cuban culture, along with the bankruptcy of the state, partly modified the terms of intellectual engagement. However, no significant change took place at the political level. In *Community and Culture in Post-Soviet Cuba*, De Ferrari looks into the extraordinary survival of the revolution by focusing on the personal, political, and aesthetic social pacts that determined the configuration of the socialist state.

Through close critical readings of a representative set of contemporary Cuban novels and works of visual art, this book argues that ethics and gender, rather than ideology, account for the intellectuals' fidelity to the revolution. *Community and Culture* does three things: it demonstrates that masculine sociality is the key to understanding the longevity of Cuba's socialist regime; it examines the sociology of the cultural administration of intellectual labor in Cuba; and it maps the emergent ethical and aesthetic paradigms that allow Cuban intellectuals to envision alternative forms of community and civil society.

Guillermina De Ferrari is Professor of Caribbean Literature and Culture at University of Wisconsin-Madison, USA. Her previous book, *Vulnerable States: Bodies of Memory in Contemporary Caribbean Fiction* (2007) studies the metaphorical power of the vulnerable body in comparative Caribbean literature.

Routledge Interdisciplinary Perspectives on Literature

1 **Environmental Criticism for the Twenty-First Century**
Edited by Stephanie LeMenager, Teresa Shewry, and Ken Hiltner

2 **Theoretical Perspectives on Human Rights and Literature**
Elizabeth Swanson Goldberg and Alexandra Schultheis Moore

3 **Resistance to Science in Contemporary American Poetry**
Bryan Walpert

4 **Magic, Science, and Empire in Postcolonial Literature**
The Alchemical Literary Imagination
Kathleen J. Renk

5 **The Black Female Body in American Literature and Art**
Performing Identity
Caroline A. Brown

6 **Narratives of Migration and Displacement in Dominican Literature**
Danny Méndez

7 **The Cinema and the Origins of Literary Modernism**
Andrew Shail

8 **The Gothic in Contemporary Literature and Popular Culture**
Pop Goth
Edited by Justin D. Edwards and Agnieszka Soltysik Monnet

9 **Wallace Stevens and Pre-Socratic Philosophy**
Metaphysics and the *Play* of Violence
Daniel Tompsett

10 **Modern Orthodoxies**
Judaic Imaginative Journeys of the Twentieth Century
Lisa Mulman

11 **Eugenics, Literature, and Culture in Post-war Britain**
Clare Hanson

12 **Postcolonial Readings of Music in World Literature**
Turning Empire on Its Ear
Cameron Fae Bushnell

13 **Stanley Cavell, Literature, and Film**
The Idea of America
Edited by Andrew Taylor and Áine Kelly

14 **William Blake and the Digital Humanities**
Collaboration, Participation, and Social Media
Jason Whittaker and Roger Whitson

15 **American Studies, Ecocriticism, and Citizenship**
Thinking and Acting in the Local and Global Commons
Edited by Joni Adamson and Kimberly N. Ruffin

16 **International Perspectives on Feminist Ecocriticism**
Edited by Greta Gaard, Simon C. Estok, and Serpil Oppermann

17 **Feminist Theory across Disciplines**
Feminist Community and American Women's Poetry
Shira Wolosky

18 **Mobile Narratives**
Travel, Migration, and Transculturation
Edited by Eleftheria Arapoglou, Mónika Fodor, and Jopi Nyman

19 **Shipwreck in Art and Literature**
Images and Interpretations from Antiquity to the Present Day
Edited by Carl Thompson

20 **Literature, Speech Disorders, and Disability**
Talking Normal
Edited by Chris Eagle

21 **The Unnameable Monster in Literature and Film**
Maria Beville

22 **Cognition, Literature and History**
Edited by Mark J. Bruhn and Donald R. Wehrs

23 **Community and Culture in Post-Soviet Cuba**
Guillermina De Ferrari

Community and Culture in Post-Soviet Cuba

Guillermina De Ferrari

NEW YORK AND LONDON

First published 2014
by Routledge
711 Third Avenue, New York, NY 10017

and by Routledge
2 Park Square, Milton Park, Abingdon, Oxfordshire OX14 4RN

First issued in paperback 2015

Routledge is an imprint of the Taylor & Francis Group, an informa business

Library of Congress Cataloging-in-Publication Data

De Ferrari, Guillermina, 1966–
Community and Culture in Post-Soviet Cuba / by Guillermina De Ferrari.
pages cm. — (Routledge Interdisciplinary Perspectives on Literature ; 23)
Includes bibliographical references and index.
1. Cuban literature—History and criticism. 2. Literature and society—Cuba. 3. Gender identity in literature. 4. Masculinity in literature. 5. Communities in literature. 6. Cuba—Intellectual life—20th century. I. Title.
PQ7378.D43 2014
860.9'97291—dc23
2013033775

ISBN13: 978-1-138-93438-2 (pbk)
ISBN13: 978-0-415-73785-2 (hbk)

Typeset in Sabon
by IBT Global.

To Mario and Paloma.

To my friends.

Contents

Figures

Preface

Like many other literary critics and students, I became fascinated in the 1990s by a curious cultural phenomenon: A huge amount of shelf space in bookstores in New York, Madrid, Seville, and Mexico City (remember bookstores?) was dedicated to novels written in a country that history seemed to have forgotten. Those novels shook my foundations. Whereas their fictionality was not in question, imagination alone didn't fully explain the power of these novels or the continuities among them. In no other literature produced at the end of the twentieth century was the context so defining of the way novels were written and the way we were consuming them. In spite of individual differences, they consistently provoked the same two expressions of incredulity: How can so much creativity happen amid so much devastation; and why is the revolutionary government still in place? It was during my first research trip to Cuba in 2001, however, that this book took root in my mind. I was puzzled by a number of contradictions that Cubans are particularly good at: scarcity and generosity, material poverty and intellectual sophistication, chaos and brilliance, isolation and cosmopolitanism, premodernity and postmodernity. But most of all, I was perplexed at the distance between the language of national dignity and the personal suffering—the indignity—I saw everywhere. The first objective of this book was to explain this distance to myself.

I wrote these pages in an effort to make sense of the paradoxical relationships that exist between national dignity, demoralization, and artistic innovation. These elements are sometimes in contradiction, but they also seem to be constitutive of each other, feeding off each other, and even fusing into each other. I chose to focus on social contracts in order to tease out how the relationship between such distinct and at times opposite categories work together to keep each other, as well as revolutionary Cuba, afloat. Hence, my interest in ethics. For unlike legal contracts, which are upheld by acknowledged rules that dictate how they are to be honored and determine the cost of breaking them, social contracts have no other founding and regulating mechanisms than those dictated by personal commitments and values. By looking into social contracts and ethics in and about literature, art, and the global cultural market, I tried to understand what Cuba had come to mean both to itself and to a twenty-first-century world.

While responsibility for the final product is entirely mine, writing a book is in many ways a communal operation. My first Cuban community was made up of the scholars who started their careers with mine and who, conference after conference, enriched my understanding of post-Soviet Cuba. James Buckwalter, Odette Casamayor, Jackie Loss, Ana Serra, Esther Whitfield: We helped build the field as the field formed us as scholars. Beyond our love for all things Cuban, most of us shared the support of an inspirational guru—thanks to José Quiroga for being such a fun and inspiring cultural critic, and generous beyond belief. My enormous gratitude goes to friends that lent their critical eye to parts of the manuscript: Alda Blanco, Glen Close, Rubén Medina, Brett White, and the anonymous reviewers. My most heartfelt gratitude goes to Mario Ortiz Robles, an amazing reader and talented editor, who read all of it—more than once. I am deeply grateful to those friends whose research I admire and whose ongoing conversation helped me reprioritize and rethink:, Gerard Aching, Mercedes Alcalá-Galán, Jossianna Arroyo, Jill Casid, Laurie Beth Clark, Susan Friedman, Sara Guyer, Ursula Heise, Paola Hernández, Marta Hernández-Salván, Alexandra Huneeus, Steve Hutchinson, Theresa Kelley, Jacques Lezra, Agnes Lugo-Ortiz, Luís Madureira, Emily Maguire, Jorge Maturano, Marilyn Miller, Marcelo Pellegrini, Juan Carlos Quintero-Herencia, César Salgado, Margarita Saona, Vicky Unruh; and to the graduate students, my captive audience, who helped this project grow: Saylin Álvarcz, Natalie Belisle, Desirée Díaz, Paula DiDío, Marcela Guerrero; to Paloma Celis-Carbajal, a great librarian and friend; to the friends I made in Cuba, and who were incredibly warm and helpful: Jimena Codina, Lillebit Fádraga, Alex Fleites, Mailyn Machado, Cristina Vives; and to the artists I discuss in this book, who were very generous both with their work and their time.

For solving some of the practical aspects of writing and publishing a book, I am indebted to a fellowship at The Institute for Research in the Humanities at The University of Wisconsin–Madison, which gave me not only research time but also my first audience for this project: scholars of all disciplines and stages in their career, who gave me faith in the value of the project; to a Faculty Development Grant on visual culture that allowed me to study the theory of photography in depth; as well as to the various summer salaries from the Graduate School at UW–Madison for freeing my time and my mind so I could write. I also want to thank the *Latin American Literary Review* for allowing me to reprint the article "Embargoed Masculinities," which appears here spread between Chapters 1 and 2, and *The Journal of Latin American Cultural Studies* for allowing me to reprint "Cuba: A Curated Culture," reproduced here with a few revisions and additions as Chapter 6. "Cuba: A Curated Culture" was also published in Spanish with the title "Consumir Cuba." I thank the Spanish journal *1616* and César Domínguez for allowing me to keep circulating it. Last but not least, I would like to thank the community of editors at Routledge (Eleanor Chan, Nancy Chen, Liz Levine, Emily Ross, Laura Stearns, and Joshua Wells) for helping make this book possible.

Thinking critically about friendship and solidarity made me appreciate my friends and family more; now I know they are not *really* supposed to always be there for me and yet, they are. To my friends, and to Mario and Paloma, I dedicate this book.

1 Socialism and Sociality

> It has been my fate to survive the failure of man's greatest enterprises and there is nothing left, I know, nothing but this, disenchantment.
>
> —Abilio Estévez's *Los palacios distantes* (2002, 99)[1]

In a 2008 essay entitled "The Incredible Decade," Cuban intellectual Ambrosio Fornet describes the revolution as a radical break with the past: "In 1959, our entire history began to be defined by the dramatic extremes *before* and *after*." What Fornet calls the "dizzying *now*" of the 1960s was due to the conviction that the world "had suddenly become sane"; that a society dominated by illiteracy, injustice, prostitution, and racism had come to an end. Those euphoric times, adds Fornet, required a distinctive ethics: "Only by encouraging *awareness* and the ability to make sacrifices for the common good would it be possible to leave underdevelopment behind and lay the foundations for a *new* society" (2008, 252; emphasis in the original). Stoicism and fraternity were the values that sustained the possibility of creating a better world, one in which the individual would feel whole and complete within a community of equals.

The profound ethical makeup of the early revolution helps explain the acute disenchantment of the 1990s. In "La crítica bicéfala" (Two-Headed Critique), one of the first panoramic articles on post-Soviet Cuban literature that appeared on the island, Ambrosio Fornet defines the disenchantment that followed the dissolution of the Soviet bloc as the growing opposition between ideology and ethics: "What happened, I believe, was a crisis of the legitimacy of ideology; a deep gap opened up between theoretical conscience and daily conscience, between public and private discourse" (2002, 20).[2] With these words, Fornet perceptively describes the affect that characterizes the early 1990s, and attributes it not so much to the overwhelming economic hardships that took place in Cuba following the dissolution of the Soviet bloc, but rather, at an abstract level, to the type of personal disappointment that comes with the realization of a heretofore ignored cognitive gap between expectations and reality.

These two isolated comments by Ambrosio Fornet alert us to the trajectory traced by the revolutionary ethics between the early 1960s, which promised the union of ethics and politics, and then, after 1991, as the moment when the failure of that promise becomes too visible to ignore. Although no doubt accurate, his observations present an incomplete view. Fornet suggestively alludes to the original union of ethics and politics within the revolutionary project, but he doesn't attempt to explain the intricate mechanisms articulating that union, its cost at personal and intellectual levels, or the role it played in the extended survival of an increasingly intransigent political regime. These mechanisms are the subject of this book, which seeks to trace in recent fiction and art the ways in which a revolutionary ethos—what Velia Cecilia Bobes has called "a set of shared beliefs and values"—has contributed to "the creation of the political" in contemporary Cuba. This book focuses on the affective intersection of ethics and politics in post-Soviet literature and art; the complex political, personal, and aesthetic social contracts such intersection produces; and the way these inherently problematic social contracts affect intellectual labor within the framework of an aged political paradigm.[3]

The purpose of this book is to study the literary and artistic engagement with what it means to be and even to call oneself a revolutionary subject after 1991. It does so mainly by analyzing the growing gap between the "theoretical conscience" and the "daily conscience" as it appears in literature and art produced on the island between the dissolution of the Soviet bloc and the formal resignation of Fidel Castro in 2008. This is a particularly fruitful time frame in literature, given that publishing abroad became a viable alternative for local authors in 1991. Once they could circumvent censorship this way, these authors became considerably more willing to examine in their writing the complex social and affective conditions of their own formation as revolutionary subjects. Cuban visual culture went further and faster than literature in embracing new ethical and aesthetic paradigms. This is largely due to the fact that Cuban artists who had gained international fame in the 1980s emigrated at the beginning of the 1990s because of the rigid state policy that prevented them from being paid in dollars. Consequently, the members of the generation of the 1990s, whom I study in this book, tend to share "beliefs and values" that are more clearly attuned to postmodern, postrevolutionary views on sociality, art, and politics.

Whereas the role of the intellectual in the revolution has historically been approached from the perspective of rights and responsibilities, I look into this question by studying the topic of literature and art production through sociology, gender, and moral philosophy. My analyses range from literature about ethics to experimental notions of community to innovative trends in the production, circulation, and reception of literature and art. First, I look at how the mechanisms of revolutionary sociality—that is, the tendency to form communities along shared personal values, political convictions, gender prerogatives, and aesthetic preferences—made possible the survival of the revolutionary government in spite of hostile economic and political conditions. Then, I examine the changing ethical paradigms in literature that, by rendering gendered cultural values visible in more or less provocative ways, help unveil the surreptitious ways in which the revolution created a specific affect while politicizing traditional notions of sociality. I then move from the personal to the aesthetic realm, by discussing the ways in which the exhaustion of ethics and politics allowed for a resurgence of artistic experimentation. Furthermore, I suggest that when the new ethical and aesthetic paradigms expose the flaws of an essentially modern political project, they question modernity itself.

My point of departure is a surprisingly recurrent type of narrative, which I call the friendship plot. I suggest that the Soviet socialist social contract took root in Cuba by imitating the mechanisms and values of male friendship. This allows for the elaboration of a theory that explains how the social mechanisms that were activated by the revolutionary social contract were based on the rhetoric of personal ethics rather than on ideology, and on a "fraternal" (masculine and equal, rather than patriarchal) gender culture. Based on this double premise, I build an argumentative arc that goes from identifying the reasons for the ethical co-optation of a mostly masculine intellectual class to the exploration of postmodern ethics, gender, and experimental communities in novels that envision forms of intellectual engagement alternative to those sanctioned by the revolutionary social contract. The discussion regarding the representation of ethics is also an engagement with the ethics of representation, which is why I also look into aesthetic responses to the question of a traumatic economic and political experience, as well as into the role that the international market played in the consolidation of a paradigmatic Cuban aesthetics that has been built on the exhaustion of socialist legality.

SOCIALIST LEGALITY, REVOLUTIONARY FAITH

Socialist legality is based on the notion of a specific type of social contract. According to the contractual model, the socialist state agrees to provide its people with a series of services—such as job security, housing, health care, and education—in exchange for their compliance and loyalty. Although there are many problems with this model, not the least of which is the sincerity with which it may be entered into, the legitimacy of the socialist government depends on the belief that it is actually based on such exchange. Implicit in the socialist contractual model, however, is that, as Linda Cook notes, "societal compliance was contingent on the regime's provision of comprehensive economic and social security" (1993, 3).[4] Historians contend that the dissolution of the Soviet bloc between 1989 and 1991 came about precisely because of the people's "withdrawal of consent" in view of their persistent dissatisfaction regarding the amount and the quality of the benefits provided.

In his book *Exit, Voice, and Loyalty*, Albert O. Hirschman defines compliance in the socialist social contract as the temporary suspension of two rights: that of voice and that of exit. In other words, the right of the members of an organization or state to express their dissatisfaction either directly or through public demonstration, and the right to abandon that organization or state if so desired.[5] In this sense, the socialist pact involves a paradox, given that in order to obtain expected goods the citizens must relinquish their individual rights as a way to ensure that the state will comply with its part of the bargain later, even though these rights are the only guarantee in their possession to ensure the delivery and quality of the service entailed. In such a situation, citizens usually have very little recourse in the case of persistent dissatisfaction. When the restitution of their rights becomes unlikely for whatever reason, the citizens can either turn trust into pure irrational faith—that is, what Hirschman calls "unconscious loyalist behavior" (1970, 93)—or else cope with "disenchantment," the natural outcome of persistent breaches of trust.

It is true that this model is modified in form when applied to the intellectual class, but it does not change fundamentally. The intellectual, a figure that emerged with Émile Zola's famous intervention in the Dreyfus Affair, is supposed to be that person whose knowledge and professional practice situates him or her "close to the central values that sustain and determine the quality of the society as a whole" (Bauman 1995, 224). Zygmunt Bauman expands on this function:

> As a group, the intellectuals hold a *responsibility* for monitoring and scrutinizing the actions of the appointed wardens of public values; and an *obligation* to intervene if they find those actions below standards. In so doing, the intellectuals transcend their own group of work-related interests. (1995, 224)

The intellectuals are bound by duties that transcend both their professional specialization and their self-interest. They speak for society as a whole. This is why Edward Said defines the intellectual as the one who speaks the truth to power (1994).

Intellectuals, who in any society use channels of expression different from those available to ordinary citizens, are bound in socialism by a unique form of the social contract. Because the medium of the intellectual is expression (voice itself), the suspension of the right to voice does not fully apply. A communist state that wants to gain legitimacy by making public, or indeed parading, its artists must grant them voice at least to some degree. This applies as well to their right to exit, at least temporarily, because it is important for the regime to show that it is not censuring or otherwise controlling intellectual exchange at home and abroad.[6] In order to ensure the intellectuals' loyalty, however, the state has to subject their expression to tight controls. Because exit can easily turn into defection, which makes for bad propaganda, the traveling artist is subject to even more surveillance. In other words, the socialist intellectual is usually provided with a means of subsistence as well as given access to public organs for the dissemination of his or her work such that state subsidies sometimes allow for a professional and personal lifestyle that proves to be more generous than that available to an artist in a capitalist setting. In exchange, the intellectual must give the impression of possessing two characteristics at all times: the full use of his or her voice and a full allegiance to the state (after all, without the first, the second would not bear any weight). The situation of the intellectual is, therefore, compromised by the fictional foundation on which it stands, a situation that was dubbed by Max Eastman as "artists in uniform" (1934).

A pact similar to the Soviet social contract was adopted in Cuba when Fidel Castro declared the socialist character of the revolution in April 1961. The Cuban revolution perceived itself as the people's liberation from a foreign-oriented oligarchy, and from a more or less informal occupation by the US, effective since the Platt Amendment in 1903. The constant possibility of an American military invasion has lent the revolutionary government a surplus of legitimacy—and it still does. What is interesting in the Cuban case, however, is that from its onset the revolution used a rhetoric more akin to religion than to politics: the revolution sought to *convert* the population to a revolutionary ethos based on the *renunciation* of material goods in the name of the *creation* of a "New Man." This is an ethos proposed and exemplified by Che Guevara, who was himself consecrated as a Christ-like figure. This phenomenon can be attributed to the peculiar legal situation of "a newly formed people," whose legitimacy, according to Rousseau, demands a certain fictional, if not outright magical, acceptance of its own existence.[7] I suggest that the revolutionary government, which emerged as the reflection of a new spirit that still had to take legal and institutional shape, promoted the idea, ideologically and rhetorically, that "being a revolutionary" was an act of faith. Damián J. Fernández suggests as much when he describes revolutionary politics as a "quasi religious crusade for moral absolutes that would redress the injustices of the past" (2000, xiii). The survival of the regime can be largely explained in terms of this Cuban particularity. As Hirschman points out, "the expectation that, over a period of time, the right turns will more than balance the wrong ones, profoundly distinguishes loyalty from faith . . . in comparison to [the] act of pure faith, the most loyalist behavior retains an enormous dose of reasoned calculation" (1970, 78–79). This is how the revolutionary contract took shape in Cuba, which helps explain why the changes that took place in Eastern Europe, and affected Cuban society to its very core, had such radically opposed consequences.

THE "POST" IN POST-SOVIET

It has been said that disenchantment is the trademark of the literature written in Cuba since 1991, a label that would at least seem justified in light of the island's recent history. For the revolutionary government, the dissolution of the Soviet Union meant the end of 100 percent of Soviet subsidies, the termination of its trade with Eastern Europe (which amounted to 75 percent of its international market), and the disappearance of a political network that had lent it meaning for several decades (Moreno et al. 1998, 2). The end of the Cold War provoked an acute economic and moral crisis that forced the majority of the Cuban population to live below the poverty line and to abandon most dignified forms of existence. This crisis received the official name of "Special Period in Times of Peace," which, as Ariana Hernández-Reguant explains, followed siege-style strategies of survival that had originally been devised for the eventuality of an invasion by US forces (2009, 4). It was a war economy without a war.

When the Cuban government could no longer provide its people with acceptable living conditions, Cubans entered a stage characterized by serious undernourishment and very significant scarcity in public-sector areas such as transportation, health care, electricity, hygiene, and even culture. People suffered these conditions with resignation and, mostly, impotence. Some counteracted them via methods that were illegal at the time—and which, therefore, constituted individual attempts of exit at a symbolic level. Among these are the black market (which predates the crisis), the establishment of small clandestine private enterprises that became legal in 1994 (such as small restaurants catering to tourists in private homes), and, most dramatically, widespread prostitution, which became a significant source of foreign currency as it swiftly followed the official development of tourism by the Cuban authorities. In addition, some Cubans tried to regain and exercise their right to exit physically—some legally by marrying foreigners and others illegally by trying to cross the Florida Straight at very great personal risk in precarious boats made of the inner tubes of truck wheels. The Center for the Study of International Migration (CEMI in Spanish) estimates that sixty thousand people left the island illegally between 1991 and 1994, of which nearly forty thousand attempts took place during the summer of 1994 alone. There is no information about how many survived the journey (Aja Díaz 2000).

In spite of these individual examples of creativity, industry, and audacity, the general dissatisfaction of the people did not lead to the end of the revolutionary contract. Much to the contrary, it led to its refashioning under the rubric of "Special Period in Times of Peace." This new name stands for a "pact" by which the government limits itself to protecting the sovereignty of the nation against the US, at least nominally, in exchange for unlimited hardship on the part of the Cuban population. This is the post-Soviet revolutionary contract. It seems fair to wonder how this arrangement lasted so long. It must be admitted that, to some degree, the tolerance on the part of the Cuban people can be attributed to fear of political retaliation, but I would argue that, most importantly, it was caused by the general opacity of the situation—a situation in which for a long time people were unable to understand the scope of the problem or to imagine what to expect next. For one thing, they may have expected the situation to rapidly change in a "natural" way, that is, as a result of Fidel Castro's death. But the opposite may also be true. The people of Cuba may have been rendered politically passive by the lack of viable alternatives beyond the all too real possibility of a return to the conditions that existed prior to the revolution, conditions that had made the revolution overwhelmingly popular in the first place. Thus, fear and opacity seem to have forced the people into accepting the unacceptable.

Cognitive clarity is often mentioned by sociologists as one of the main goals of friendship. In his essay "The Psychology of Affiliation," Stanley Schachter notes that "people will seek one another out when their opinions are shaken and that an otherwise uninterpretable event leads to a search for social reality" (1974, 9). The intellectual plays a similar role in that he or she is expected to help "lay" people interpret their social reality. Indeed, the Cuban situation is in serious need of decoders; even the nomenclature used to name the historical period shows a good deal of confusion. Some people talk of transition, although it is not clear what comes next or what measures are being taken to that effect, which leads Ariana Hernández-Reguant to talk about "an irresolute transition" (2009, 2). Strictly speaking, the phrase "Special Period" refers to the moment of the harshest economic crisis in the early '90s, but even Raúl Castro acknowledged in a speech on July 26, 2007, that it wasn't yet over.[8] For literature, the phrase "novel of the 90s" is often used, despite also encompassing works produced in the twenty-first century. Hernández-Reguant uses the term "late socialism" to refer to the strategic dissociation of socialist politics from socialist economics, which was devised precisely to avoid the fate of the Soviet Union (2009, 8); and uses "Special Period" to name a defining epochal culture or ethos (2009, 3). At the local level, many of the intellectuals who are now "called to order," as it were, seem to be nostalgic for an era of comfortable state sponsorship and, at any rate, see the generous cultural politics of the revolution as the aspect most threatened by a regime change. The conflicts undergirding the real-life intellectual class remain hard to grasp given that they exist under a convenient veil of silence meant to protect the social and economic position of the artist. In addition, and this is my main point, there is a general lack of vocabulary and values for bringing clarity to a situation that is rendered opaque by the compelling rhetoric issued by the theoretical conscience of the revolution in everyday life.

Given the contemporary nature of the situation and the many conflicting interests that are at stake, I would suggest that the shared cultural values and ethical co-optation that allowed for the creation of a compromised intellectual figure became most visible in literature, particularly the literature produced and disseminated after the 1990s, when new publishing venues outside Cuba allowed writers to speak by rules different from those established by the State. Literature is particularly well suited—more so than any other media—to the task of representing a reality repressed by official discourse. As the writer Arturo Arango notes, "When the Special Period began, it became clear that the true state of affairs was much closer to what was reflected in our work (frequently declared to be pessimistic or skeptical) than to the idealized depictions of the press" (1997, 124). This accords well with Pierre Bourdieu's statement that "the literary work can sometimes say more, even about the social realm, than many writings with scientific pretensions," precisely because it "says it only in a mode such that it does not truly say it" (1995, 32).

Narrative, a privileged medium for ethical dilemmas to be discussed in the abstract, can also be a privileged vehicle for nostalgia. When Ambrosio Fornet traces disenchantment to "a crisis of the legitimacy of ideology; a deep gap opened up between theoretical conscience and daily conscience, between public and private discourse," one can sense a certain longing for that foundational moment in which political and private conscience were united, a situation he calls "a teleological dream" (2002, 21). It is not without irony that Ambrosio Fornet traces the separation between official ideology and private ethics to a specific historical moment: the dissolution of the Soviet bloc. Whereas this moment did in fact force the collapse of the Cuban economy, which lowered the island's living standards across the board, and the reconfiguration of its geopolitical situation, which further isolated the regime, it was really an event that was external to the revolution itself. In other words, Ambrosio Fornet is reluctant to consider earlier instances of political tribulation such as the censorship of the film *PM* by Saba Cabrera Infante (the event that prompted Fidel Castro's famous speech "Palabras a los intelectuales"); the Padilla Affair; the Quinquenio Gris; or the Ochoa Affair in 1989.[9] These are just a few instances of real or symbolic violence toward the Cuban intelligentsia that were justified by the Cold War and demonstrated in no uncertain terms that the government expected a militant disposition from its artists as much as from its soldiers. Ambrosio Fornet's nostalgic view differs from that of his son, Jorge Fornet. As is well known, Ambrosio published "La crítica bicéfala: un nuevo desafío" in *La Gaceta de Cuba* in 2002 in response to an article published by Jorge Fornet in *La Gaceta de Cuba* the previous year under the title "La narrativa cubana entre la utopía y el desencanto." In contrast with his father, Jorge Fornet does consider some of the events that took place in the 1980s as marking a point of divergence in revolutionary sentiment (e.g., the Mariel exodus, the Ochoa Affair, the loss of the Sandinistas in the 1990 election, and above all, the fall of the Berlin Wall and the economic disaster that ensued in Cuba), but he claims that the true source of literary disenchantment is ultimately a general postmodern feeling (J. Fornet 2006, 63). He may be partially right.

The divergence between the theoretical and daily conscience alluded to by Ambrosio Fornet could point not so much to a historical moment, but rather to a change in what is considered the "truth." If one were to see contemporary Cuban literature in its entirety as a dramatized revision of the revolutionary conscience, then an appropriate framework to interpret this would be Alain Badiou's notion of a "truth-process." The Cuban revolution was what Badiou calls an "event," meaning an occurrence that produces a radical break in both the political and the ethical domains, or rather, in the symbiotic combination of the two. The triumph of the Sierra Maestra rebels in 1959 produced a radical separation between the dictatorship that preceded it, which, as Velia Cecilia Bobes shrewdly notes, was characterized by "the absence of virtue," and the socialist society that followed, which was dominated by the ideals of stoicism, fraternity, and justice (2000, 49). Thus, the revolution constituted a "truth-process"; a process that generated new values and a new language, and which would have had no meaning according to the values and languages of the "situation" that preceded it. Truth, defined as fidelity to the original event, entails a discursive and hermeneutical coherence with the new paradigm of knowledge and values produced by the break itself.[10] Badiou consequently defines the ethical subject as "the bearer [*le support*] of a fidelity, the one who bears a process of truth" (2001, 43). As such, the subject cannot exist prior to the event, because it is the event that creates the subject, not the other way around.[11]

Following Badiou's elaboration of subject production, we can interpret Ambrosio Fornet's words to point to a moment when the revolutionary subject comes face to face with the end of its own truth process in 1991. The fall of the Soviet bloc had the potential to become a second event capable of altering the rules of engagement of the Cuban intellectual according to a new truth. No longer immersed in the same "situation" created by the revolution, Cuban intellectuals would be free to reposition themselves both ethically and politically. The problem, however, is that no new truth was generated by that second event. From a political perspective, the revolutionary socialist social contract was not radically altered by the dissolution of the Soviet bloc. On the contrary, what we may call "the post-Soviet revolutionary social contract" demands from Cubans an intense austerity in exchange for fewer services and a strictly rhetorical defense against imperial powers. Whereas the fall of the Berlin Wall in 1989 was an event (in Badiou's terms) *in Berlin*, it is not clear it meant a new ethical and political situation *in Cuba*. In an interview with Peter Hallward that appears at the end of *Ethics*, Badiou had this to say regarding Cuba:

> I respect Cuba as a figure of resistance, for we should respect all the forms of resistance to the hegemony of the global market, and to its principal organizer: American imperialism. But Cuba provided singular testimony of an outmoded conception of politics. And so Cuba will have, unavoidably, very serious problems, internal problems, because it bears witness, with incontestable grandeur, to a figure of the Party-State that belongs to another political age. Everything that exists is born, develops and comes to an end. After which we move on to something else. (Badiou 2001, 107)

One could say that the revolutionary project is an exhausted event—one that has lost its original meaning—without yet having been replaced by anything else. Because a new political age has not yet started, the post-Soviet period is an empty situation, which is what Badiou calls a simulacrum of truth. The revolutionary ethical subject has for the most part become a duplicitous subject (i.e., a subject bound by a truth that no longer is). I contend here that the existence of a post-Soviet revolutionary (i.e., inherently paradoxical) subject today can be attributed to the generous terms of engagement of a compromised intellectual activity as well as to a particular gender culture that has helped shape the relationship between socialism and sociality in Cuba.

CULTURAL VISION, POLITICAL BLINDNESS

The relationship between gender, culture, and politics during the Cuban revolution began on an auspicious note. Immediately following its triumph in 1959, a series of laws protecting women and gender equality were implemented, effective literacy campaigns were carried out (thus creating a new readership class), and many important institutions were founded in order to promote the production and distribution of art. Institutes such as ICAIC (Instituto de Cubano de Arte e Industria Cinematográfica), UNEAC (Unión de Escritores y Artistas Cubanos), and Casa de las Américas were housed in the homes that were abandoned by the fleeing Cuban bourgeoisie who were now exiled in Miami. There was the impression among Cuban and international artists and intellectuals that for the first time the political vanguard and the artistic avant-garde had a common cause (Franco 2002, 86).

But by the end of the 1960s politicians had grown more suspicious of local intellectuals. In *El socialismo y el hombre en Cuba*, Che Guevara famously pointed out that the original sin of the intellectuals was to not be truly revolutionary (2007, 25).[12] As Desiderio Navarro notes, international events such as the Prague Spring and the Brezhnev Doctrine "would contribute to the idea held by many politicians that intellectuals were unreliable fellow travelers, if not a political opposition in their own right" (2002, 693–694). This attitude of suspicion animated the dissolution of the journal *Pensamiento Crítico* in 1968 and culminated in the Padilla Affair in 1971. Heberto Padilla was a well-known writer whose collection of poems *Fuera del juego* (Off the Field) won a national literary prize in 1968 even though it was considered a seditious text by the government. This act of defiance on the part of Padilla and, by implication, the members of the prize jury had to be punished. Thus in 1971 Padilla was briefly imprisoned until his jail sentence was commuted to house arrest and he was forced to confess in a public *auto-da-fé*. Padilla's self-incriminating testimony included naming other like-minded intellectuals. This televised event contributed to the disillusionment of a large part of both the international and the local intelligentsia, whose support had lent legitimacy to the revolutionary government. In spite of the international outcry, Cuba continued to subject its own intellectuals to tight controls in accordance with the principles outlined by Fidel Castro in his 1961 speech "Palabras a los intelectuales," in which he described, and in doing so prescribed, the intellectuals' responsibilities toward the revolution. Not surprisingly, Padilla's confession was followed by a decade of limited cultural development. The climate of censorship and self-censorship that ensued led to a period of considerable cultural poverty that Ambrosio Fornet conservatively named "Quinquenio Gris" (Gray Five-Year Period), but that in fact spanned from 1967 to 1981, a stretch of about fifteen years that Mario Coyula playfully calls the "Bitter Trinquennium" (2011, 31).

However, it was the repression of homosexuals by the state that contributed the most to the disenchantment vis-à-vis the revolution that took place among international intellectual circles.[13] The implementation of a series of laws aiming to control any expression of taste, fashion, and lifestyle perceived by the government as a threat to the revolutionary spirit—such as "la ley de la vagancia" (law against loitering) that effectively made cruising an actionable offense—was seen by foreign intellectuals as an overtly repressive gesture against homosexuals. As these measures were put into place, sexual and ideological reeducation camps called UMAPs (Unidad Militar de Ayuda a la Producción) were established between 1965 and 1968, with the double function of ensuring the loyalty of all citizens and of homogenizing Cuban citizenship under the appearance of an ideal militarized masculinity. The notion of citizenship was clearly defined in terms of those who were willing and capable to sacrifice their body for the nation. Although the persecution of homosexuals seemed unbelievable at first to the international intellectual community, who for the most part sympathized with the Cuban cause, it eventually became known through personal testimonies, thus creating the first wave of disenchantment.[14]

In "To Write in Cuba, Today," Arturo Arango reflects upon the ongoing role of the intellectual in Cuba from the perspective afforded by the Special Period. Originally, he claims, the revolution promoted a higher degree of freedom of expression in Cuba than in other socialist countries, and the government assumed the role of a *de facto* patron of the arts, providing artists with a basic livelihood and adequate means to practice their craft. Arango notes, however, that even though Cuba failed "to establish an official aesthetics," it did follow "an authoritarian concept of ideology," understood as the obligation "'to direct' society" in a rigid top-down bureaucratic structure, which was obviously restraining the freedoms the state otherwise granted (1997, 121). This statement contradicts other opinions, but even if it were an accurate assessment, it stands to reason that to have *more* freedom than other socialist countries is not necessarily the same as having absolute freedom of expression. In fact, this situation of support was always accompanied by a variable but persistent mistrust of the artist.

In *La balsa perpetua* (The Enduring Raft) Iván de la Nuez points out the fact that the relationship between culture and politics was articulated *for* the intellectuals, but not *by* them (1988, 57). The citizens' loyalty to the revolution was controlled daily by institutions such as the "Comités de Defensa de la Revolución" (Committees for the Defense of the Revolution) and other disciplinary tools including voluntary work, restricted access to higher education, and camps of sexual and ideological reeducation.

As soon as the revolutionary contract was consolidated—that is, at the time of the most fervor in favor of the cause—the first case of open censorship took place when the film *PM*, by Saba Cabrera Infante, was released in 1961. Because this measure was taken only six weeks after the military invasion of the Bay of Pigs, it was easily rationalized as the continuation of the war against imperialism on a different front. The dissatisfaction that ensued led to the organization of a conference held at the National Library in June 1961 during which Fidel Castro delineated an ethics for revolutionary intellectuals with the cryptic phrase "dentro de la Revolución, todo; contra la Revolución, nada" [inside the revolution everything; outside the revolution, nothing] (1961, 11–12). After that, all intellectual activity had to fit within that vague yet unforgiving premise. As Desiderio Navarro explains in his article, "*In medias res publicas*: Sobre los intelectuales y la crítica social en la esfera pública cubana" [On intellectuals and social criticism in the Cuban public arena], the intellectuals of the 1960s considered themselves a critical force from within, although they were always rather timid to venture outside those topics they considered inherently their own. In other words, while they believed themselves to be free to give opinions pertaining to the aesthetic realm, they tried to stay away from social and political problems. According to Navarro, this sets the Cubans apart from other socialist intellectuals who did use a critical voice in, for instance, the *Literaturania Gazeta*—a statement that explicitly diverges from Arango's stated opinions about Cuban intellectuals having more freedom of expression than their Eastern European counterparts. More revealing, perhaps, is Jean Franco's observation that the fate of various publications shows the contradictions of the revolutionary cultural project in Cuba: *El caimán barbudo*, edited by Jesús Díaz (a "dissonant" rather than a dissident supplement), and *Juventud Rebelde* saw themselves as the new media giving voice to the new spirit, whereas *Lunes de Revolución*, directed by Guillermo Cabrera Infante, published young writers of all stripes and was closed in 1961. When Lisandro Otero, secretary of the UNEAC, wrote in 1966 that "conformity, consent and using freedom to accept the revolution are the attitudes of the revolutionary writer," he seemed unaware of any inherent contradictions (quoted in Franco 2002, 92).

As the incidents related to both the UMAPs and the Padilla Affair illustrate, the cultural project of the revolution sustained itself on a masculinist view of the nation, on the one hand, and on an unquestionable loyalty to the cause, on the other. These topics became partly open to discussion following the fall of the Berlin Wall, and although the political structure did not change substantially, the cultural landscape of the island suffered dramatic modifications. The changes became immediately visible on two fronts. First, the search for new forms of revenue led the island to open itself up to tourism (mostly ideological and sexual), which led to an unprecedented degree of cultural exchange at an individual level. Second, the insolvency of national publishing houses encouraged local writers to seek publication opportunities abroad, mostly in Spain, with the consequent loosening of both censorship and self-censorship. This would seem to have been a change for the better. Publishing abroad, however, is not always well regarded by Cuban writers, who perceive the need to accommodate their writings to the laws of the marketplace—a foreign market, at that—as a form of "selling out."[15]

It would seem that the early efforts to socialize the administration of culture failed in the long run. For instance, if asked, a member of the general population might say that the current literary boom I have suggested does not exist. Cubans, who used to consume subsidized books avidly, can no longer afford to buy a book regardless of its place of publication. New books have become quite invisible for the general public. Whereas the new European editions are simply not found on the island—both for economic and political reasons—locally produced texts can only be purchased in clandestine bookstores on the island (stores that are usually run in the homes of official bookstores' employees). When sold privately, books sell for as much as US$10 or US$20, a prohibitive amount in a country where a university professor makes US$14 a month or less.[16] The main way in which books circulate, then, is in manuscript form as they pass from hand to hand among friends, who are usually other writers. This reinforces the notion that the intellectual class is formed by a few closed social networks providing their own systems of validation. Culture in the Special Period, as it turns out, produces more exclusive groups with a high-priced membership than ever.

It is therefore ironic, and all too uncomfortably real, that local critics usually neglect to take into consideration the production and circulation of culture. As Navarro writes:

> At a time when non-Marxist theorists and critics around the world are increasingly acknowledging the sterility of an "ergocentric" type of criticism—that is, criticism focused on literary works as if they were suspended in a social and communicational void—and stressing the need to study literature in the context of their production, dissemination and reception processes, Marxist critics in socialist Cuba are expected to disregard the social aspects of art, to deny its role as social communication. Criticism by Marxist critics in Cuba is expected to be less sociological; that is, *it is expected to be either less Marxist or, even, not Marxist at all.* (2002, 698–699; emphasis in the original)

Navarro's comment points to the often-conservative stance of Cuban writers and literary critics, which he attributes to the fear of government censorship. But this attitude, I suggest, can also be attributed to an acute notion of aesthetic value, which carries in itself a sense of social prestige. I am following Pierre Bourdieu's notion that taste and aesthetic judgment are related to the administration of social capital (see, e.g., *Distinction*). For aesthetics to be judged as pure in the Kantian sense, it must be disinterested (i.e., noninstrumental), ethically neutral, and governed by reason. Aesthetics so defined is seen as a superior social practice in many places, not excluding, I would argue, socialist Cuba. Chief among the implications this may have for the role of the intellectual in the Cuban context is that this aesthetic practice conveniently positions the intellectual within an apolitical role. This is another way of putting Navarro's claim; but it also has other implications. First, it helps the intellectuals separate themselves from the material conditions of their present existence, which are more deeply felt in popular sectors. And second, that these conditions become most apparent when attending domestic needs, such as the daily difficulties of obtaining food or trying to cover other necessities, "naturally" forces a gender gap, as women are more likely to be the ones carrying along the household rationing card.[17] Pure aesthetics, then, defines membership in a group that effectively excludes many women and most of the working class, as both are more in contact with the hard conditions of daily life and are often socially conditioned to judge a work of art from either an utilitarian, moral, or sensorial point of view.

I claim, then, that what remains unsaid in Navarro's otherwise accurate statement is that the Cuban intellectual class conforms to a sort of "masculine aristocracy" of culture, one that has remained ideologically decontextualized from the revolutionary structure that sponsored it, and which has subscribed to its own elitism in the name of making peace with the revolution. It is not entirely surprising that this form of elitism has been further consolidated by the changes in cultural management that took place between 1991 and 2008. The circumstances are such that artists and intellectuals can often accept invitations by foreign universities and cultural institutions to travel outside the country, thus "legitimately mak[ing] money that can radically affect the everyday lives of our families," as noted by Arturo Arango, who uses the phrase "soft exile" to describe this flexible situation (1997, 123). One should consider that not only does the possibility of partial exit allow intellectuals to improve their personal living conditions, but it also makes them actively dependent on a government that has the right to either grant or deny their permission to travel. Although I agree that, in many cases, personal gain in "soft exile" can condition the intellectual's use of voice today, I doubt that it alone can explain why the intensification of the social contract in post-Soviet Cuba did not immediately lead to an overt loosening of the traditionally conservative stance by most local intellectuals. I believe that other cultural factors should be taken into consideration, factors that are more clearly seen in the literature about friendship produced in recent years. I contend that intellectual labor is conditioned by a set of defining values and practices that equally intersect the socialist social contract and the bond of male friendship.

THE REVOLUTIONARY POLIS

In an essay dedicated to the ruins of Havana, architect Mario Coyula describes the revolutionary city as a failed polis. The society forged by the revolution shared a new ethical community built on moral responsibility and social justice. However, the foundations of the new society needed to be protected until they became solid and stable, and to do so, the ruling class needed to be implacable. Coyula discusses the political administration of culture by tracing the policies of architecture schools and unions. Under the motto "the university is for revolutionaries," government and academic leaders fostered an "aberrant climate fed off of suspicion, opportunism, and envy, unleashing the instinctive cruelty of the human being upon the weak member of the tribe" (2011, 42). Coyula eloquently sums up the mentality of the time by explaining how certain citizens, especially gays, hippies, and religious people, were used as scapegoats. Generalized corruption of morals resulted from a generalized state of fear:

> Fear led to a double standard that then spread to those who were purged and those who purged them. It is possible that some of the proponents of that policy and even the victims themselves were convinced that the sacrifices of a few would benefit the whole society. *In fact, atheist heterosexuals and revolutionaries were collateral victims of these witch-hunts because they made us worse people.* I was there, and I did not rise up to object. As did my colleagues, I weighed the pros and cons of the great social project to which I was dedicating my life. I took stock, and I shut up. (2011, 42; emphasis added)

Coyula's statement renders visible a slow process by which the union of public and private ethics becomes increasingly more difficult to sustain. With the phrase "I took stock, and I shut up," Coyula helps explain the reluctance on the part of local intelligentsia to see the problem for what it is. Unlimited personal concessions in favor of a larger notion of community is a structural requirement in revolutionary Cuba. Full participation in an ethical and political project and the right to exercise one's personal virtues at one's discretion are not always possible in what Hirschman calls a "loyalty demanding organization" such as the socialist state (1970, 92). The highly idealized project puts even the most loyal, nonreligious, heterosexual intellectuals at a moral and political crossroad.

It is important to note in this context that there have been moments of significant freedom for intellectual activity that is critical to the government. First, the distinctive atmosphere of the early days after the triumph of the revolution in the early 1960s was characterized by the enthusiastic harmony between local and international intellectuals and the revolutionary project. A second moment occurred at the end of the 1980s, when the Cuban intelligentsia was invited to participate in the ideological design of the country as a way to prevent some of the changes that had started among socialist countries in Eastern Europe. This moment of openness was particularly evident in the visual arts. Overall, however, intellectual labor as a concrete social practice is persistently restricted in the name of the "health" of the revolutionary project. Besides open censorship, the fact that intellectuals often depend on government sponsorship for the creation and dissemination of their work tends to compromise their work. They must be accountable for their work vis-à-vis governmental expectations that, although not clearly spelled out, are binding, and powerfully so. Frequently, the exercise of intellectual labor, as Navarro notes, becomes "the target of all kinds of political and ethical accusations" (2002, 697). Authors see their access to voice and exit severely curtailed through the loss of manuscripts, the rejection of travel-permit requests, and excessive, unexplained delays. An additional form of censorship takes place through stigmatization, defamation, and official neglect. These practices are popularly called "estrategias de ningunificación," strategies that often amount to the moral and even civic death of the artist. The silence surrounding these practices earned them the popular name of "síndrome del misterio." Among these strategies is the not always veiled threat of government retaliation, which effectively forces artists and intellectuals to lead their lives and carry out their work in a state of perpetual anxiety (Navarro 2002, 697). The implicit threats of losing channels of distribution for one's work, public recognition, membership in the national intelligentsia, access to college education, or simply one's job are all unacknowledged forms of coercion that condition intellectual labor in Cuba.

In 1992, writers write. According to Arango, they write despite the shortage of paper, publication outlets, and intellectual freedom. They even write in spite of "the loss" of several prestigious writers to exile. However, even though he insists on the tenacity of writers, Arango is far from stating that nothing has changed. In fact, the government's dire financial situation following the dissolution of the Soviet bloc curtailed the possibility of state sponsorship, forcing writers to seek publication outlets abroad. In my view, this radical change has had three important consequences in the practice of intellectual labor: It gives writers full access to their voice; it enables Cuban writers to join an international republic of letters, a republic that conditions the intellectual labor by the laws of the free market, but not by the explicit and implicit laws of the state; and, finally, it results in a dramatic change of readership. If the weakening of censorship offered unprecedented opportunities for publishing, the foreign market has largely dictated the rules of engagement by demanding an immediate, descriptive, and rather crude prose. One could argue that the literature of the 1990s served as a testimonial to a reality to which the world at large had no access and, in its most daring examples, as an open celebration of an abject state of affairs. This type of literature could be seen as the Cuban "destape" or "outing" that was only made possible by the existence of new international publication outlets with a specific taste. However, this type of literature is often criticized in local intellectual circles as being commercial, opportunistic, and simply bad. As I have argued elsewhere, this reveals a conservative view of art—"good" art understood as a national sign of distinction that effectively determines membership in local intellectual circles. Furthermore, the importance of group validation suffers structural changes with the entrance into a larger and much better remunerated readership.[18]

Because writers have lost most of their local readers, who cannot afford the cost of a book published in Spain, books published abroad often circulate around the island in manuscript form among the author's friends (i.e., other intellectuals). This helps explain Arango's comment regarding the fact that local writers lost their natural interlocutors and their valuable feedback after the exile of several artist friends. On the other hand, however, exile itself has changed. Writers like Jesús Díaz, later Abilio Estévez, and more recently Antonio José Ponte, who began publishing in Spain, eventually chose to relocate to cities like Madrid and Barcelona, which shifted the traditional Havana-Miami axis of political exile and thereby complicated the Manichean view of intellectual labor as ideologically inflected. The establishment in Spain and Mexico of a new type of intellectual who is no longer aligned with the American exile of the 1960s has further helped feed a nostalgia for island culture, which often results in contradictory images of Cuba as the last socialist utopia, as a failed tropical experiment, as a corrupt Republic, and so on. These are the conditions of a rich cultural production that competes with and frequently outshines the artistic work that is currently being sponsored at the local level (in Havana but also in Miami). In Madrid, writer Jesús Díaz founded *Encuentro de la cultura cubana*, a journal that quickly became the new epicenter of Cuban culture. Hence, Díaz's statement in 1989 that Cuban literature "está de fiesta"—a phrase that prompted critic James Buckwalter-Arias to clarify: "If Cuban literature 'está de fiesta,' the *fiesta* is not, by this account, taking place in Cuba" (2005, 362).

The revolutionary social contract and the way it affects the intellectual class has changed since 1991. Government sponsorship has declined, freedom of speech increased, and intellectual voice found new venues through foreign publishers. Attracted no doubt by new funding opportunities, some have turned to scriptwriting and others are guest speakers in academic circles outside Cuba, whereas "undoubtedly, the most traumatic individual response to the crisis has been exile" (Arango 1997, 122). A peculiar form of exile, "soft exile" designates the prolonged stays of Cuban artists and intellectuals in other countries for work. Even though writers haven't had the same opportunities as musicians in this respect, invitations for colloquia or occasional teaching jobs by American and European universities have given writers access to hard currency, allowing them to support their families above the Cuban average, particularly above the average of those who do not have access to hard currency.

Considering the new relative freedom of expression, intellectuals have been somewhat timid in expressing a critical view of the current ideological structure. As Iván de la Nuez points out in *La balsa perpetua*, this may be due to the fact that writers would rather hold on to some of the economic privileges available to artists and intellectuals that have come with the opening of the cultural sphere to a market economy, than to be confrontational to the government (1988, 63). Arango, for instance, advocates for unspecified changes that could help revive the national economy while preserving the achievements of the revolution, particularly those found in the cultural sphere. This is a view common among older, established intellectuals, who express the desire for another type of socialism, one that is economically more effective and more democratic. In literary and artistic circles, this phrase usually reveals the truly utopian desire to maintain cultural activity simultaneously free of the pressures of an international market and of the ideological restrictions historically imposed by the government.

Somewhat understandably, intellectuals living in Cuba prefer to maintain the *status quo*. Even though state support for intellectuals has diminished or even disappeared, their membership in national cultural institutes still provides them with more than symbolic capital. Indeed, these institutions provide accreditation, personal validation, group affiliation, and a built-in local readership insofar as they are responsible for the production and dissemination of cultural products. These psychological and affective goods often compensate for financial scarcity. However, material gains can also be substantial: Being an accredited intellectual favored by government officials is the only way to obtain a travel permit during this period. Without a travel permit, intellectuals cannot accept invitations by foreign institutions and therefore miss the opportunity to earn hard currency. From the point of view of the artist, the fear of losing these privileges may cause the intellectual laborer to embrace official policy regardless of personal conviction. It is, no doubt, a period of transition for writers, who manage their voice within the limits and contradictions offered by the system. In fact, most writers writing in Cuba make an effort to label themselves post-Soviet socialist intellectuals, which is a compromised, if not outright contradictory, situation.

The ethical impossibility contained in the figure "Cuban socialist intellectual" informs Rafael Rojas's question "What do local intellectual and political élites understand by *socialism*?" In an essay aptly entitled "A Question for Cuban Socialists," Rojas confronts contemporary intellectuals who define themselves as socialist, a category that includes most publishing intellectuals who reside on the island and who are recognized by the authorities as such. Rojas notes that even though Cuban socialism is undergoing the same "theoretical precariousness as all the other political projects of the Latin American left" since the 1980s, it could still be described as a "totalitarian, Soviet-style socialism; that is, one that maintains the centrally-planned economy and the single-party system." That this label is at least partially anachronistic doesn't exactly help intellectuals who confront the ethical dilemma that comes today with the label "Soviet socialist" intellectual. The problem, according to Rojas,

> lies in the fact that, institutionally speaking, Cuban socialism is still totalitarian. Therefore, those intellectuals claim an "organicity" that would only be attainable following a regime change and the establishment of a democratic left government. To call oneself "socialist" in Havana today, and to pretend this label means an affiliation to a Neo-Marxist platform, is a contradiction given that the official power sees it as evidence of unconditional loyalty. It is very likely that some of those intellectuals actually desire the detotalization of the regime, or the abandonment of all traces of Stalinism on the part of the state, and that they use the label "socialist" so as to negotiate narrow margins of agency. (2008)[19]

The strategic adoption of a misnomer simultaneously speaks of and further complicates the question of what it means to be a post-Soviet revolutionary subject. This takes us back to Alain Badiou's formulation of evental truth. There is no doubt that the Cuban revolution was the most significant cultural and political event of the twentieth century not only in Cuba but in all of Latin America. It was an event whose reach extended beyond a change of social and political structures and sought to name every aspect of reality on the basis of a truth it had generated itself. Hence the paradox pointed out by Rojas. The ethical situation of the Cuban intellectual cannot be easily resolved, but rather gets more complicated in the indivisible unit that comprises the phrase "socialist intellectual." As an ethical subject, the Cuban intellectual must officially remain loyal to an original event that produced the current situational truth—the revolution—an event that has not suffered any significant political reformulations in spite of the changes that have reshaped the political world. It is only in private that intellectuals may feel safe to acknowledge that they no longer feel fidelity to the revolution as a truth-process. One could say that intellectuals seem to be trapped in an ethical "double citizenship" of sorts, given that they maintain a duplicity (in a Badiouian sense) that, necessary as it may be for their survival as intellectuals, is automatically canceled out by the public use of their voice.

Badiou warns us against the conflict that is intrinsic to any individual affiliation to a communitarian identity: "The subject of a revolutionary politics is not the individual militant . . . To be sure, the militant enters into the composition of this subject, but once again it exceeds him (it is precisely this excess that makes it come to pass as immortal)" (2001, 43). One could understand the revolution as the producer of two identities superimposed upon the figure of the revolutionary individual, who considers himself as an individual being, bearer of his own truth, but who is at the same time the bearer of a collective identity that exceeds him. He is part of a collective ethos, which makes him "immortal." This paradox is unlikely to change as long as intellectuals remain caught within the language and values of the revolution. Fiction written by these very same intellectuals, which features characters who are intellectuals like themselves and who fight, compete, and demand explanations from other intellectuals, is particularly revealing in this regard. Ultimately, the interpersonal conflicts staged in and by these texts attest to the sorts of personal negotiations in which intellectuals as a group must engage as they move in and out of different fields of social meaning. In staging these conflicts, post-Soviet novels expose the cultural values deeply ingrained in the gender and cultural politics of the revolution, which constitute veritable blind spots in the utopian society it tried to create.

SOCIALISM AND SOCIALITY

Alain Badiou's description of the dual identity of the revolutionary subject (i.e., the notion that several truths that operate simultaneously can coexist within an individual) is helpful in coming to terms with Ambrosio Fornet's claim that the origin of literary disenchantment can be located in the separation between the private and the collective conscience. As this dual identity becomes more evidently unsustainable after 1991, we still find that local artists and intellectuals cannot rid themselves of this label without bringing upon themselves a professional catastrophe. It is illuminating in this context to note that many Cuban novels published between 1991 and 2008, which have now become the "classics" of the post-Soviet era, are constructed as narratives of personal tragedy in which the individual's dual identity comes into conflict with the demands the community places on him to sustain his membership in the group. Although one can only assume that conflictive fidelities pervade the real life of Cuban intellectuals, these dilemmas are eloquently unraveled, metonymically, in these post-Soviet novels. Hence my claim that to approach contemporary Cuban narrative and art from the perspective of ethics can help us attain a deeper understanding of the current state of affairs in Cuba.

The theme of conflicting loyalties, central to the formation of the revolutionary intellectual as a subject, is the focus of novels by Jesús Díaz, Leonardo Padura, and Abel Prieto. In these texts, friendship among intellectuals appears as a structural impossibility vis-à-vis the sublimated ethical demands of political identity. Indeed, Díaz, Padura, and Prieto treat in different ways the relation between pure aesthetics—disinterested, politically neutral art that is governed by reason—and the elevated ideals that define artistic labor as a superior social practice. At the same time, the ethical values that appear most prevalently in their fiction are those of honor, fraternity, and loyalty, all of which are closely associated in their narrative elaboration with a heightened performance of masculinity. What these works suggest is that, even though Cuban society is male oriented, its cohesion does not depend on a patriarchal notion of authority, but rather on fraternal bonds. In reading them, one could argue that, in terms of its gender culture, Cuba falls into a category aptly described by Gayle Rubin in these terms: "There are gender-stratified systems which are not adequately described as patriarchal . . . The power of males in these groups is not founded on their roles as fathers or patriarchs, but on their collective adult maleness, embodied in secret cults, men's houses, warfare, exchange networks, ritual knowledge, and various initiation procedures" (1975, 168). In other words, it is what Carole Pateman has called a fraternal social contract (2002, 129). The revolution was largely possible thanks to a manly and fraternal vision of society, a vision that becomes all-absorbing when the revolution is seen to be threatened by the perpetual enemy of American imperialism. Fraternity and masculinity are military values that also help define friendship between men, which is best articulated in these novels through the notion of loyalty.[20]

Published just before what I have been calling "the post-Soviet period," the short story "El lobo, el bosque y el Hombre Nuevo" (The Wolf, the Forest and the New Man) by Senel Paz was one of the first literary attempts to expose the rigid gender structure of the revolution. Particularly significant in Paz's story is the moment when David, a young militant, flashes his Communist Youth party membership card to fend off Diego's sexual advances. The fact that the card can simultaneously indicate ideological *and* sexual allegiances exposes the deeply ingrained cultural values that equate militancy to manliness. What is perhaps more telling, however, is the neglect with which this connection was received among critics. For instance, Jorge Fornet discusses this scene in detail and even alludes to the connection between ideological affiliation and sexual preference in his essay "La narrativa cubana entre la utopía y el desencanto." However, he fails to question the lack of distinction between the two categories, which is all the more shocking given that the story seeks to emphasize the distinction between sexual orientation and politics in no uncertain terms when the gay character Diego explains to David, his militant friend, that one can be both gay *and* revolutionary. The indifference of a perceptive local critic like Jorge Fornet to the deeply ideological meaning of this scene further demonstrates the questionable gender politics dominating intellectual circles.[21]

Iván de la Nuez describes the revolution as a project that equated modernity and emancipation (1988, 57). From the point of view of its gender and ethical culture, however, the revolution is a modern utopia that has outlasted both its relevance and its own modernity. Indeed, whereas many of the fictions considered in this book (by Padura and Díaz, for instance) seem to navigate among values that are shared by both private and public spheres, other works (by Portela, Estévez, and Ponte) situate themselves beyond the revolutionary project itself in both ethical and political terms. These three writers, I argue, are bearers of a different kind of truth. What constitutes them as ethical subjects is not their faith in a utopian project but rather the *fin-de-siècle* understanding that utopias are not only not possible but also dangerous; that principled causes are not only not worth dying for but may not even be worth living by. Their truth-process originates in a shift in the international ethical landscape. According to moral philosophers Zygmunt Bauman and Gilles Lipovetsky, postmodernity has effected a radical change in the configuration of ethics, one that, under the name "crepuscular ethics" (Lipovetsky's term), shuns "hyperbolic imperatives" in favor of subjective rights.

I suggest in this book that the divergence of discourses mentioned by Ambrosio Fornet can be understood not so much as the separation of ideology and ethics within the revolution but rather as the liberation of literary conscience thanks to a structural change in contemporary ethics. The change, moreover, reached the island through a cultural and aesthetic evolution that is separate and/or alternative to official ideological discourse. This is why various forms of "perversion" in novels by Abilio Estévez, Antonio José Ponte, and Ena Lucía Portela—authors that are not aligned with the heterosexual, virile, and, according to Guillermo Cabrera Infante, the bourgeois ethics of revolutionary culture—seem to effectively revise the ethical economy of revolutionary virtue. Furthermore, evil may be said to be a productive social force inasmuch as it produces a short circuit in the ethical mechanisms of a co-opted society. If, as Judith Butler claims, "collective ethos is always invariably a conservative one" because it "postulates a false unity that attempts to suppress the difficulty and discontinuity existing within any contemporary ethos," one can see how evil can be inherently liberating (2005, 4). Badiou contemplates this possibility when he suggests that evil destroys the situation because it "interrupts the truth-process in whose name it proceeds, since it fails to preserve, within the composition of its subject, the duality [duplicité] of interests" (2001, 85). Even though this disruption, for Badiou, would seem to be negative, it is possible to envision the ways in which new truths emerge in certain contexts by means of disruption itself. In other words, whereas writers who are not aligned with the cultural politics of the state and who would probably never call themselves "socialist" intellectuals seem to participate in the same or at least similar gender and ethical values, "perverse" authors negotiate their anxiety over personal alliances through the paradoxical ethics of the revolution from an entirely different position. They too fall prey to a collective notion of identity and the univocal ethics of a project, but their project resides either outside, or in direct opposition to, a male-oriented revolutionary culture.

Given that disenchantment is not possible among those who never had any hope, Jorge Fornet states in "La literatura cubana entre la utopía y el desencanto" that Portela and other "novísimos" "were born in another country, as it were" (2001, 45). With this phrasing, he banishes from the literary establishment those authors whose membership in the exclusive circle of political disenchantment is ruled out by the accident of age. I believe that the true frontier of the revolutionary lettered city is more ethical than generational; it is, in fact, conditioned by radically alternative notions of gender, ethics, and even subjectivities. In this book, I suggest that most of the texts that, according to Jorge Fornet, are "legitimately" disenchanted, share values inherent to revolutionary masculinity. Such a view frames all affective conflicts among characters within an ideology that is both residual and inoperative. By contrast, those texts that position themselves against such notion of masculinity propose emergent alternative models of civil society.

In varying degrees, all the writers and artists I study in this book become what Judith Butler describes in *Giving an Account of Oneself* as one's own social theoretician, that is, as a person who studies in her own artistic production the conditions in which she was constituted as an ethical subject (2005, 4). Taking the notion of the ethical subject as a point of departure, we can talk about the coexistence of two distinctive ethical and aesthetic languages in literature produced between 1991 and 2008. In the first group, we find writers that operate within the rules of revolutionary engagement, even when, politically, they do so from a critical perspective. These writers ostensibly seek to reclaim the distinction between public truth and private virtue, a distinction that had dissolved in and with the revolutionary social pact. On the other hand, another group of writers includes subjects whose epistemological world is informed by the fluidity of their gender and ethical values—it is this fluidity, not their age, that makes them alien to a revolutionary ethos. Therefore, I examine the coexistence of two types of ethical subjects, a modern one that, albeit politically critical, is inadvertently revolutionary in its ethical constitution, and a postmodern one that sees through, and aesthetically disavows, the ethical claims of the revolution. Post-Soviet literature can also be said to follow two main trends. Whereas a significant number of writers write within the same language and aesthetics of the revolution regardless of their loyalty to the specific ideological project, another group is not only aware of the post-Soviet breach between the ethics and politics of the revolution as event, but inhabits this space beyond the revolution. The writers in the latter group constitute in their radicalization what Blanchot calls an unspeakable or "unavowable community," a community that doesn't acknowledge itself as such, at least not in most traditional terms, but that is open to new forms of relationality.[22]

In an effort to address the different aspects informing the distinctive conflation of ethics and politics in the revolutionary social contract, I study the rules of engagement of the intellectual in the period between 1991 and 2008. By looking into what has been called an "aesthetics of frustration" in visual culture, or into an "aesthetics of disenchantment," the term preferred in literary criticism, I will pursue three interrelated questions: How does post-Soviet literature and art address their own rules of engagement at the twilight of the revolution? What ethical and aesthetic paradigms emerge at this time and what do they mean? What administrative (institutional and/or "curatorial") innovations are at play in the production, dissemination, and consumption of a post-Soviet art and literature? It is my aim to reflect on these topics so as to illuminate the ways in which fictional sociality and artistic experimentation help us envision alternative forms of civil society.

Although its treatment varies widely, the theme of sociality usually appears either in the context of competing loyalties to the state and to other friends, or, at a more abstract level, as a social configuration of art, community, and ethics. The analysis of friendship has two related objectives in this study: First, it helps unmask a foundational strategy of the revolutionary state that consisted in fusing ideology with the rhetoric of personal ethics, a gesture that, I contend, largely explains the survival of the socialist social contract in today's Cuba. Second, by analyzing the problem of divided loyalties among intellectuals with ties to the state, these novels help us interrogate the relation between the individual as an autonomous cultural producer and a social project of collectivity that would tend to subsume the subject. Friendship, art, and revolution imply the existence of a subject that, according to Alain Badiou, is exceeded by collective identities with their own inherent truths. When this (structurally impossible) collective subject comes into conflict with the individual, it poses a series of problems that tend to be formalized in the contemporary Cuban narrative as either a dramatization, reformation, deformation, or experimental reformulation of the utopian sociality that has historically defined an originally idealized but now deteriorated political project.

The chapters of this book follow a progression within the argument I have just outlined. In Chapter 2, "The Friendship Plot," I address the intersection of artistic excellence, loyalty, and honor in novels by Jesús Díaz, Leonardo Padura, and Abel Prieto, following in part Derrida's *The Politics of Friendship*. I contend that the revolutionary social contract mimics the structure and values of male friendship. Feeding off the same values of loyalty and fraternity, masculine friendship seems blind to the moral traps structurally imbedded in revolutionary rhetoric, thus paralyzing a mostly male intellectual class. Chapter 3, "Ethics after Dark," looks into perversion as a systematic metaphor that promotes disidentification, defined by Cuban philosopher Emilio Ichikawa as the "moral emancipation of the individual from his subordination to the transcendental ends of a deteriorated polis" (2001, 66). Through readings of novels by queer authors like Abilio Estévez and Antonio José Ponte, as well as part of Ena Lucía Portela's work, I follow Foucault, Judith Butler, and Leo Bersani in urging for a "utopian" view of homosexuality and perversion as an unsettling form of relationality that facilitates the creation of disenfranchised pacts of solidarity. Chapter 4, "The Poetics of Evil," studies the literary production of Ena Lucía Portela, Wendy Guerra, Pedro Juan Gutiérrez, and Guillermo Rosales vis-à-vis a social contract that has become politically and morally unhinged. Following Nietzsche, Badiou, and Beaudrillard, I argue that evil (evil as both an ethical category and as an aesthetic device) puts an end to the revolution as a truth-process. The failure of communism to deliver community exposes the unviability of the modern social contract. Unlike perversion, which reflects on the incompatibility of interests that characterizes the revolutionary subject, the power of evil resides in the fact that it destroys all social contracts. Chapter 5, "Ethics Is the New Aesthetics," addresses the search for new aesthetic paradigms within the ethical crisis I have outlined in previous chapters. More specifically, it looks into hyperrealism as a representational mode that dismantles the modern social contract regarding artistic immanence while advancing a postmodern ethics regarding the production and consumption of art. I study novels by Pedro Juan Gutiérrez and Abilio Estévez, the film *Suite Habana* by Fernando Pérez, photography by Abigail González and René Peña, and installations by José Manuel Fors, among others, from the point of view of the theory of photography. I propose that these authors/artists cultivate an aesthetics of barely mediated sensory provocation in literature and art—of what art critic Eric Rosenberg has called "the abdication of metaphor"—in order to force the reader/spectator to translate a visceral reaction into instantaneous moral judgment. Chapter 6, "A Curated Culture," focuses on post-Soviet Cuba as a cultural trend. Taking a closer look at the production, administration, and reception of culture, Chapter 6 proposes to see post-Soviet Cuba within an ethics of consumption. By following the consecrating agents and institutions that determine the circulation of artistic objects and aesthetic meanings, I analyze the social contracts that were created between artists and nonproducing cultural agents as the socialist state tried to reinvent itself. These new social contracts shape the aesthetic and ethical conversations of the previous chapters by casting the question of intellectual agency and responsibility today in light of the interplay between an ethics of representation, local politics, and an international artistic community. Not only does the global market create notions of taste and consumers, but it also claims to exist, according to Baudrillard, beyond good and evil.

I situate my analyses of fiction and art produced between 1991 and 2008 within the framework of sociology, gender, and moral philosophy. Taking as a point of departure the social functioning of certain values such as loyalty and truth from various perspectives—literary, artistic, political, and philosophical—I analyze contemporary trends in Cuban culture as well as the role of intellectuals in a Soviet-style socialist model that seems eroded.

Sociologically, I am interested in exploring how certain values have the capacity to either articulate or disarticulate communities, justifying their existence and determining the relationship between the group in its artistic, gender, and political specificities and the society that contains it. Politically, the communities I analyze here can be seen as groups that are aligned either in favor of or against the socialist social contract, while experimenting with different models of civil society. Philosophically speaking, the issues are more complex, for what is ultimately at stake is a triad of notions—namely community, subjectivity, and truth—that are capable of producing a radically different ethos. In this sense, literary and artistic debates assume ideologies that are either residual or emergent, reflecting paradigms that are either modern or postmodern. It is largely the adherence to these paradigms that determines the tone and scope of each of these conversations. Undergirding all of these positions is a notion of gender that is capable of envisioning different ethical and aesthetic modes of being together in the peculiar situation that is post-Soviet Cuba. It is by discussing gendered notions of community that post-Soviet literature and art reveal the fissures lurking beneath the dreams of the twentieth century.

2 The Friendship Plot

> All revolutions presuppose a vortex of vicissitudes in which every detail is transcendent to the point of exhaustion. Within revolutions, every single individual has an epical dimension.
>
> —Iván de la Nuez (2002, 39)

In *El socialismo y el hombre en Cuba* (Socialism and Man in Cuba), first published in 1965, Che Guevara promised that "in socialism, Man, in spite of his apparent standardization, is more complete. His capacity to express himself and to become part of the social apparatus is infinitely higher, even though there is no perfect mechanism to this end" (2007, 17; see also Serra 2007). In a somewhat contradictory fashion, however, Guevara suggests a few pages later the existence of a chasm between intellectuals and the political class: The original sin of the intellectuals, according to Guevara, was that they were not truly revolutionary; it was not in their nature to fight for a common cause. Guevara aptly illustrated his view of the organic intellectual with a reference to a commonplace botanical metaphor: "We can try to graft the elm tree so that it bears pears, but at the same time we must plant pear trees" (2007, 25). Whether intended or unintended, the political consequence of such persistent ideological interpellation on the part of the state was the compromise of the intellectual's public voice. This situation was all the more crippling given that public voice is what defines the very essence of the intellectual's labor. This state of affairs largely explains why, when trying to understand the role of the intellectual in post-Soviet Cuba, we need to look into works of fiction.

J. Hillis Miller wonders how the nonlinguistic world of ethics can become language (1987, 7). His response has two parts. First, he states that "ethics and narration cannot be kept separate, though their relation is neither symmetrical nor harmonious . . . morality cannot be discussed in the abstract. It *must* be analyzed and demonstrated in terms of specific cases. Hence moral philosophy requires textual interpretation" (1987, 2–3). Second, he proposes that ethics becomes apparent through figures of speech, which elaborate complex relations between referent and language (1987, 6). Within Hillis Miller's premise, some of the fiction written by Cuban artists featuring characters who are intellectuals like themselves and who fight, compete, and demand (personal) explanations from other intellectuals, is highly revealing. Ultimately, the interpersonal conflicts staged in and by these texts attest to the sorts of personal negotiations in which intellectuals as a group must engage as they move in and out of different fields of social meaning. For, in staging similar conflicts in novels that mimetically reflect the world of the engaged male revolutionary intellectual immersed in his social circle, these narratives expose ethical values deeply rooted in the gender and cultural politics of the revolution and that, I suggest, constitute significant blind spots in the utopian society it tried to create.

I would like to propose that what these novels reveal, often in spite of themselves, is that the degree of commitment expected of the individual to the production and maintenance of collective good required by the socialist social contract, evokes the structural characteristics of friendship. A fraternal bond based on idealized notions of equality and reciprocity, friendship offers the social template within which the soldier, the artist, the teacher and the politician would cultivate their best selves in the common pursuit of what Aristotle called "the good life." Structural similarities between friendship and revolutionary rhetoric, I suggest here, help explain why immediately after the fall of the Berlin Wall, when the insolvency of publishing houses on the island allowed for new publishing opportunities in Spain, thus opening up new levels of freedom of expression for Cuban writers, a series of novels appeared that focused on the topic of friendship. These novels discuss friendship among men as an affective bond, as a strategic artistic alliance, and,—as I suggest here,—as an ideological trap. What makes the discussion of friendship in and about literature so relevant to the intensely ethical position of the Cuban revolution is the paradoxical role that friendship plays in revolutionary culture; the social and political mechanisms that become exposed when friendships go wrong; and the personal tragedies that unveil the ultimate disunion between art, ethics, and politics.

I will call this model the friendship plot, partly following Peter Brooks's definition of plot as "a structuring operation peculiar" to a specific historical problem to which it seeks to provide an affective "form of understanding and explanation" (1984, 10). The post-Soviet friendship plot can be described as follows: Several young male artists who become friends in light of a common notion of pure aesthetics have a strong desire to produce such art and a comparable level of talent. Yet, for various reasons, they are never fully equal to the task at hand. They all depend on the group both for intellectual growth and for reassurance of their worth, two aspects of their formation that will presumably help them attain the unquestionable artistic recognition they seek. In order for success to be legitimate, the individual artist in these novels has to pass a double moral test: He must neither surrender to the pressures of the government nor betray any of his friends.[1] Standing against the government means that his sense of value is ultimately measured by his sense of courage, which Alasdair MacIntyre defines as "the capacity to risk harm or danger to oneself" for a cause or a person (2007, 192). Both value and courage have the same etymological origin. They are both called "valor" in Spanish, thus putting his very sense of masculinity at stake. In this context, I use "manliness" (the notion of behaving like a true man) and "manly virtues" (the values of stoicism, assertiveness, honor, and courage that define manliness) in a sense similar to that expressed by Harvey Mansfield, who sees these ethical principles not only as inherent to maleness, but also as endowing masculinity with a heightened notion of value (where value equals worth). By contrast, I use "masculinity" following Leo Braudy, who uses it as a critical term that looks into how a gender models itself and what ethical principles it holds in high esteem. I am interested in analyzing the way in which those who believe in these principles are conditioned to behave in specific—and often paradoxical—ways, as well as the role such attitude plays in shaping the social and political world.

Crucial to the friendship plot is the concept of narrative-based identity elaborated by Neo-Aristotelian philosopher Alasdair MacIntyre. To the question of who we are, we respond with our life stories. Loyalty dilemmas hold a privileged role in the process of giving shape to an individual's life story. Following MacIntyre, Michael J. Sandel states:

> To live a life is to enact a narrative quest that aspires to a certain unity or coherence. When confronted with competing paths, I try to figure out which path will best make sense of my life as a whole, and of the things I care about. Moral deliberation is more about interpreting my life story than exerting my will. It involves choice, but the choice issues from the interpretation; it is not a sovereign act of will. (2009, 221)

Ethics in general dictate how we relate to our own personal stories, to our historical context, and to our social situation. More concretely, loyalty dilemmas define who we are, for we make choices according to how we would like our lives to be interpreted.

Similarly, Australian philosopher John Anderson says that it does not really matter what purpose any given social institution serves, but "of what conflicts is it the scene?" Anderson's question leads MacIntyre to develop a "Sophoclean insight": "that it is through conflict and sometimes only through conflict that we learn what our ends and purposes are" (2007, 163–164). Exploring this insight in the context of institutions and social formations such as art, friendship, and socialism, I suggest that what becomes evident through the friendship plot among artists in the Cuban setting is that all three formations feed off the same values of loyalty and courage. This is why, in the novels I study, the freedom of artistic creation that is so adamantly defended at a rhetorical level soon loses its focus at the level of representation. As James Buckwalter-Arias notes, "what we see instead is a thoroughly politicized literary environment in which artistic freedom is encroached on not only by the state but also by peers, in which the notion of freedom is both constituted in and delimited by ingrained cultural expectations" (2005, 369).

In this chapter, I will try to define such "ingrained cultural expectations" and to elaborate upon their importance in defining the role of the intellectual during the post-Soviet era in revolutionary Cuba. In what follows, I will read Jesús Díaz's *Las palabras perdidas* (The Lost Words), Leonardo Padura's Mario Conde series and his novel *La novela de mi vida* (The Novel of My Life), and Abel Prieto's *El vuelo del gato* (The Flight of the Cat) against the sociological and philosophical background of male friendship and the virtues associated with it, such as loyalty, courage, honor, and stoicism. I will discuss how the mechanisms of these virtues intersect the revolutionary social contract and permeate not only personal bonds but also the role of the intellectual. Due to the structural interdependence between accountability and narrative, as well as to the intimate connection between politics and friendship in philosophical discourse, I will look into how the literary conversation about male friendship in post-Soviet Cuba withstands a Neo-Aristotelian reading of the loyalty paradigm. I hope to show that, by pitting essentialized loyalties against one another, the romanticized thematization of literary creation in its double framework (that of friendship and that of the socialist state) helps us understand the perpetuation of the socialist government in Cuba due to a suggestive series of structural and thematic parallelisms between the virtues and cultural expectations that inform the bonds between men in revolutionary culture.

In my readings, I will look into various genres, such as the bildungsroman, the detective story, and a postmodern allegory, and will trace four ethical aspects elaborated in the friendship plot: the incompatibility between excellence in art and revolutionary commitment; the triangular structure required by the tests of loyalty; honor as the all irreducible category of manliness; and stoicism as a revolutionary value that confines the political to the rules of heroic societies. I will discuss these values (excellence, loyalty, honor, and stoicism) so as to prepare the ground for two complementary hypotheses regarding the Cuban intellectual class and the survival of the socialist social contract. The first relates to the political and ethical aspects of friendship and art production as they appear in the post-Soviet Cuban novel. The second, which I will elaborate at the end of this chapter, suggests a philosophical misunderstanding within the revolution as ethical project.

THE VALUES OF FRIENDSHIP

Legitimacy in both friendship and socialism is determined by high ideals such as loyalty and fraternity, values that, regardless of their quality and function in real life, help define them as social formations. Concretely, I suggest that these structural similarities have allowed the official rhetoric of the revolutionary state to co-opt the values commonly associated with friendship, mostly male friendship, to the point of paralyzing the labor of a mostly male intellectual class. Two related premises contribute to this reading. The first is a strictly literary premise based on the consistent representation of an intellectual world that presents friendship, political legitimacy, and artistic integrity as what Pierre Bourdieu calls "structurally irreconcilable possibles" (1995, 20). As I show in my discussion of *Las palabras perdidas*, the formation of the revolutionary artist consists not so much in learning the craft and maturing emotionally, as is the case in the traditional *Künstleroman*, but in identifying the incompatibility of social allegiances and having to choose the object of betrayal at a high moral and/or political cost. The second premise refers to the social world: I understand that underlying the structural impossibility of maintaining these allegiances is a rigid gender structure that only endorses a limited number of acceptable forms of being a man in Latin America. In other words, what prevents the successful coexistence of these three fields of social meaning (friendship, revolutionary compliance, and artistic creation) is not only the high demands placed on individuals by the socialist government, but also the fact that all three "practices" feed off a common fund of internal virtues, such as reciprocity, equality, loyalty, and courage. Although these virtues are considered essential to guarantee the quality and even the survival of many social formations, they have also traditionally been considered to constitute the very definition of manliness.

The rhetoric surrounding the commitment to a revolutionary ethics echoes the highly idealized values of friendship in a tradition that goes back to Aristotle. Graham Allan concisely summarizes the Aristotelian tradition by defining friendship in these terms:

> The solidarity of the friends, based solely on their personal and voluntary commitment to each other, is taken to be unfettered by any selfish or instrumental concerns. Each gives what the other needs, without thought to cost or reward, simply because of the fact of their friendship. From this perspective, such friendship can be recognized as a bond of enormous moral significance: as one of the highest expressions of voluntary, altruistic commitment there can be between people. (1989, 13)

In contemporary sociological terms, friendship is defined as a voluntary personal relation, expressive in nature (i.e., noninstrumental), informal (i.e., not contained within an institutional structure), established between equals, reciprocal, and based on high ideals such as loyalty and solidarity. Even though disinterestedness is one of friendship's main characteristics, sociologists agree that they "*are* used instrumentally [although] it is true that friendship must not be defined in these terms" (Allan 1989, 20; emphasis in original). One could say that friendship, like pure aesthetics, is disinterested, and that friendship, like the revolution, is defined in terms of its ideals, not on the grounds of its real practice.

In *The Politics of Friendship*, Derrida brings this paradoxical quality of friendship to the fore by suggesting that there is something inherently utopian in this human activity:

> "Good friendship" supposes disproportion. It demands a certain rupture in reciprocity or equality, as well as the interruption of all fusion or confusion between you and me. By the same token it signifies a divorce with love, albeit self-love . . . "Good friendship" is born of disproportion: when you esteem or respect [achet] the other more than yourself. (2005, 62)

In this passage, Derrida follows Nietzsche's views on the topic of friendship to uncover one of the hidden truths about this highly valued form of association. Contrary to common perceptions, friendship is not so much a bond with others as a rupture with oneself. It is because of this disproportionate quality that friendship most resembles utopianism.

According to sociologists, friendships are classified based on the nonmaterial benefits sought by the participants. The friendships among young intellectuals depicted in the novels I mentioned seek, in the first place, social integration, a feeling of belonging to a group with common interests and values expressed in terms of aesthetic choices, artistic talent, and social values. Second, friendship also allows access into a social network that provides "reassurance of worth" by confirming the competence of a given individual in a specific social role (R. S. Weiss 1974, 23–24). Accordingly, friendship provides the fictional intellectuals I analyze in this chapter with a double form of membership. The first is supranational: Friends belong to a world of letters that is based on an intransigent adherence to pure aesthetics. The second matters at the national level: Friends form part of a fraternity endowed with social power and which is ruled by an ethics different from that of the state as well as from that of the home. In light of the values upheld, the double membership afforded by these friendships provides male protagonists with a sense of moral superiority.

The bond of friendship among men is a suggestive illustration of Cuban society as a whole. Cuba's gender culture falls into a category that, as I mentioned in the previous chapter, is best described by Gayle Rubin, who claims "there are gender-stratified systems which are not adequately described as patriarchal . . . The power of males in these groups is not founded on their roles as fathers or patriarchs, but on their collective adult maleness, embodied in secret cults, men's houses, warfare, exchange networks, ritual knowledge, and various initiation procedures" (1975, 168). This seems to be a particularly illuminating description of the masculinist system as it appears in the novels under consideration in this chapter. The most obvious case, perhaps, is Leonardo Padura's *La novela de mi vida*, which follows two parallel time lines, establishing a clear analogy between contemporary friendship among male intellectuals and nineteenth-century Freemasonry. The parallelism is very telling, as the lodge houses a society of men forming a fraternity of equals that is, in fact, quite exclusive. It holds its own initiation practices and rituals, and produces its own laws that separate its members affectively and morally from both the demands of the state and those of the home. Freemasons are subject to the requirements of loyalty and secrecy upon which their membership stands. Interestingly, many of the values just described cross into other institutions and social formations, the most exacerbated of which is, of course, the army.[2]

Indeed, the 1959 revolution was very much made possible thanks to the formation of popular armies, which were commanded by four men: Fidel Castro, his brother Raúl, Che Guevara, and Camilo Cienfuegos. According to Leo Braudy, not only does military masculinity offer the "prime way of being a man," but war also offers the most pure way of being patriotic, and even just (2003, 7).[3] The aura of militarism in the name of social justice was consolidated by Cuba's perception of itself as waging a perpetual war against American imperialism, and with a very immediate effect. As Edward Said has noted, war forcefully limits the critical stance that defines the role of the intellectual given that "to debate the justice of a war [is usually] construed as the equivalent of treason" (1994, 45). The masculinist postulates used by the revolutionary project to first define and then promote itself even until today informs the nation's main prerogatives, such as the expectation of a strong male population (courage), the justification for extreme material sacrifices on the part of its people (stoicism), and the demand for uncompromising adherence on the part of its intellectual class (loyalty).

Loyalty in friendship is codified according to the very terms undergirding political loyalty—voice and exit. This has been extensively elaborated upon by Albert O. Hirschman, who defines loyalty as permanence in an organization or state in spite of unhappiness. A paradoxical aspect of loyalty stands out, given that, as Hirschman shows, "loyalty is at its most functional when it looks most irrational" (1970, 81). Among other aspects, postponement of exit is determined by the price of entry into or exit from an organization. In most cases, membership that is hard to come by—like friendship in artistic and intellectual circles—is considered valuable and, therefore, elicits a higher degree of loyalty. This has consequences within the dynamic of the relations. In a deteriorating friendship postponement of exit helps to activate voice as a recuperating mechanism, with voice being all the more effective in view that the threat of exit is possible or even imminent. Loyalty also tends to last longer when the price of exit is high.

In the case of nations, entry is usually free. Today's Cuba, however, has a high-priced exit. Not only is exit rarely possible, but the mere desire to exit is automatically perceived as desertion or betrayal. Actual exit or even desired exit can subject the person to all sorts of bureaucratic, moral, and political complications. The socialist state is, in Hirschman's words, a "loyalty demanding organization," which, by setting the price of exit—or of the threat of exit—very high, helps effectively eliminate voice alongside exit (1970, 92).[4] In compensation, however, it seeks to create an irrational type of loyalty, looking for "devices converting, as it were, conscious into unconscious loyalist behavior" (93). In general terms, patriotism and a rather essentialist mixed-race pride—which includes the notion and promotion of a certain innate superiority at several levels, particularly in the area of sexual appeal and performance—has long helped Cubans harbor a sensation of exclusivity and pride of membership at a national level. Unconscious loyalty to the revolution, however, requires an appeal of a moral kind that begins with, but is not limited to, the pride elicited by the heroism of the Revolution.

At a political level, I argue, the friendship plot reveals that, in order to create ever renewing amounts of unconscious loyalty, the revolution framed its social contract in terms of an idealized friendship—that is, as a personal commitment to a fraternity of equals based on an altruistic belief in solidarity and justice—while disregarding the structural differences between the two formations, not the least of which is the difference in access to voice and exit. Neglecting the differences between the two did away with, among other things, the notion that a social contract is political, not moral, and that altruism is hardly expected in a political system for any extended period of time. In addition, the revolutionary social contract tried to actualize prerogatives of friendship that, ultimately, were never meant to be fully actualized even in private relations—after all, what friendship is about in the abstract cannot always be demanded in reality without putting the friendship under "unendurable strain" (Eisenstadt and Roniger 1984, 12).[5] The appropriation of personal ethics on the part of the state under the revolutionary contract was all the more invasive given that friendship could or should have had the potential to protect the citizen from the all-encompassing pressures of the socialist state (Misztal 1996, 187).[6] In other words, what I call the friendship plot can be read as an attempt on the part of Cuban intellectuals to hold the revolutionary project accountable for the nationalization of friendship as a "political crime" in the sense given by Derrida in *The Politics of Friendship*, that is, as a "crime *against* the possibility of politics, against man *qua* political animal, the crime of stopping to examine politics, reducing it to something else and preventing it from being what it should be" (2005, ix; emphasis in the original).

JESÚS DÍAZ'S EXCELLENCE

A particularly compelling account of friendship among artists can be found in Jesús Díaz's novel *Las palabras perdidas*. The story begins in 1967 when an up-and-coming intellectual, called el Flaco, is assigned the task of producing a cultural supplement to a journal. El Flaco envisions the journal as a compendium of poetry and fiction that, under the title *El güije ilustrado*, will revolutionize the world of letters. He recruits two other young men who share his elevated aesthetic notions, el Gordo and el Rojo, and eventually a woman, emblematically called Una, who is appreciated for her intelligence and her arrogance—in brief, she is valued for her "manly" characteristics—and is nonetheless often relegated to a nurturing role. All four *güijes*, who consider themselves the very offspring of the revolution, aspire to renovate the cultural landscape of the island through the symbolic "burial" of the greatest writers of the preceding generation—Alejo Carpentier, José Lezama Lima, Nicolás Guillén and Eliseo Diego—whom they nevertheless imitate passionately. The *güijes*, who are very different from one another, aim to find a nurturing community that will foster their production of art, that will reassure each of them of their worth, and that will provide them with a social network that will distinguish them from all others.

As young bohemian artists, the *güijes* belong to two opposed groups. On the one hand, they consider themselves the children of the revolution, and therefore "natural" heirs to their principles and ideals. They even feel authorized to criticize the revolution "from within." At the same time, however, their artistic affiliation establishes them as free spirits "who, strong in their cultural capital and the authority born of being *taste-makers*," reign over family members and less talented peers, to borrow Pierre Bourdieu's phrase (1995, 56–57). For example, the art of living that is their trademark leads one of the young poets, el Rojo, to describe cigarettes as "very delicate Persian poems that burn as they are read, bestowing an ineffable happiness" (Díaz 1992, 265). Their creative and often frivolous way of seeing the world is essential to who they are. More important, however, they share an elevated notion of avant-garde aesthetics, a notion that above anything else, defines them as a cohesive group. Thus, it is not surprising that the *güijes* are convinced that their journal will be judged exclusively on the grounds of its novelty and aesthetic value, only to find out that they are fatally wrong. The journal that was conceived of as a parricide soon becomes a fratricide (1992, 100). The production of the first and, as it turns out last, issue begins by generating friendship and literature, but ends up giving way to large doses of rivalry and envy. These passions are even stronger among a second tier of friends, the aspiring *güijes* who are occasionally invited to admire the original *güijes*' talent. Given this atmosphere of arrogance and jealousy, it seems inevitable that the first issue is banned because of a secret report turned in on the eve of publication. After the official condemnation of the supplement, the *güijes* fall into literary sterility, guilt, suicide, and death.

A telling scene takes place at the newspaper's office, where el Flaco's former protector discusses the impossibility of publishing the journal in its present form. The tone of the interview is set by the director's first question: "Do you have enemies?" (1992, 330). El Flaco, who realizes that the entire project is at stake, shows a surprising willingness to compromise that could not have been predicted given his previous unbending adherence to aesthetic principles. He now finds himself going back on his editorial decisions and remaking the supplement as the director questions different aspects of the project. El Flaco's goal at this point is not to produce the supplement that he wants, but merely one that can be published. In spite of his efforts, however, the supplement is banned and the *güijes* are sanctioned. At the climax of this meeting, the boss praises the humiliated *güije*'s mature attitude; even his friends admit that he behaved "like a politician" (1992, 341). During the interview with the editor, el Flaco abruptly learns the incompatibility between the two worlds, the political and the intellectual, which is all the more poignant in the context of a revolution that had promised its youth the union of the political vanguard with the artistic avant-garde.

Literarily, *Las palabras perdidas* is a novel of initiation in the manner of Gustave Flaubert's *Sentimental Education.* In both texts a group of young men who are equipped in different ways to achieve social power must understand the rules of society in order to better play the social game. In *The Rules of Art*, Pierre Bourdieu explains Frédéric Moreau's "sentimental education" in the capitalist world of nineteenth-century Paris as

> the progressive learning about the incompatibility between two universes, between art and money, pure love and mercenary love; it is the story of structurally necessary accidents which determine social ageing by determining the telescoping of structurally irreconcilable possibles. (1995, 20)

Similarly, for the young writers in *Las palabras perdidas*, the writing of the first issue of *El güije ilustrado* points to that privileged moment in which intellectual success, social power, long-lasting friendship, and sexual fulfillment all seem to be possible at the same time. During their education, the young artists in Jesús Díaz's novel must negotiate and often renounce certain expectations, as their devotion to art, friendship, and politics frequently pulls them in different directions. They must learn, in sum, that art and power are not possible at the same time due to the constraints placed on them not only by limited but calculable resources such as time, energy, capital, talent, or reputation, as is the case in the social world depicted by Flaubert, but by the introduction of the unpredictable demands of loyalty, instead.

The paradigm that posits loyalty at the heart of what Bourdieu calls "structurally irreconcilable possibles" in Jesús Díaz's plot can better be understood when seen through the lens of Alasdair MacIntyre's notion of "practice." MacIntyre calls a practice

> any coherent and complex form of socially established cooperative human activity through which goods internal to that form of activity are realized in the course of trying to achieve those standards of excellence which are appropriate to, and partially definitive of, that form of activity, with the result that human powers to achieve excellence, and

human conceptions of the ends and goods involved, are systematically extended. (2007, 187)

Art is a "practice"; that is, a "socially established cooperative human activity" defined by specific virtues that not only distinguish the activity in itself but, to the extent that they are exercised properly and with the correct spirit, make that activity reach its highest possible degree of excellence. Therefore, the good artist is the one who, having the proper skills and quality of form as well as a deep understanding of the internal goods defining such art—that which makes a particular type of art what it is—can actualize those internal goods so as to reach, or aspire to reach, the point of excellence that characterizes the practice. This aspiration, in turn, cultivates the artist's own happiness. For "virtues are to be understood as those dispositions which will not only sustain practices and enable us to achieve the goods internal to practices, but which will sustain us in the relevant kind of quest for the good" (2007, 219). The best possible expression of art as a practice would then be that which simultaneously makes the artist and his art find the highest expression of that art's—and that man's—internal virtues.

When MacIntyre explains that virtues will sustain us in the course of our individual quest for the good, he refers to the fact that the human agent that is the support of a certain practice is himself improved by honoring the excellence of the practice. Because every practice is a social activity, the notion of excellence in any practice is inseparable from the well-being of the community. In principle, this view largely justifies the development of the arts within a political project—such as the Cuban revolution, at least originally—that was so deeply defined by its ethical goals. Indeed, to produce literature requires not only the proper set of skills and talents, but also a clear conception of what constitutes excellence in literature and what virtues such excellence requires.

Concretely, writing can be seen as a practice whose exercise is expected to honor literature as well as to improve both the writer and the reader, for, according to MacIntyre, "what the artist discovers within the pursuit of excellence in . . . the fine arts in general—is the good of a certain kind of life" (2007, 190). Given the moral stakes in this enterprise, a caveat needs to be mentioned. You can plagiarize, or even imitate, the greatest poets, but that action only has an oblique relationship to excellence in literature—one that is very remotely related to the practitioner. Plagiarizing in literature constitutes what MacIntyre would call a simulacrum of virtue (2007, 149–150). As opposed to external goods—be it fame or prestige—an internal virtue is something without which that practice becomes something else, something other than what it is. Both art and artist are degraded when that art's defining virtues are substituted with their simulacra.

An Aristotelian view of art like the one offered by MacIntyre is an apt lens through which to read Díaz, not least because it advances the notion that art improves the quality of one's life, that specific virtues are intrinsically attached to that practice, and that artists participate in its exercise and honor those virtues both individually and collectively. Indeed, the friends in *Las palabras perdidas* call themselves poets because they are driven by the mad desire to reach "an idea of poetic perfection for which they were all responsible" (1992, 142). Furthermore, their friendship largely depends on a shared aesthetic vision. Regardless of their actual individual literary production, they all adhere to the fact that only internal aspects of their writing will produce excellence in literature. Immediate financial or political gains are to be seen as not only irrelevant but probably even damaging, a view they uphold in spite of occasional instances of personal ambition. Each *güije* has little doubt about what constitutes excellence in literature ("gran literatura"), even though its internal virtues are as hard to uphold as they are to define.

In his book *Cuba and the New* Origenismo, James Buckwalter-Arias devotes his chapter "*Gran Literatura* and Socialist Cuba" to *Las palabras perdidas*. Buckwalter-Arias points out that, although the four friends endow literature with a mystical aura (2010, 59), it is not so much in the *güijes*' actual literary production as in their conversations and rounds of critique that the values of the four artists become explicit (56). Whereas el Flaco aspires to write "a *total* novel" (Díaz 1992, 36) and seeks to maximize the aura of his production by combining various formal techniques, el Rojo values poetry when it encapsulates the best of Western tradition but is, at the same time, capable of transcending it (114). In turn, el Gordo's conversational literature, which according to Buckwalter-Arias "is more democratic, and certainly more consistent with the socialist ethos," often borrows from folklore, a strategy that incites el Rojo's disdain (2010, 63). For el Rojo, the experiential does not have a place in "great literature." Even Piotr, the uneducated stepfather of el Flaco's Russian son, reveals his own vision when he asks el Flaco whether his writing is true to reality. For Piotr literature should speak the truth. Establishing what level of truth, how, and with what purpose would determine the difference between defining literature on the basis of either internal or external virtues.

In turn, the official view, which becomes evident when el Gordo is denied a position in the university and later during the interview between el Flaco and the newspaper editor, is that literature is valuable when it praises the country (Díaz 1992, 97). To praise the country constitutes an external virtue and therefore lies outside, and even corrupts, artistic excellence. The official view of art finds its most exacerbated version in a Social Realism conference that takes place in Prague, where el Rojo meets Roque Dalton, the Salvadoran poet and activist who appears as a character in the novel. During the conference, Dalton satirizes such instrumental views of literature in his poem "After the A-Bomb," in which he appropriates Quevedo's famous verse to suggest that politics kills poetry: "They will be dust, but will they be dust in love?" ("Polvo serán, mas ¿polvo enamorado?"; Díaz 1992, 166).[7]

While confusion may arise about what constitutes excellence in literature when defining it as a practice, there seems to be a consensus among the protagonists that literature must remain free from extra-aesthetic determinations and political requirements.[8] Accordingly, *Las palabras perdidas*, which was originally staged in homage to the dead friends, can be said to be an elegy to a collective dream. At least on the surface, the drama for the young writers of *Las palabras perdidas* is the violent awareness of the illusory character of the fusion between art and politics in revolutionary Cuba. The political project seems, in fact, to leave little room for excellence in art. However, rather than their incompatibility, I suggest, it is their similarities that prevent their coexistence. Literature so defined demands from the artist a great deal of loyalty to an abstract notion of what makes literature what it is, as well as the courage to defend his views against external pressure and cooptation. The same can be said about both friendship and political commitment.

Loyalty and courage are internal virtues to all three practices in this critical moment in Cuban history: friendship, art, and politics. Friendship, like literature, is a "socially established cooperative human activity," defined by a set of internal goods without which it can become a simulacrum of friendship. The virtues that define friendship are that of reciprocity, equality, loyalty, and even courage, for, as MacIntyre suggests,

> To be courageous is to be someone on whom reliance can be placed. Hence courage is an important ingredient in friendship . . . The other ingredient of friendship is fidelity. My friend's courage assures me of his power to aid me and my household; my friend's fidelity assures me of his will. (2007, 123)

It is interesting that these structural characteristics of personal friendship strongly resemble the terms of the socialist social contract. In other words, that in the name of equality and justice for all (the internal virtues that help define and even advance excellence in socialism), the government requires from its citizens unconditional loyalty and courage.

This structural similarity partly explains why the topic of friendship often displaces that of literary production. Considering that *Palabras* is a novel built on two time lines that frame the beginning and the end of the period of extreme censorship, which came to be known in Cuban history as Quinquenio Gris, it is particularly interesting that the artistic production that occupies the characters so intensely in the early story line soon loses narrative power. Instead, the narrative focuses on the rivalry among the four *güijes*. The complex emotional bonds among them range from jealousy (who is closer to whom) and competitiveness (who is more talented) to calculations and power trips (who manipulates whom). Within this affective landscape, however, the main question is who will remain loyal to literary excellence. After the failure of the project, Una and el Rojo accuse el Gordo and el Flaco for having betrayed both friendship and literature: "But it is death, and only death, which reunited them by el Rojo's deathbed" (Díaz 1992, 345).

Indeed, in addition to denunciation, which lies at the very heart of the narrative structure I am calling the friendship plot, two other types of betrayals are worth considering in some detail. First, and most importantly, is the guilt of having survived his friends, which consumes el Flaco—"Who could blame him for choosing to live, even in silence?" (1992, 348). A philosophical tradition that goes from Cicero to Maurice Blanchot and Derrida treats the fundamental call for friendship as the elimination of death. Simon Critchley summarizes this view: "Although it is indeed 'difficult to say,' it is because of friendship that the *dead live* (*mortui vivunt*), and the condition of possibility for friendship is memory." He concludes in bold fashion: "In this sense, *philia* is *necro-philia*" (1999, 257–258). The promise of writing a novel in his friends' memory seems to el Flaco the only way to live up to his friendship.

The second betrayal is more earthly, pervasive, and clearly gendered, as it refers to several instances of the "traffic of women" between men. The first instance concerns "la dama del perrito," who used to date el Flaco, but makes out with el Rojo at the party at Roque Dalton's house, and ends up marrying el Rubito. Although she is a minor character, or perhaps precisely because of it, her sentimental itinerary speaks solely to the dynamic of jealousy and rivalry between the young writers. Like literary fame and political power, the girl with the glorious behind—after which she is nicknamed—is a trophy all the more desirable because another one desires her. There is little doubt that el Rubito ends up with both power and the girl out of desire for that which is valued by the young men whose respect he fails to win in the literary field. A more dramatic variation of a similar pattern can be seen in the fact that el Flaco sleeps with Una, who has been el Rojo's lover for a long time, three days after el Rojo's death from cancer. El Flaco's betrayal is the culmination of his long-established envy of el Rojo (for his artistic talent, his class superiority, and his nonchalance). This kind of male-male-female erotic triangle is inherent to male homosocial desire as described by Eve Kosofky Sedgwick, who suggests, advancing René Girard's argument, that the bond of rivalry is more powerful than that of love (1985, 21). I will elaborate this in more detail below; however, let's say for now that the gender prerogatives of the friendship plot are further underlined by the male friends' common desire for the only prominent female character in the text. This is the case of Una in *Las palabras perdidas*, as well as Tamara in Padura's detective series, Delfina in *La novela de mi vida*, Amarilis in *El vuelo del gato*, and so on. This vision of triangular desire further underlines friendship as an androcentric institution (Derrida 2005, viii) and insinuates that particularly Cuban notions of masculinity lie at the heart of the conflation of the political and social structures. It is very ironic that el Rubito's double betrayal originates in Roque Dalton's house, playfully tagged "la roquicueva" in a humorous reference to Batman and Robin's hideout, which was one of the most suggestively queer spaces in the popular culture of the time.

We learn from the frustrated social structures in *Las palabras perdidas* that loyalty and courage are internal virtues to all three practices novelized in this critical moment in Cuban history: friendship, art, and revolution. Friendship, which is defined by equality and reciprocity, is supposed to follow a binomial structure. However, because friendship is measured by loyalty and courage, which need tests to be actualized, friendship becomes triangular by necessity. What is more, the structural characteristics of friendship mentioned above strongly resemble the terms of the socialist social contract insofar as the government requires from its citizenship unconditional loyalty in the name of equality and justice for all, the virtues that determine excellence in socialism.

LEONARDO PADURA'S LOYALTY

First published in 1991, *Pasado perfecto* (literally Past Perfect, translated as Havana Blue) inaugurates Leonardo Padura's crime series "Las cuatro estaciones," (The Four Seasons), a tetralogy that focuses on the adventures of Teniente Mario Conde during the fateful year of 1989. Sure enough, the end of the fourth novel, *Paisaje de otoño* (Autumn Landscape or Havana Black), which leaves the protagonist bracing himself for a disastrous hurricane, has been read as an announcement of the fall of the Berlin Wall and its aftermath (J. Fornet 2001, 43). In this account, the apocalyptic image of the unstoppable forces of nature battering the island aptly represents the historical moment in which the social and political world that Cuba so closely depended upon would be destroyed overnight. Conde also looks into this destruction with a glimpse of hope for himself: While he guards his house against the powerful winds, he also prepares his desk for the writing of that novel he has always dreamt about, which, convention *oblige*, is none other than *Pasado perfecto*. It is perhaps surprising that the novels in this series, which are set in such terrifying yet auspicious moments of potential cleansing and renewal, are not so much concerned about the future but about the past.[9]

Unlike Flaubert's Frédéric Moreau or Díaz's el Flaco, Mario Conde is not transformed by time and experience as mandated by the laws of the bildungsroman. On the contrary, he remains unchanged even amid the most degraded reality that he, as a policeman, has to face on a daily basis. The dignity of his character is rooted in an unbending sense of loyalty that appears formally justified through frequent intrusions of personal details in the generic conventions of the detective story. According to Tzvetan Todorov, detective fiction is built on two story lines, the story of the crime and the story of the investigation. Each, in turn, presupposes two distinct literary conventions: The story of the crime is a story of action oblivious of the book it has become, whereas the story of the investigation is a self-conscious "slow apprenticeship" (1977, 44–46). In Padura's "Las cuatro estaciones," the stories of the four investigations, which take place during the course of a very emblematic 1989, and the stories of the crimes, which happen just before the beginning of each investigation, are supplemented by a third story line. This additional narrative line returns the action to the 1970s, a time when young Mario Conde and his friends live in that glorious moment in which everything is still possible—Conde wants to become a writer comparable to Ernest Hemingway; he will always be friends with his friends; and he will love beautiful Tamara forever. In the storyline of 1989, we find Mario Conde retaining the same friends, still in love with the same woman (after decades of not seeing her), and still aspiring to write a novel "escuálida y conmovedora" (torrid and squalid) like Hemingway. In brief, Mario Conde has never really changed. As a policeman who remains a policeman in spite of his contempt for the institution—he simply cannot tolerate the idea that a criminal could literally get away with murder—he has certainly learned a great deal about the baseness of humanity, but this only seems to help him reaffirm the values of his youth. Mario Conde remains fixated in that moment of infinite possibility even after it is long gone. The best way for him to avoid choosing between dignity and prestige is to perpetually postpone the choices and disillusions that would allow him to mature both socially and affectively. This, I think, is at the heart of his immense popularity as a character: Mario Conde stands for the right to not compromise any of his ideals for any reason at any point, regardless of the social sacrifices such attitude may entail.

The true test of Mario Conde's loyalty is the test of time. Only through time can the characters truly show their unbending adherence to the ideals of their youth—which is how Conde understands integrity. His effortless capacity to conjure up the past instantaneously accounts for the distinctive texture of Padura's detective novels. The present and the past often coexist in the protagonist's mind, making the narrative adopt the double perspective of Mario Conde's nostalgia. "El Flaco que ya no es flaco" (Skinny, who's no longer skinny) is an emblematic character that embodies the visible mark of time. Like the wheelchair to which he is now relegated, due to a wound inflicted on him as a soldier in Angola, "el Flaco que ya no es flaco" is a name that encapsulates the history of someone who has been deprived of his dreams. Hence the suggestion that el Flaco's body is in itself a betrayal (1995, 99). Conde, who sees el Flaco almost daily, treats him like a brother and even acts like an adoptive son to el Flaco's mother, very much defines his own life in terms of his loyalty to his ill friend. Loyalty, originally defined as permanence in spite of dissatisfaction, does not even include dissatisfaction in Mario Conde's case. In this sense, Conde's ethical makeup can be said to be purely Aristotelian. He does not do the right thing by fighting his inclination (the Kantian view), rather he has shaped his inclination to follow virtue.

In *Pasado perfecto*, the third story line is justified insofar as it informs both the crime and the investigation. The story of the crime that inaugurates the series and gives birth to Conde as a protagonist is, at heart, an old personal matter, which I will develop in more detail later in this chapter. Consider for now, however, that the personal subtext of the third story line provides an additional layer of identity and accountability. This is probably why the first novel in the Mario Conde series, with its triple temporal structure, is suggestively built on a series of triangulations of desire and betrayal that follow in many ways those suggested by René Girard, who sees the triangle as "a systematic metaphor, systematically pursued" that aspires to make the mystery of intersubjective relations intelligible (1976, 2–3).

In what follows, I will discuss two such triangles. The first includes Rafael Morín, the promising militant who married Tamara, the love of Conde's youth. As a high school student in the '70s Conde is in love with Tamara, who ignores his silent devotion and chooses, instead, to date and eventually marry Rafael Morín, an ambitious member of the Juventud Comunista. For Conde, Morín came to embody the rival to Tamara's heart: "What always bothered you is that he fucked Tamara while you jerked off for her," el Flaco summarizes eloquently (1995, 98). In the present time of the investigation, Morín has also come to embody everything that was wrong with the revolution (i.e., the opportunism of its leaders). Sure enough, it becomes clear in the course of the investigation that Morín, who held a top position in the revolutionary government, had often used his position and traveling privileges to smuggle, steal, and betray. About to be caught, Morín tries to leave the island by boat but is killed on the eve of his escape. At the political level, Morín's disappearance offers a human explanation for the fall of socialism, at least in Eastern Europe in 1989. In Padura's narrative, the revolution is endangered because its leaders have become corrupt—it is a human error, not a structural betrayal.[10]

The fact that Rafael's fall from power and Conde's rise in Tamara's heart is negotiated, almost literally, over Tamara's body, advances the notion that their rivalry is never really about her. As René Girard explains, "the impulse toward the object is ultimately an impulse toward the mediator" (1976, 10).[11] If in the 1970s, Rafael appears as Conde's rival, in 1989 he is eliminated both physically and morally. It is significant that, even though Mario Conde may have loved Tamara for seventeen years, it is Morín he thinks about at the culmination of his love story. When he finally crosses the door to Tamara's bedroom, Conde "desires the woman as much as that Rafael Morín come in at that very moment so he can see his proverbial smile melt" (1995, 146). The degree of intimacy Conde reaches with Morín through his newly gained access to Tamara's body is highly suggestive. As Sedgwick explains, "'to cuckold' is by definition a sexual act, performed on a man, by another man" (1985, 49). She suggests that literary rivalry between two men means that "heterosexual love" appears "chiefly as a strategy of homosocial desire" by which men protect the interests of men (2). Sedgwick, who digs deeper into Girard's triangular model, suggests that "the men's heterosexual relationships . . . have as their *raison d'être* an ultimate bonding between men; and that this bonding, if successfully achieved, is not detrimental to 'masculinity' but definite of it" (50).[12]

I would like to propose a reading of Padura's loyalty from the perspective of what Sedgwick calls homosocial desire, and to argue that such desire generates the true cohesion of the community produced by the Cuban revolution. In order to elaborate upon this idea, I will first recall Jean-Luc Nancy's definition of community:

> Distinct from society (which is a simple association and division of forces and needs) and opposed to emprise (which dissolves community by submitting its peoples to its arms and to its glory), community is not only intimate communication between its members, but also is organic communion with its own essence. It is constituted not only by a fair distribution of tasks and goods, or by a happy equilibrium of forces and authorities; it is made up principally of the sharing, diffusion, or impregnation of an identity by a plurality wherein each member identifies himself only through the supplementary mediation of his identification with the living body of the community. (Nancy 1991, 9)[13]

Nancy's words stress the complexity of identity within community, and the importance of a "supplementary mediation of identification" that ultimately "seals the deal." This form of mediation, it follows, makes a community more than the sum of its members. Community resides not just in the numbers, but in the "glue" (to use Sedgwick's term) holding them together. Jean-Luc Nancy calls this "*clinamen.*"[14] In the Cuban case, along with the shared hatred for a common enemy, which sparks a necessity for the solidarity and the fraternal bond of the army, male homosocial desire is the truly invisible "glue" holding together the remnants of a highly idealistic project. This glue is actualized in every instance that manly virtues are called to order, and is therefore frequently materialized in the triangular structure of erotic relations.

In a variation of formal expectations, Padura's detective novel *Pasado perfecto* begins not with a corpse, as is customary of the genre, but with a disappearance—Morín's character, whom we never see alive in the 1989 story line, only shows up dead at the end of the story—thus the learning process entailed in the story of the investigation is merely a corroboration. These two "imperfections" are revealing at two levels—the political and the ethical. The novel begins with a query: Where is the blameless, competent, and idealistic party leader? There is a suggested continuity between Tamara's loneliness and confusion, a kind of orphanhood, and that of the revolutionary project at this point in time. Both Morín's character and the political situation seem to have degraded, whereas Conde emerges as remaining proudly unchanged. For those living in the present, however, Conde's innocence is a form of insult. A mature Tamara reproaches Conde: "Why are you so embittered? Why do you speak as if everyone else were a scoundrel and you, the most pure and humble?" (1995, 91). As Morín becomes a traitor, Conde's pride, seen as his refusal to change, proves inoperative. He can't keep Tamara, and can't write a novel. His superiority is, like Morín's, partly delusional.

It is not just that Mario Conde is loyal to his friends; he is also loyal to friendship itself. This is most evident in Padura's novel *Adiós, Hemingway* (Good-bye, Hemingway), an unexpected sequel to "Las cuatro estaciones" in which Mario Conde, now retired (he has become a self-employed bookseller), investigates a murder that took place in 1958 in Finca Vigía, Hemingway's house in Cojímar. When a big storm uncovers a corpse buried in Hemingway's garden, the detective is concerned about the writer's reputation. This case brings up intense feelings in Mario Conde, who used to admire the writer's talent and male bravado. In a suggestive scene, Conde appropriates Hemingway's masculinity, at least metaphorically, when he steals a black lace panty left by Ava Gardner in the writer's house and then used by Hemingway to wrap his .22 revolver. However, Conde's admiration for the writer has long turned sour. In fact, the mixture of admiration and contempt that Conde feels for the writer is constantly reevaluated during the course of the investigation. Given the many years that have elapsed between the crime and the investigation, it is difficult for Conde to corroborate his leads and the now private investigator has to face a choice: He can either condemn Hemingway publicly or he can honor his memory. In the end, Conde chooses to leave the case unresolved in the name of his past admiration of the American writer. This action responds to two ideals that define Mario Conde: honor and loyalty. First, Conde's decision follows the rules of honor, which dictate that one cannot fight against someone who is not an equal; Hemingway, being dead, cannot defend himself, and, therefore, is not an equal to Mario Conde.[15] Second, with this act, Conde chooses to remain loyal to his own past devotion to the American writer, not to Hemingway himself. Such attitude suggests that Conde has forgiven Hemingway at a personal level because the investigation has unearthed, along with the corpse of an FBI agent, Conde's lasting contempt for the American writer, a contempt in large measure fueled by Hemingway's disloyalty to a friend.

Beneath the fictional story of Finca Vigía lies the real story of the friendship between Hemingway and John Dos Passos, and of their friendship with José Robles, Dos Passos's Spanish translator. Robles, who fought for the Republic during the Spanish Civil War, was executed as part of what is now understood as a Stalinist purge of the Republican side. After Robles's disappearance, both Hemingway and Dos Passos, who were in Spain to work on Joris Ivens's film *The Spanish Earth*, tried to find out what had happened to Robles because nobody really knew why he had disappeared. In contrast to Dos Passos, who condemned Robles's execution, Hemingway publicly accepted the official charge of treason against Robles, probably because it better suited his own political positioning. This was perceived as an act of personal betrayal by Dos Passos, who never forgave Hemingway's unwillingness to condemn the execution. Although the novel fails to mention it, Dos Passos also perceived Robles's execution as an act of political or institutional betrayal and became disenchanted with communism as a result. Hemingway's role in the "Robles affair" is similarly viewed by Mario Conde. Hemingway's opportunism and betrayal explain Conde's aversion, evident in his efforts to "find a clue pointing to Hemingway's guilt; it would be quite appropriate if he were a lowly murderer" (2001, 39).[16]

Conde forgives Hemingway at the end of the novel, but this forgiveness is to be read as a celebration of his early admiration for the American writer, as well as a whole era, that is now gone. Conde's acceptance of Hemingway's disloyalty is possible because Conde understands personal betrayal as only secondary to the betrayal of time, in this case aging and death. The signs of decay are visible in Hemingway's most personal writing, that which records his ever-diminishing weight on his bathroom wall:

> Hemingway's real drama was written on the bathroom wall in a way that revealed the man's fears better than any of his novels, his letters or his interviews. On that wall, alone with his own body, with no other witness than time and a fateful scale, Hemingway had chronicled the proximity of his own death with numbers that were far more eloquent than any adjective. (Padura 2001, 107)

Conde interprets Hemingway's impending death as a liberation of the constraints posed by the character the American writer had invented for himself (2001, 129). Forgiveness is owed to a man whom another character, Sergio of *Memorias del subdesarrollo* (Memories of Underdevelopment), describes as "an unbearable guy." It is in this frame of mind that a forgiving Conde closes the case. Interestingly, even though Conde's generosity toward an aged, weakened Hemingway is certainly honorable, it is also suggestive of a political reconciliation with another formerly strong man—an old man who also sported a beard and that famously flirted with the American actress, and who has historically epitomized revolutionary masculinity: Fidel Castro. In this novel about long overdue accountabilities, Padura seems to suggest that it is time to let go and to move on.

The novel ends with a pilgrimage undertaken by Conde and his friends to Cojímar, Hemingway's Cuban enclave, in order to hear the story of the investigation and to commemorate their past visits to this place of shared literary nostalgia. In so doing, the friends pay homage to a specific moment in their youth in which everything was possible because nothing had yet happened. The physical and emotional journey culminates with the staging of a ceremony of acceptance. They begin by taking stock of their present situation as well as that of their lost friends—lost to exile, to death, or to betrayal and self-destruction. After accepting that their childhood friend Andrés, now living in Miami, "is indeed like us," they write a letter addressed to "Andrés, somewhere up north," in which Conde asks him to clarify who he, in turn, has or has not become. By including Andrés's life story alongside their own, they accept his exile as one of the many accidental turns of life, not as a political stance, which allows the friends to reincorporate him into the group. In the same spirit, Conde asks Andrés to embrace Hemingway in his name "if you see him down there," suggesting that exile can also be a form of death. They then insert the letter (together with Ava Gardner's fetishized underwear) into the bottle of rum they have just drunk, and, after carefully closing it, they let the bottle float freely in "an infinite sea of memory and desire" (2001, 130–135). This message to Andrés can be seen as providing a hasty closure not only to personal grudges, but also to the very spirit of the twentieth century that the Cuban revolution still conjures.

As the title suggests, *Adiós, Hemingway*, a phrase first uttered by Mario Conde as a small child, is a nostalgic farewell to a century of heroic dreams now grown stale and to a series of unforgettable betrayals that, Conde seems to believe, should now be forgotten. However, that their offering to Andrés is the Ava Gardner fetish suggests a nostalgia for a notion of masculinity that is dismissed as no longer relevant but still proves to be an infallible method to rekindle the friendship between men.

LEONARDO PADURA'S HONOR

Whereas loyalty appears to be the most prominent aspect of masculinity governing the social world presented in the Mario Conde series, Leonardo Padura's *La novela de mi vida* emphasizes the complexity of honor as a precondition of both manliness and political allegiance. Honor—defined by Mansfield as the need to defend one's turf (2006, 64)—is characterized by Leo Braudy as "an internalized code of personal behavior, whose principles partake of spiritual truth" (2003, 56). Honor, then, is a form of ethics, materialized through iterative behavior as well as through the consistent defense of values perceived as superior and shared only by a few men. Honor, which is exclusive and therefore aristocratic, has long been considered a mark of manliness. One of the structural characteristics of honor is that, in order to be actualized, it needs to be tested, and thus is potentially required to be defended by force or even war. Honor always implies courage; that is, the willingness to risk harm, for in the end "it is armed combat [or its possibility] that turns this individual honor into a social fact" (Braudy 2003, 56). As a personal value that involves the constant "policing of boundaries," to use Braudy's expression, honor is often metaphorically extended to family, land, and nation. In this sense, it often involves either giving or demanding loyalty.

As we saw at the beginning of this chapter, loyalty dilemmas are crucial to the concept of narrative-based identity because they help shape our life story and redefine its interpretation. Like loyalty, honor has the capacity to redefine the meaning of social actions, sublimating pain and transforming an apparent defeat into an act of glory. This is possible as long as an inner sense of self remains intact despite, or precisely because of, the magnitude of the difficulties it has overcome. In fact, in its efforts to ensure the proper interpretation of a person's life or actions, honor may go so far as to demand death.

Since 1959, Cuba has claimed honor as both cause and consequence of its most defining moments. It played an essential role in the success of a revolution that was made possible by the sheer justice of its cause and by the bravado of its young warriors. What seems more controversial, however, is that honor has also been invoked in justifying the Special Period. Indeed, during the crisis of the 1990s, honor effectively helped sublimate a national narrative that appears otherwise deprived of glory. The preservation of health, the most precious value during the Special Period, is in itself neither honorable nor dishonorable, for honor always entails a social supplement. Nevertheless, hunger and indignity, once incorporated into a narrative of simultaneously resisting an embargo by the most powerful of enemies and the sudden betrayal of the country's former allies, shows a resourcefulness and will on the part of the civilian population worthy of a truly heroic population. As Braudy remarks,

> The most lasting cultural mediator between the individual soldier and his social group, between violence and civility, between war and peace, is the concept of honor . . . Historically, it is the concept of honor that mediates between individual character and the pressure of outside forces, as well as between the body that wants to survive and the mind that seeks other goals, including glorious death. In terms of masculinity, the invocation of personal honor—with its links to family, tribe, and nation—gives eternal justification to an act of immediate violence. (2003, 49)

As a privileged mediator between a man's character and social and political pressures, honor helps Padura's protagonists negotiate the competition of loyalties doubly staged in *La novela de mi vida*.

The novel follows the return to Havana in 1997 of Fernando Terry, an intellectual and ex-"marielito" now residing in Madrid, in search of an autobiographical manuscript by José María Heredia, Cuba's most famous poet of the nineteenth century. In truth, Terry is looking for someone to blame for his doomed career and subsequent exile. In spite of having been called "the first non-detective story by Padura," *La novela de mi vida*, which uses the double structure of all detective novels and is, like them, animated by a search for knowledge, seeks to illuminate Terry's drama in light of Heredia's tragic life. It is not surprising that Terry's favorite films are Alfred Hitchcock's *Vertigo* and *Psycho*, two detective stories in which the crime is resolved by unmasking an impersonation. In the novel, it becomes clear that Heredia's painful exile, like Terry's, had been brought about by a denunciation. As the text suggests, Heredia's childhood friend Domingo del Monte reported the poet to the colonial authorities for his alleged participation in a seditious plot. Heredia's political sin originated in his membership in "La Logia de los Caballeros Racionales" (The Lodge of Rational Gentlemen), a lodge sponsored by Simón Bolívar that sought the independence of Cuba from Spanish rule. Although, as historians have noted, independence was quite unlikely until abolition became an acceptable option for the slave-owning *criollos*, and Heredia's participation in this lodge seems, in the novel, to have been more social than political.

The double story line in *La novela de mi vida* has a paradoxical quality. Heredia's story, which helps describe the political intransigence of the revolutionary regime as an illegitimate force corrupting all aspects of private life, also makes Terry's personal drama all but insignificant. Indeed, Heredia's alleged crime was plotting a revolution; the denunciation of his intentions took the future national poet to an exile that would achieve mythical proportions; and the traitor was Domingo del Monte, a prominent figure whose protagonism in the political and cultural life of nineteenth-century Cuba leads to the belief that betrayal may, actually, pay. Heredia's story even seems to suggest that the strong bond between del Monte and Heredia was one in which admiration and envy were not deprived of homoerotic desire. In contrast, Terry's exile and thwarted ambitions, sad as they are for him, seem petty and inconsequential, for his crime merely consisted of knowing of a deceased friend's desire to escape, and no one had really denounced him; he fell into a trap and denounced himself. Terry's experience is all the more banal given that he brought such fate onto himself by mere stupidity or, worse, by his gender misconceptions. In the course of his investigation, Terry learns that he may have actually denounced himself because he thought Enrique, who was gay, had turned him in. It just seemed to Terry at the time that such a dishonorable act would not have been unnatural to a gay man. What is more, much to Terry's shame, his exile is not particularly uncomfortable: His life as a teacher in Madrid is far better than that of his family and his poet friends (the "Socarrones") who stayed on the island, many of whom try to support themselves by selling their first editions of treasured local novels to foreign intellectuals. Unlike Heredia's, Terry's exile has neither made history nor literature.

Whereas writing in Heredia's time is powerful and rich, there is almost no production of literature in the present story line. Not many Socarrones write in 1997, including Terry. Even those who have achieved some literary fame are inherently compromised by their allegiance to the state to the point at which their writing—which is never represented—is a source of suspicion. The only finished manuscript that promises "to speak truth to power" is Enrique's. Enrique, the gay friend now dead, completed *La tragicomedia cubana*, a text that remains buried in Terry's chest of nostalgia with no hopes of publication.

Although this novel is structured like a detective story, the real crimes it narrates can best be described as violations of an honor code. These crimes include a friend turning in another friend in the 1800s; the possibility of blackmail in the 1930s, which appears as the probable cause for the vanishing of Heredia's text; and an apparent denunciation in the 1970s. The plots are such, however, that the cause of dishonor can be safely traced to a specific villain only in the story lines that take place in the distant past. In the present, by contrast, obscure circumstances create dishonorable situations. Impersonal either by accident or by nature, these offenses cannot be properly avenged. Terry is therefore left with the urge to defend his wounded honor, but with no one to fight against. It is not surprising, then, that he finds himself morally, artistically, and politically maimed.

In the context of the main argument developed in this book, I see that Padura's text illustrates two vital points about the literary production during the Special Period. First, I find that the stillness of the second story line vividly attests to the devastating effects of the appropriation of personal ethics by the revolutionary state. This is largely due to the fact that although the post-Soviet social contract sought to mobilize the same principles and virtues of the 1960s, its specific conditions, which included severe scarcity and political staleness, make the empty promise of state-sponsored safety in exchange for civic freedoms a simulacrum of a social contract. In its 1990s incarnation, the revolution cannot hide that its ethical foundation is severely degraded. Honor is seriously compromised when the main goal of the state is the protection of its political class. We could even go as far as Braudy and state that "when honor becomes separated from personal integrity, it becomes not an aspect of identity but a commodity" (2003, 53).

The idea of honor as a commodified value informs my second point. I would like to suggest that, even though Padura's text reveals how the antagonistic structure of honor helps generate both artistic and political legitimacy in the past, this is not the case in the present. The specular relation between state power and intellectual activity in the present obtains in the manner in which the moral and even the artistic superiority of the young intellectual is confirmed by the challenges posed to it by the state, not by the works he creates. In this way, we see that Terry's claim to artistic creation has been replaced by a life devoted to the administration of a tainted honor that cannot be restored. What is much worse, his life only has meaning in view of this sacrifice. In other words, Terry's honor has been soiled not only by false accusations prompted by corrupt state agents, but mostly by a revolution that has commodified its own. This is a degree of debasement that Terry, as the opponent of an unworthy enemy, cannot escape.

In the end, *La novela de mi vida* cannot be read without keeping this faulty, vampiric economy in mind. For, as Braudy notes regarding commodified honor, "like anything else in a commercial society, it is part of a world in which there is only a limited amount, and the only way to gain your own is take it away from someone else" (2003, 53–54). The novel's implicit, yet significant, intervention in the politics of power resides in its representation of the irrelevance of Terry's life—his broken friendships, his thwarted writing, his invisible exile, and his loneliness—which is there only to prove that, in order to perpetuate its honor and maintain irrational loyalty, the dictatorial regime must create its own crimes.

ABEL PRIETO'S STOICISM

In October 2000 Abel Prieto, the long-haired, middle-aged Cuban Minister of Culture, publishes his first novel, *El vuelo del gato*, in Spain. The story follows a group of friends from the early 1960s to New Year's Eve 1999. It is narrated by a minor character, one of the friends surrounding an unlikely pair formed by charming and carefree Freddy Mamoncillo and stoic and somber Marcus Aurelius Escobedo, a.k.a. "El Pequeño." That the all-male gang loves to listen to the banned Beatles would hardly be worth mentioning—after all, all the *piñas* discussed so far obsessively listen to smuggled copies of the legendary band—if it weren't for their distinctive preference for John Lennon, whom they consider the true soul of the group, over a sentimental Paul McCartney. In high school, the friends have acquired some fame thanks to their complex disquisitions not only about the better Beatle, but also about the philosophical implications of playing chess Cuban style (i.e., surrounded by commentators and jokesters as in domino games), about Cuban Laughter and Cuban Guilt, and about the true ideology behind students' passionate adoption of 1960s fashion (is it frivolity, philosophy, or a truly dialectical synthesis of form and content?). Their passion for sophisticated discussions about local social practices—what we could call, after Roland Barthes, "Cuban Mythologies"—makes Prieto's characters enlightened cultural critics of their own time. In contrast, the nostalgic groups of friends in the other novels sound sentimental, even elegiac, to a point of critical paralysis. There is no doubt that Prieto's characters appear to both readers and fictional peers as hard-core intellectuals, mainly thanks to Marcus Aurelius, who was named after the philosopher emperor whom he emulates both intellectually and ethically.

Two female characters accompany the friends throughout the forty-year span. However, they only acquire protagonism in the 1990s reincarnation of the gang. One is Lourdes, crowned beauty queen of "el Pre de Marianao" in 1964, who, thanks to her unsuccessful obsession with looking young and with rekindling the group's affective cohesion of the early days, has become a parody of her old self in ways that evoke, not without irony, the ungraceful aging of revolutionary slogans. The other is Amarilis, a very thin and silent woman who had rarely called any attention to herself in the early days, but ends the novel occupying both Freddy's and Marcus Aurelius's beds as wife and lover, respectively. The last night of the year 1999—or of the millennium, or of the fourth decade of the revolution, depending on how you are counting—finds Amarilis living in a comfortable *ménage à trois* and, most importantly, about to give birth to a multiply-fathered child (or children) of the future. This could be construed as a "dishonorable" end for Freddy when seen from the perspective of the manly values cherished in the other novels I have been mapping here, novels that would fall more squarely within the post-Soviet, modernist impulse that James Buckwalter-Arias has called "New *Origenismo*." It could also be seen merely as another instance of the male-male reproduction fantasy destined to reaffirm a perfect homosocial world. However, the erotic triangle in Prieto's novel is resolved in truly innovative and productive ways, as it trades potential rivalry for cooperation, discards fixed notions of masculinity, and underscores the allegorical weight of a yet unthinkable futurity. For the child of the new millennium is expected to follow the logic of "the flying cat" offered by José Lezama Lima in the poem "Universalidad del roce" (Universality of Contact) that lends the novel its title, and which suggests the magic potential of unexpected combinations:

> The cat copulating with the sable
> begets neither a cat
> of Shakespearean and starry fur,
> nor a sable with fluorescent eyes.
> They beget the flying cat.[17]

Before I discuss what Lezama Lima's metaphor of the "flying cat" means to *El vuelo del gato*, as well as to the topic of manly virtues more generally, I will briefly discuss the allegorical structure of the novel.

In terms of genre, the novel subscribes to the metaphorical impetus of Lezama Lima's fantastic hybrid. Technically an allegory, the novel includes elements of fable, emblem-book, and even myth. Each chapter opens with the description of an imaginary frieze presenting the characters in emblematic moments of their lives. The use of this technique is simultaneously ludic and didactic. Three aspects of the novels contribute to this dimension: the symbolism of the frieze, Marcus Aurelius's cultural analyses, and the use of capital letters to elevate common nouns to the status of abstract concepts—for instance, the Special Period, defined in the text as "the profound ethical and cultural crisis that invaded everything during the 1990s" (Prieto 2000, 293) is called La Cosa. These narrative strategies dignify the characters by calling attention to their dimension as archetypes whose conflicts respond to the fateful logic of classical mythology. With his humorous use of allegory, Prieto elaborates a complex discussion about friendship and ethics through the different stages of revolutionary society, a society that, like the "flying cat," is an unexpected combination of popular, national, and international forces in the economic, political, ideological, and ethical spheres.

The chapter "Our Fable," gives an interesting overview of the strongly ethical impulse of the early revolutionary years. However, by telling this story from the perspective of the Escobedo family, it suggests that what can be recognized as revolutionary ethics in fact predates revolutionary politics. In this chapter, the reader finds out that Marcus Aurelius got both his name and his Stoic education from his father. Serafín Escobedo, a fervent admirer of the Roman emperor, was unhappily married to Marcus Aurelius's mother, a woman who loved to acquire Things and to cultivate in all possible ways the "Fictitious Life." Her character is reminiscent of pre-Castro Cuba and its Americanized values—values that will be periodically revivified during visits with her family in Miami in the 1990s. Their personal differences, however, were taken over by politics. The war between Marcus Aurelius's parents, which began in the late 1950s, was settled when Marcus Aurelius's younger brother was born, and with him,

> a forceful revolution that, like a hurricane, went through the True and the Fictitious Lives of all Cubans. Enlightened, Serafín Escobedo came out to the streets and joined that storm of transformation and foundation with unusual fervor. After that, the war between Serafín and his wife became political. (2000, 30)

Indeed, "that storm of transformation and foundation" ("aquella tormenta de trastocamiento y fundación" in the original) can be seen as an instance of what Badiou calls an "event" which, by breaking with the ideological and interpretive tools of the past, would initiate a totally new truth-process. However, the idea that Serafín joins this truth-process is misleading, for, even though he becomes the loyal bearer of the new truth, we realize that, in fact, it is the political process that joined *him*. Nonetheless, the similarities between them justify the strategic displacement of Marcus Aurelius's mother's original anger against her husband to the much more powerful new government. Revolutionary items such as "la Libreta de Abastecimiento" were, in fact, a call for virtues like austerity and self-control that had been insistently promoted by Marcus Aurelius's father. It is part coincidence that Serafín Escobedo's admiration for Stoicism aligns him with the ethics and the politics of a revolution that promised the harmonic marriage between the two. However, if revolutionary ethics existed before the revolution, it could also exist outside it. This view decouples what used to be seen as one of the main achievements of revolutionary ideology.

In his own learning process over the forty-year textual span, Marcus Aurelius Escobedo's commitment to Stoic ethics overtly transcends any political stance. Although open political criticism is conveniently left out of Marcus Aurelius's famous speeches, it is the image of the "flying cat" that best illustrates an unhappy political association. One can see the friends' obsession with the horrible child that their friend Angelito *el Chino* had with a Russian woman from Novosibirsk as a suggestive comment on the political and cultural experiment that was Soviet Cuba. Angelito's daughter, nicknamed "la rusita," a high-pitched, blonde *mulatta* with toad-like features, points to the only Caribbean *métissage*—"a species ignored until today" (2000, 225)—that produced scary results. Genetic lotteries are never predictable and, it turns out, not always desirable.

Marcus Aurelius, too, has a physical defect. He suffers from strabismus. This condition is the physical manifestation of his philosophical commitment. His lazy eye allows him, at least metaphorically, to better gauge the distance between surface and truth. It is only partly ironic that this tale of revolutionary accountability presents history through Marcus Aurelius's eyes. In truth, for El Pequeño, the revolution didn't go far enough—didn't succeed—because it mainly focused on the surface of things. Contrary to others in his generation, Marcus Aurelius regards the official attacks against "la Moda-Lennon, el Mensaje-Lennon y sus derivados" during his university years as the manifestations of a false ideological avant-garde:

> No effort was spared in their attempts to Cubanize the cosmopolitans, to humiliate the proud, to proletarize the intellectuals, to toughen up the softies. Or else, they would all be banished from the Pure Revolutionary University, from the University of the Future that was being built from the present. By then, Little Marcus Aurelius had already drawn his own conclusions: that was not a real ideological vanguard, and their meetings could hardly be called "radicalization," given that they rarely sought to reach the root of any problem. They merely occupied themselves with the branches and invested all their strength on the external. (2000, 204)

Instead, Marcus Aurelius dreams of the "Superior University," which would cultivate stoic indifference to the material world in order to progress ethically, ideologically, and spiritually. In an environment that cultivated the true virtues, the revolution would bring the young into "the Collective Soul of a New University Community," that is, to a deeply innovative community of learning that would be free from vanity and empty slogans (2000, 205). It attests to the perhaps excessively high idealism of Marcus Aurelius's vision that this, one of his most famous speeches, becomes known by both friends and foes as "el discurso de la Paja Estoica" (The Stoic Masturbation Speech).

It may not be surprising that a novel so deeply invested in the potentialities of the hybrid consistently operates on the basis of contrasting opposites. Stoic Marcus Aurelius's best friend, Freddy Mamoncillo, is a voluptuous and generous Epicurian who doubly militates in the "Party of Decadence" and in the Communist party. He loves to acquire things, to throw parties, and to help out friends and family in need, which he is able to do thanks to a successful career in the Ministry of Interior Commerce (MINCIN). Freddy is the product of the not-so-unlikely combination of an Afro-Cuban father and a white mother who is a devoted follower of Allan Kardec, a nineteenth-century French teacher who believed in spiritism, reincarnation, and the notion that the visible and the invisible worlds feed off each other. Freddy inherited in part his father's dignity, self-sufficiency, and poise. He also learned a vampiric notion of life cycles and social bonds from his Kardecist mother. The notion that for someone to gain something another has to lose something makes Freddy surprisingly comfortable with inequalities in life. The 1990s find Freddy as a "rich" man, dedicated to business deals with foreign countries, traveling abroad, and bringing all sorts of novel items to Cuba, such as a VCR. Even though he is a convinced militant of the Fictitious Life, Freddy's heartfelt generosity makes him a worthy citizen in Marcus Aurelius's view of the True Life.[18]

Marcus Aurelius never gives up the ideals of the 1960s. However, he does not believe that such ethical society can only be actualized through revolutionary politics. On the contrary, he is the character best prepared to see the revolutionary union of ethics and politics as momentary and even opportunistic. In turn, Freddy seems to understand that survival is accomplished by an attitude that he calls "estar en la viva," which means to be alert but also to be opportunistic, and which is amply compensated for by his generosity. The utilitarianism of the 1990s is not demonized in Prieto's novel, which is why, when Freddy invites a homeless Marcus Aurelius to move to his house so that el Pequeño may better admire his economic success, he also truly wants his unlucky friend to live a better life.

Alluding to the allegorical texture of the novel, Rafael Rojas states in *Tumbas sin sosiego* (Restless Tombs) that,

> Rather than a decade, the Nineties in this novel is a metaphysical character that attests to the decadence of revolutionary values. Whereas the Sixties were the domain of Little Marcus Aurelius, archetype of austerity, spiritualism and culture, the Nineties belong to "Freddy Mamoncillo," paradigm of frivolity, selfishness and joy. With or without nostalgia, contemporary Cuban narrative witnesses a gigantic social mutation in which the figure of the communist comrade is dissolved into many fragmented communities. (2006, 370)

Rojas interprets the two protagonists as allegories of the two most defining moments of revolutionary history. Although I would also add Lourdes's personal trajectory into the mix, I generally agree with Rafael Rojas's view: This novel attests to the profound social mutation of the post-Soviet era, like Padura's *La neblina del ayer* (The Mist of the Past) and many others.

However, I would argue that this mutation is more far reaching than Rojas actually states. Ending the novel with the mythical reproduction of Freddy and Marcus Aurelius through Amarilis turns betrayal into hope. The novel, I believe, advocates for creating a society less grand and more inclusive, one that would bring together the best of both worlds, that would soften the sharp ends of both ideology *and* ethics, and that would be overall more forgiving. This view can be seen as a hybrid of two philosophical views of friendship as politics.

Prieto's protagonists adapt classical ethics to the Cuban context by embodying two forms of friendship that occupy important allegorical positions. In his book *Politics as Friendship*, Horst Hutter suggests that Stoic and Epicurean theories of friendship follow Aristotelian principles, which they adapt to their own respective core beliefs. On the one hand, the Stoics' notion of *philia* appears as deprived of affect, it is guided exclusively by reason, and is extended to all human kind—a form of *philanthropia* that makes true and exclusive friendships immoral. For Stoics, *philia* is not an ethos but what Horst Hutter describes as a "disposition of character which is motivated by insight and virtue based on right reason" (1978, 127). However, the Epicureans have a notion of friendship that is both private (it is not connected to politics) and utilitarian given that "friendship is indispensable to a happy life" (117). In the utilitarian cosmovision, it is the state's responsibility to answer the need for security, whereas friendships answer the individual's need for happiness (118). In the novel, the counterpoint between these two views, friendship based on virtue versus friendship based on pleasure, enriches the intellectual world of *la piña* throughout its history—which is, following Rojas's thinking, a personal history of the lived revolution. When projected into a future, however, the result of this theoretical combination is an unknown instance of the "flying cat."

The flying cat is an image elaborated by Lezama Lima in his poem "La universalidad del roce." Lezama uses a fantastic biological reproductive imagery to envision infinite poetical combinations, resulting in what the poem endearingly calls "el nuevo monstruo," a metaphorical "new monster" that Prieto will appropriate in significant ways. Like Lezama, Prieto uses genetics as a structure of combinations that deliver unpredictability within certain coordinates.[19] The novel, however, seems more interested in what Claudia Card has described as the "unnatural lottery" of moral luck, which are in the many ways in which one may rise to the challenges of history, of which most citizens have no control, and still live "a life in accord with the virtues" (1996, 2–3). In the context of moral luck, Lezama's "new monster" becomes a poetic alternative to the "New Man," because he is a creature more free to err, but also more free to achieve a life that is happy and praiseworthy.

The plot reserves some of its twists to narrative "luck"—it helps the novel's denouement that Marcus Aurelius has lost his apartment in a divorce and has no other place to live, that he runs into Freddy the day he abandons his marriage and apartment with his very few possessions, and that once in Freddy's house he falls head over heels for Amarilis, Freddy's wife. However, it is through their choices that characters define themselves. Freddy, Marcus Aurelius, and Amarilis all seem to have consented not just to the adultery, but to an adulterated form of community. While their *ménage à trois* is an experiment in social bonding, their common procreation ("the copyright of the guilty spermatozoon" remains a mystery) advocates for a "moral *métissage*," to use Marcus Aurelius's words (2000, 290), that marries Freddy's utilitarianism to Marcus Aurelius's stoicism. The result of this marriage is, like Lezama's "flying cat," ultimately unfathomable.

In a famous "lecture" he delivers to the reunited *piña* while looking at postcards featuring a monument to the Emperor Marcus Aurelius and his son, Commodus, Little Marcus Aurelius evokes the pattern offered by Lezama Lima's poem and analyzes the value of the "flying cat" against the background of the Special Period, defined in the novel as a profoundly ethical and cultural crisis, as I noted previously. Regarding Commodus, the unworthy son of the Great Emperor, the stoic friend proposes,

> "The point isn't to criticize Commodus," he said, "but rather to understand him as a symbol of the Great Leap Backward and as a symbol of the authentic monster, of the *possible monster* (that's what he said). And, as a synthesis, (he added) we should learn something from the double crisis that can result from all that." (2000, 295; emphasis added)

As a fable, this novel is an invitation to learn of a world of possibilities brought about through narrative. Freddy's hospitality (the offering of his house and, particularly, of his wife as a shared and commonly valued possession) toward Marcus Aurelius is an invitation to rethink male virtues and male homosocial bonding at the abstract level. In the vampiric economy governing Freddy's mind, things may even out in the end. In Marcus Aurelius's cautionary tale, however, Commodus appears also as a warning against the "possible monster" that could be born in a society deprived of dreams. *El vuelo del gato* playfully suggests (although, in Marcus Aurelius's thinking, this may be more of an indictment) that ethics and politics may have more novel ways of coming to fruition than those imagined by artists in the uniform of revolutionary virtues.

THE GOOD LIFE

Frequently in the post-Soviet novel, we find "characters," themselves intellectuals, in the process of negotiating interpretations of their personal stories and often holding their friends and, indirectly, the state accountable for their fate. Part of the drama facing these characters arises from finding themselves in the rather surprising situation in which aspiring to write, to "criticize from within," to love and to befriend—what in traditional ethics would amount to aspiring to improve themselves both in their human relations and their professional expectations—seems to have the potential effect of endangering their position in the community. This human aspiration to the good life is not alien to the original revolution as a truth-process. Sure enough, the revolution was founded on the intention to create a community of equals "whose shared aim is the realization of the human good" (MacIntyre 2007, 155). However, the exact meaning of "the good" in the good life is not always clear.

As MacIntyre explains, to define what constitutes "the good" presupposes "a wide range of agreement in that community on goods and virtues" (2007, 155). As I see it, the Cuban intellectuals aligned with the revolution believed at first that they would participate in such dialogue. In other words, they assumed the revolution favored the creation of a true *polis.* The government assumed, in turn, that their moral views constituted the *raison d'être* of the revolution. Revolutionary values of equality and justice were so fundamental to their mission that they were either considered a given or they were estimated to trickle down to the less committed sector of the population, who were in any case bound by loyalty *a priori* as per the socialist social contract. From a moment that could, for the sake of convenience, be pinned down to the Padilla Affair, it became clear for the first time that there were in fact two different views at work in the task of defining those values. In other words, whereas the intellectuals understood the revolution as enabling a conversation over the good life, a conversation that they, as intellectuals, had both the right and the responsibility to lead, revolutionary government officials saw themselves as constituting an Aristotelian aristocracy (see Cooper 2005, 77); that is, as the government of those who are morally superior to the rest of the population. Such superiority had its basis on the justice of the war just fought, as much as on the heroism they showed in fighting it in the first place. Therefore, the values that the revolution rhetorically, at least, expected from the population are similar to those demanded in a heroic society. That heroic values are deeply taxing to a civil society was pondered by Sergio in the film *Memorias del subdesarrollo* when, in reference to the Cuban Missile Crisis, he points out that "this is a very high-priced dignity." In turn, Cuban philosopher Emilio Ichikawa suggests that post-revolution, a term with which he encapsulates the moral exhaustion that follows the institutionalization of all revolutions, invariably leads to the disintegration of the *polis* (2001, 66).

Hence the importance of friendship in these novels. To some degree, in both the heroic and the "political" stance, the definition of the moral good is closely related to the notion of friendship: the heroic, fraternal bond of the military, on the one hand; and the Aristotelian friendship that is at the center of the search for the good life, on the other. By the latter I mean that type of friendship that is neither inspired by mutual benefit, nor by the search for pleasure—although both may be present in some way—but by "a common allegiance to and a common pursuit of goods" (MacIntyre 2007, 156). In other words, it is the kind of friendship animated by a shared commitment to what the good is and by a desire to make it happen. It is also uncannily similar to the revolutionary project in those instances when it has come very close to achieving its own excellence. By thematizing a social bond that is so intricately related to both ethics and politics, the novels about friendship do not question the Cuban revolution from a utilitarian point of view—socialism doesn't work because not enough people benefit enough—but from an Aristotelian point of view: The revolutionary social contract has not worked because it falsely pretends that it enables the pursuit of the good life.

The friendship plot reveals that loyalty and courage are internal virtues to what constitutes excellence in art production, male friendship, and the revolutionary social contract. It is only through triangles that we come to define and actualize our loyalties, and only through rivalries that we can test both the intensity of our commitments and our courage to defend them. The transition from binomial (friendship) to triangle (rivalry) is a transition from loyalty in the abstract to the actualization of loyalty through a number of tests (what I am capable of in order to defend my friend) and then to tests of honor (what I am capable of in order to defend my turf), tests that measure courage and define manliness. Ultimately, by pitting essentialized male loyalties against one another, these novels expose the cultural traps of the revolutionary social contract, which uses the language of friendship, loyalty, and courage in order to generate its own legitimacy. At the very least, the thematization of friendship and betrayal in the post-Soviet Cuban novels analyzed in this chapter can be seen as the staging of a symbolic "withdrawal of consent"; that is, as a timid attempt on the part of the intellectuals to renegotiate on new and better terms the rules that have governed the formation of social bonds as well as the production of art for over five decades.

In this chapter, I have mapped some of the basic elements of friendship as they appear in the post-Soviet novel. Taking some of the most representative examples, I have pursued a number of triangles that define the homosocial space of male friendship in Cuban revolutionary culture. In doing this, I sought to bring to light the social bonds among men, how they become constituted, and what forms of social contracts they produce and imitate. In the next chapter, I will explore a counterintuitive but complementary course of inquiry: the possibility that perversion may, by virtue of not subscribing to the gender values of the socialist social contract, have the capacity to generate truly operative communities, even if only as a seductive metaphor.

3 Ethics after Dark

> Institutional codes can't validate these relations with multiple intensities, variable colors, imperceptible movements and changing forms. These relations short-circuit it and introduce love where there's supposed to be only law, rule, or habit.
>
> —Michel Foucault (1981, 38)

> Collectivization, sociability, indecency and promiscuity were, in Cuban socialism, ways to live the freedom of the flesh; to fill with desire the void left by the spirit of the law.
>
> —Iván de la Nuez (2001, 13)

Disidentification, defined as the "moral emancipation of the individual from his subordination to the transcendental ends of a deteriorated polis," is the process that, according to Cuban philosopher Emilio Ichikawa, best describes postrevolutionary societies (2001, 66). In an article that compares contemporary Cuba and Hellenistic Greece, Ichikawa seeks to reconfigure the moral landscape of Cuba on the basis of "self-love." Even though he notes that such a process has already taken place in many circles of Cuban society, Ichikawa is concerned that serious current discussions about a democratic future for the island are often based upon the same expectations of excessive personal sacrifice that have traditionally informed the revolutionary ethos. In suggesting that "the alternative to the totalitarian logic of the revolution is individualism, not antirevolutionary totalitarianism," Ichikawa advocates for an apparent paradox: Collective well-being will be possible only through the cultivation of self-interest. Philosophically speaking, he estimates that, following a long period dominated by the Kantian legacy of Hegel and Marx, it is David Hume and Adam Smith who can best illuminate the postrevolutionary path that will lead the individual to live closer to pleasure and happiness (2001, 66–67).

In "Cuba helenística," Ichikawa does more than explain a contemporary Cuban predicament in light of classic liberalism. Perhaps inadvertently, he is pointing to a transition in ethical thinking toward a view that, partly rooted in the culture of "self-love," is characterized by the autonomy of pleasure from moral rules. Indeed, ethics today has abandoned both its traditional prerogative of providing universal rules of conduct destined to govern interpersonal relations, and the modern expectations of individual moral responsibility towards the nation. This is why Ichikawa's championing of a society that endorses a multiplicity of allegiances, moral relativism, and individualism suggestively aligns postrevolutionary Cuba, not so much to a capitalist ethos, as with what contemporary philosophers have called postmodern ethics.

To be sure, contemporary ethics everywhere is undergoing a process that, under names like "*après-devoir*" (after-duty) or "crepuscular ethics," advocates against sacrificial values in ways similar to what Ichikawa calls disidentification. In his *Postmodern Ethics* Zygmunt Bauman postulates that "what is assumed here [that is, in contemporary ethics] is that being-for-the-Other rather than for-itself is 'contrary to nature,' and that two modalities of being are in opposition" (1993, 13). In turn, in a book entitled *Le Crépuscule du devoir* (The Twilight of Responsibility), French philosopher Gilles Lipovetsky encapsulates the current moral landscape in the phrase "we no longer recognize the obligation to join anything other than ourselves" (1992, 15). Based on the similarities between postmodern moral philosophers in capitalist societies and Ichikawa's suggestions regarding post-Soviet ("Hellenistic") Cuba, we may pose two provisional hypotheses. First, a large part of the world lives in post-utopian times. One could say that we are all "post-Soviet" in the sense that the entire world has lost the main historical alternative to capitalist hegemony (see Badiou 2007). However, we must remain aware that such notion—the suggestion we are all "post-Soviet"—can too easily overlook the considerable gap that exists between Europe or the US and Cuba in areas such as access to political representation and consumerism. Second, we may speculate that the highly educated Cuban artists produced by the art schools founded and, until 1991, funded by the Cuban revolution may be particularly well positioned to combine a postmodern aesthetic sensibility with the actual experience of the failure of utopia. While a comprehensive comparison between postmodernism in capitalist societies like the ones Bauman and Lipovetsky study and that of post-Soviet socialist Cuba is beyond the scope of the present argument, I want to suggest that contemporary discussions on postmodern ethics may provide a broader and more accurate context for exploring the social mechanisms, potential consequences, and limitations of postrevolutionary disidentification.

In their description of the current moral state of affairs, Bauman and Lipovetsky agree on a number of key issues. First, they both understand that the rise of neo-individualism does not mean amorality. On the contrary, while neo-individualism in a pluralistic society implies a larger variety of available causes, it also presupposes a more passionate adherence on the part of each individual to her selected values. Such predicament makes postmodern moral imperatives less imperative yet all the more moral because they are the result of an active personal commitment. This tendency, combined with today's political landscape in general, leads Lipovetsky to proclaim that the only utopia that is possible in the twenty-first century is of the moral kind (1992, 12). Second, both thinkers suggest that the underlying mission of postmodern ethics is to unmask the traps of modern morality, which they claim was based on an illusory idea of the common good that is "neither attainable nor, for that matter, desirable" (Bauman 1993, 3). Third, they both view moderation and tolerance as the only current "universal" values, for they guarantee not only respect for the other but also an element of self-doubt, both of which are necessary to sustain the good life. In part, the importance of moderation lies in the fact that it helps soften both the universalism of modern ethics and the philosophy of self-interest. Furthermore, it suggests that postmodern ethics may be more indebted to Aristotle than either philosopher would like to admit. We may borrow Lipovetsky's words to suggest that, in stark opposition to revolutionary modern values, postmodern ethics "does not prescribe the eradication of personal interests but its moderation, does not necessarily demand heroism and disinterestedness, but the search for reasonable compromises, of fair play and fair measures adapted to real circumstances and real people" (1992, 22). It follows that, if one of the main goals of postmodern ethics is to denounce the moral traps of utopian thinking, the Cuban revolution is today a modern utopia that has not only outlasted the validity of its utopian premises, but even outlasted its own modernity.

While, historically speaking, disenchantment can be traced to the gradual institutionalization of the Cuban revolution in the 1970s, it is more clearly understood as a 1990s process that results not only from a rejection of the violence with which some revolutionary ideals where implemented, but also from a shift within the social appreciation of some of those ideals. It is instructive in this context to consider Adorno's meditation on the corruption of ideology. He states,

> nothing is more degenerate than the kind of ethics or morality that survives in the shape of collective ideas even after the World Spirit has ceased to inhabit them—to use a Hegelian expression as a kind of shorthand. Once the state of human consciousness and the state of the social forces of production have abandoned these collective ideas, these ideas acquire repressive and violent qualities. (2000, 17)

The metaphor used by Adorno to describe the life cycle of ideas is analogous to a Christian conception of human death in which physical corruption begins when a spiritual dimension abandons its material support. Similarly, when ideas lose the faith vested in them by a social force at a given moment, they become void, empty of meaning. For Adorno, an ethics with a will to persist once its spiritual life has expired is particularly violent. It is the assumption underlying this chapter that the union of ethics and politics that was promoted by a nationalistic, heroic project such as the Cuban revolution, and which implied a strong conviction on the notion of "being-for-the-Other," to use Bauman's words, has lost its validity in face of world changes in both the political and the ethical arenas. Having lost its original spirit, the Cuban revolution has now become what Badiou would call a simulacrum of truth (for more on this concept, see Chapter 4).

Given that the ethical imprint of the revolution was from the beginning so eminently masculinist, the literature produced by women and, especially, by gay writers is a rich site for examining the validity of some of its social and philosophical premises. The new ethics that values relativism and pluralism, seeks the autonomy of pleasure from moral rules, and has as its main political agenda that of unmasking the hidden violence of universal values, is of course not entirely new. Interestingly, queer theorists have anticipated some of these ideas by finding in homosexuality a vantage point to unveil the oppressive forms in which society operates and to articulate new social forms of connectivity.

Queer theory has not only paved the way for what is now called postmodern ethics, but has also articulated forms of relationality that are both innovative and revisionist. In an interview published in a gay French magazine, Foucault invites us to consider "what relations, through homosexuality, can be established, invented, multiplied and modulated?" Because homosexuality is at the intersection of intensely private and affective, but also of social, ethical, legal, and political forces, it signifies for Foucault a space in which to actualize unexpected forms of "relational virtualities." The "slantwise" position of the homosexual has an inherent capacity to disturb "the social fabric," allowing "these virtualities to come to light" (1981, 39). As a point of departure for the ethical analyses included in this chapter, I will look at a "utopian" notion shared by Foucault, Michael Warner, Judith Butler, and Leo Bersani, among others: the understanding of homosexuality as a socially unsettling form of relationality, and as a producer of a "queer ethics," an umbrella term including what various authors have called queer, lesbian, or postmodern ethics that facilitate gender and moral disidentification.

In *The Trouble with Normal*, Michael Warner argues that "queer culture has long cultivated an alternative ethical culture that is almost never recognized by mainstream moralists as anything of the kind" (1999, viii). In a section of the book called "The Ethics of Queer Life," Warner further argues, "In those circles where queerness has been most cultivated the ground rule is that one doesn't pretend to be *above* the indignity of sex" (35). Such acknowledgment of a common humanity enhances empathy and limits the desire to control others. Like many other theorists, Warner celebrates the theoretical power of homosexuality when he states "the term 'queer' is used in a deliberately capacious way in this book, as it is in much queer theory, in order to suggest how many ways people can find themselves at odds with straight culture" (38).

While in his book *Homos* Leo Bersani protests that the term "queer" has been made to refer to political rather than erotic tendencies, he willingly admits that "the elaborating of certain erotic preferences into a 'character'—into a kind of erotically determined essence—can never be a disinterested scientific enterprise." While Bersani warns against the "restrictive and immobilizing analyses" that may encourage queerness to repeat what it set out to resist (1995, 2–3), he nonetheless celebrates the utopian nature of homosexuality suggested by its mobility within and outside subject positions: "This mobility should create a kind of community, one that can never be settled, whose membership is always shifting. It is also a community in which many straights should be able to find a place" (1995, 9). He goes as far as to challenge the notion of community itself, because queerness allows for "an anticommunal mode of connectedness we might all share, or a new way of coming together: that, and not assimilation into already constituted communities, should be the goal of any adventure in bringing out, and celebrating, 'the homo' in all of us" (10).

To be sure, there are a number of issues that divide queer theorists: Should queerness refer to something other than a sexual preference? Should it be seen as political? If so, should it be about resisting normativity or about destroying social patterns (a position that Lee Edelman argues in *No Future*)? It matters to this discussion that queer theorists have seen homosexuality as politically productive and even "utopian." Such "queer" spirit informs the ethical position of this chapter, which explores the productive force of homosexuality and other irreverent forms of sexual and textual associations, which I will group under the larger term "perversion." Indeed, perversion, which advocates for multiple, individual understandings of what is right outside both the Oedipal Complex and the Lacanian Law of the Father, is deemed by Molly Anne Rothenberg and Dennis Foster, editors of *Perversion and the Social Relation*, to be clearly anti-Kantian, for it rejects the reason of Reason in favor of acting on inclination and pleasure, a notion that has chaotic social consequences (2003, 7).

In this chapter I suggest that, by promoting values that disrupt the militarized ethos of revolutionary Cuba, perversion produces unexpected pacts of solidarity. I call queerness and other transgressive sexual behaviors "perversions" in an effort to highlight the unsettling character of unorthodox sexuality in the social fabric; that is, the capacity of homosexuality and other associations based on pleasure to transform the sign of moral values. With this suggestion, I seek to advance three notions that are relevant to my view of the socialist social contract and the role of the intellectual in post-Soviet Cuba. First, I understand that perversion facilitates the moral emancipation of the individual from a collective project that conflates ethics and ideology along gender lines. Second, it also implies the alignment of the individual with a more varied set of values, thus promising a mobile community that is temporarily and partially (yet passionately) committed to those values. And third, by encouraging both the disidentification with a collective project and the formation of alternative alliances, perversion helps the creation of an anticommunal community on the basis of jouissance.

In my reading of "pervert" texts, I will discuss the ethical values and the creative social bonds that can be reinvented through disidentification with gender and moral normativity, and which directly speak to the moral emancipation that marks the demise of a deteriorated polis. Given that "the queer of Queer Ethics," as philosopher Claudia Card claims, "encompasses many varieties of sexual heresy, not only gay and lesbian ones," I will explore various forms of "deviations" that are politically unsettling to what I have called the revolutionary socialist social contract (1995, 76). One such "deviation" is queerness, a "perversion" that is no longer one in the eyes of either psychoanalytic circles or most contemporary societies, but that still retains a metaphorical force that many theorists would rather not do without. More importantly, I will also analyze other "perversions" that have managed to keep their pathological pedigree almost intact, even in postmodern times such as promiscuity, masochism, and necrophilia.

In this chapter, I view "perversion" as a "systematic metaphor, systematically pursued" (to use René Girard's phrase) that, like what the figure of the triangle does for Girard in *Deceit, Desire and the Novel*, helps advance the narrative in the novels I study while speaking to an emergent, "inverted" ethical world with precise political ramifications in the Cuban context. In my readings of the queer novels *Cien botellas en una pared* (One Hundred Bottles) by Ena Lucía Portela, *Los palacios distantes* (Distant Palaces) by Abilio Estévez, and *Contrabando de sombras* (Smuggling Shadows) by Antonio José Ponte I refer to theories by Monique Wittig, Leo Bersani, and Brad Epps, among others. I argue that perversion allows us to formulate, articulate, advance, and even perform disidentification—and a double disidentification at that because it breaks away from both revolutionary gender and moral prerogatives—and to thereby envision, through literature, the formation of a subject that is antithetical to the social truth offered by revolutionary values.[1]

THE CIVILITY OF PERVERSION

The need for moral emancipation becomes inexorable when read against the co-optation of the language of personal ethics by official ideology. As I have been arguing in this book, the revolution in its inception radically altered the sociopolitical structures of 1950s Cuba largely thanks to its ethical component, a feature that helped it become what Badiou calls an original truth-process. The moral superiority of the revolution was defined both by what it fought (corruption, oligarchy, and imperialism) and by what it sought (equality and justice for all). In order to succeed, the new political project required from its population the manly virtues of heroism (courage and stoicism) and loyalty between men. The exchange of loyalty, courage, and stoicism for sovereignty and basic services is, in a nutshell, what I have been calling the revolutionary socialist social contract.

As I suggested in the previous chapter, when read from the perspective of community and friendship, contemporary Cuban fiction reveals that the survival of the socialist social contract in its harsher post-Soviet incarnation survives not so much due to its enduring validity as to the social value of the values it helped sublimate and which still define the revolutionary mission at a rhetorical level. The thematization of friendship and betrayal in the novels I analyze in the previous chapter suggests that the same "internal virtues" define male friendship, art production, and revolutionary ethos. I argued that the affective and ethical negotiations between intellectual protagonists staged in these novels, which reflect mimetically the social world in which the authors move, are compelling narratives of artistic and personal political co-optation. While no doubt critical, these novels betray a nostalgic adherence to a residual ideology that is modern (attached to the utopian socialist project) and manly (informed by the strict gender prerogatives of a fraternal social contract). Regardless of the explicit disenchantment shown in novels by Jesús Díaz, Leonardo Padura, and, to a lesser extent, Abel Prieto, they can be said to share both the aesthetic and ethical DNA of the revolutionary project. The writers represented in these novels can be described as "pure intellectuals" in Julien Benda's characterization (2007). Indeed, as Amauri Gutiérrez Coto explains in *Orígenes y el paraíso de la eticidad* (*Orígenes* and the Paradise of Ethics) the "pure intellectuals" in recent Cuban novels do not feel inclined toward much moral or sexual experimentation. While they do not renounce sex altogether, they consider it of secondary importance. Theirs is a new form of asceticism (Gutiérrez Coto 2010, 18). I suggest that the reason why these novels have considerable difficulty unmasking the strategic coupling of ethics and ideology, which sustains the revolution even as it loses some of its original force, is that they operate within the same framework of "manly virtues" of the revolutionary project. Thus, they are unable to envision a social imaginary that is not contained within the truth-process initiated in 1959.

By contrast, the novels I explore in this chapter base their aesthetic force and ethical creativity on the cultivation of various forms of sexual and formal "perversions" that allow postmodern and/or queer authors to analyze the social conditions and structural values of revolutionary masculinity as well as to suggest emerging models of civil society. While deliberately ironic, my use of the term "perversion" derives from its traditional definition. According to the Oxford English Dictionary (OED), "perversion" refers to a "sexual behaviour or preference that is different from the norm; that which is considered to be unacceptable or socially threatening, or to constitute a mental illness," a definition that has traditionally included, but is by no means limited to, homosexuality. I consider the aspects of "different from the norm" and "socially threatening" as ethically productive forces following the lead of the queer critics discussed earlier in the chapter. Interestingly, "perversion" also extends into other stubborn transgressive behaviors, such as "the action of turning aside from what is true or right; the diversion of something from its original and proper course, state, or meaning; corruption, distortion" (OED); an example of such deviation would be the notion of "perversions of justice." Notably, a brand of *formal* perversion already occupies a central place in Cuban letters. Indeed, when understood as a diversion from an original course, perversion constitutes one of the defining characteristics of Caribbeanness for Neo-Baroque aesthetics, according to which European scientific instruments, philosophical ideas, and notions of decorum "naturally" lose their original signification when entering the tropical waters of the Caribbean Sea.

Even more interesting is the fact that "co-optation" also means a diversion from an original course or function. The similarities between the meaning of "to pervert" and "to co-opt" facilitates the "magical inversion"—to use Žižek's term—that operates between the "perverted" ethics I analyze in this chapter in contrast with the "co-opted" virtues I study in the previous one. For Žižek, "magical inversion" is "a fundamental operation" mobilized when the intervention of a supplementary negative emotion "momentarily changes" earlier negative emotions "into their opposite, . . . turn[ing] chaos into a 'new harmony' and suddenly mak[ing] 'comprehensible' what was up to then a meaningless and even terrifying disturbance" (1991, 29).[2] We can say that a form of magical inversion is put in motion by the harsher demands of the Special Period, which changed the terms of the socialist social contract. Following the dissolution of the Council for Mutual Economic Assistance (CMEA) led by the Soviet Union, the state was no longer able to provide basic services and only nominally guaranteed sovereignty. At the same time, the current conditions push the demands for loyalty, stoicism, and the heroism of the revolution to nearly impossible limits. By casting a shadow of suspicion on revolutionary virtues, the post-Soviet social contract turns old negatives—homosexuality and perversion, formerly viewed as foreign and ideologically corrupt—into new positives. I doubly invoke Foucault and Žižek, then, to suggest that in today's Cuban novel moral virtue facilitates political co-optation whereas perversion often leads to the invention, multiplication, and modulation of civic virtues.

In one way or another, contemporary Cuban literature has long reflected the values and gender myths of a society that, politically speaking, is dominated by the idea of "war as a permanent social relation," to borrow Abel Sierra Madero's words (2006, 16). This refers to the fact that Cuba has waged an ongoing war—occasionally real but mostly symbolic—against foreign domination, a war that is exacerbated with the advent of the revolution. Immersed in such premise since its inception, Cuban nationalism has demanded a virile population, creating what Sierra Madero has called a "homophobic *habitus*" (2006, 243). This can be defined, adapting Pierre Bourdieu's idea to the Cuban context, as a social law that, materialized in everyday practices, pays homage to the virtues of honor and courage. This *habitus*, which has been inherent to the construction of the Cuban nation, has culminated in the cult of the virtues of masculinity by revolutionary society. It is this structural homophobia that leads Emilio Bejel "to conclude that Cuban nationalism is an abomination" (2001, xxiv).[3]

In his article "Proper Conduct: Reinaldo Arenas, Fidel Castro, and the Politics of Homosexuality" Brad Epps aptly illustrates the degrading status of homosexuality vis-à-vis the community spirit of the Cuban socialist project:

> Since, in theory, the "natural function" of the phallus is that of active penetration, any man that is penetrated assumes an "unnatural" position . . . Even though he possesses a phallus, he abdicates not only this capacity but also the symbolic power associated with it. Interestingly, . . . when the revolution demands from a man his submission to a collective mission—that is, to sacrifice his own ego for an ideal one—this is understood as neither the material nor the psychological subjection of one man to another. While political subjection is seen in terms of strength (I subject part of myself in order to become part of a more powerful entity), sexual subjection is understood in terms of weakness, degradation and abjection (I subject myself to someone who is stronger than me) . . . The man who "is taken" by another man is left with an indelible mark; he will forever be known for his inferior, subordinate, negative and weak position in society. (1995, 233–234)

In this passage, Epps reveals an uncanny analogy between the subjection to the common good that is expected in socialism and the subjection of a man to another in the sexual act. He notes, however, that while the Revolution's demand of individual subjection to a collective will is seen as a means to achieve greater collective moral and physical strength, it still sees sexual "subjection" as an unequivocal sign of civic weakness and moral degradation. In his analysis of Arenas's *Antes que anochezca* (Before Night Falls), Epps anticipates three notions that I expect to advance in my readings of "perversion" in contemporary Cuban literature, which I will call anti-honor, the politics of pleasure, and anticommunal community. As a result of the "magical inversion" that has taken place since post-Soviet economic and political hardships changed the moral sign of virtues and sins, notions of honor, stoicism, and community have lost their luster. In what follows, I will develop in more detail these three categories that I believe to be crucial to an understanding of the role played by perversion in the process of disidentification.

Anti-honor. The most forceful of Epps's ideas is the view of homosexuality as the abdication of political power, a notion that was also developed by Leo Bersani, albeit in a different context. In an essay on AIDS entitled "Is the Rectum a Grave?" (I discuss this article in more detail below) Bersani can be said to further Epps's statement regarding the intimate connection between sex, politics, and honor when he states that "the self is a practical convenience; promoted to the status of an ethical ideal, it is a sanction for violence" (1988, 222). In light of Epps's and Bersani's discussions, I would like to propose that we see queerness as a form of relationality that defines itself against the view of "war as a permanent social relation." What is more, queerness disrupts the cult of virility not only by "feminizing" society but, most importantly, by desecrating the notion of honor—the self "promoted to the status of an ethical ideal"—that justifies violence in order to protect a sublimated conception of self. By weakening the masculine imperative of "pursuing glory and distinction in the public sphere," to borrow Bourdieu's words, queerness changes the rules of the political game. I understand that, in post-Soviet Cuba, literary queerness exalts the virtues not so much of "negative honour," seen as feminine honor and which can only be lost, but as "anti-honor," a term that speaks of honor that could be gained but is deliberately rejected.[4]

The Politics of Pleasure. By suggesting that sex between men disarticulates paradoxical assumptions regarding virility and compliance dear to the revolutionary project, Epps can be said to allude to "enjoyment as a political factor," a notion more explicitly elaborated by Žižek in *For They Know Not What They Do: Enjoyment as a Political Factor*, a book intended to supplement his earlier *The Sublime Object of Ideology* (1989) with a new, post-Soviet understanding of ideology and politics. Žižek, who combines Lacanian psychoanalysis and Hegelian dialectics to study the status of the Left today, is concerned with "the status of enjoyment in ideological discourse" (1991, 3), and proposes that "*pleasure*" is an "uncanny excess" that speaks to the "hidden truths" and the "short circuits" that operate between duty and desire in social and political life (239; emphasis in the original). Using the concept of "magical inversion" I mentioned earlier, Žižek seeks to understand how ideological stances can be seen as pathologies related to sexual enjoyment.

Žižek asserts that perversion "implies its own ethical attitude." Under this injunction, he discusses current "pathological" attitudes toward the Left. In this context, the post-Soviet Cuban political situation can be described in terms of what Žižek calls "the Narcissism of a Lost Cause." This is most evident in the novels I discussed in the previous chapter, which show nostalgia for both the ethical promise of the political project and of the real possibilities of male intellectuals to take an active role in it. Žižek's pathologies include the obsessive desire to sacrifice oneself for the Other that becomes explicit in "the Stalinist pervert position of an instrument serving the enjoyment of the big Other of History" (1991, 271–272); a sacrificial view of the self that is suggested by Epps and is most visible in the figure of Trotsky's assassin, Ramón Mercader, explored in all its Cuban resonances by Padura in his novel *El hombre que amaba a los perros* (The Man who Loved Dogs; 2009).

Ultimately, these two pathologies (narcissism and extreme self-sacrifice) participate in "the ethical compulsion which compels us to mark repeatedly the memory of a lost Cause" (Žižek 1991, 272); that is, to revisit history as a trauma that results from the distinction between the ideal of the socialist revolution and its reality, constituted as either a human or a philosophical betrayal. True to his premise, Žižek finishes the book with an instigation against the drive to revisit, again and again, the lost Thing, which in this case is the moral betrayal of the revolutionary social contract. Instead, Žižek finds in enjoyment, not sacrifice, a more worthy ethical position:

> The point is *not* to remember the past trauma as exactly as possible: such "documentation" is a priori false, it transforms the trauma into a neutral, objective fact, whereas the essence of the trauma is precisely that it is too horrible to be remembered, to be integrated into our symbolic universe. All we have to do is to mark repeatedly the trauma as such, in its very "impossibility," in its non-integrated horror, by means of some "empty" symbolic gesture. (1991, 272)

Žižek urges us to look into pleasure as "an 'empty' symbolic gesture" that fails, *a priori*, to reconstruct and absorb the "reality" of the trauma. Because enjoyment, "far from confining the Left within a nostalgic infatuation with the past, is the only possibility for attaining a distance on the present, a distance which will enable us to discern signs of the New" (1991, 273). Enjoyment as a political factor is Žižek's anti-Kantian proposal.[5]

Anticommunal Community. In his comparison of the physical homosexual act with the metaphorical possession of a self by a sublimated ideal, Epps alludes to a paradox implicit in the apparent similarities between communism and community, similarities that help lubricate what Žižek calls the sacrificial stance of the Left. Žižek undoes this paradox by posing sexual pleasure as the negative of a useless sacrifice—therefore as a new positive. As Bersani notes, homosexuality and, by extension, perversion is always already an "anticommunal mode of connectedness"; that is, a form of relationality that aspires to building temporary communities that are unthinkable within the normative side of "community" (1995, 10).

Foucault endorses a similar stance when he states that "homosexuality is not a form of desire but something desirable" because of its capacity to modulate a multiplicity of relations outside institutional patterns of sociability (1981, 38). Foucault's "friendship" is a creative force behind uncharted relationalities. Foucault insists that to speak about friendship in relation to homosexuality is to address a lifestyle beyond the sexual act. For sure, he defines friendship as "the sum of all the things that two men can do to make each other happy," but this goes beyond immediate pleasure, as he seems to be more concerned with what happens "when men share meals, beds, concerns, knowledge and secrets" (38); a relationship that is "neither the purely sexual encounter nor the loving fusion of two identities" (39). *Intimacies*, a book of essays written by Leo Bersani and Adam Philips—an essayistic dialogue in which authorial authority can be said to be itself promiscuous, devious, and "deformed"—takes the vision of promiscuity even further by discussing homosexual multiple relationalities as a utopian society: "A wonderful world, where everyone has been to bed with everyone else, is a world where no one is interested in penetrating—invading and possessing—anyone else's desire" (2008, 41).[6]

What I would like to call the civility of perversion depends on how we stylize—situate, produce, or shape—ourselves as ethical subjects. For Foucault, morality is more than a code of conduct. By ascribing to a set of prohibitions, values, and rules, the subject positions itself in relation to a particular social truth. A person defines herself as ethical subject in relation to some "technologies of the self," which Foucault considers a form of *ascesis*, that yield specific identity practices (1990, 28–29). When seen in the context of Foucault's technologies of the self, disidentification from a collective moral project would imply the exploration of nontraditional practices, so as to position oneself as an ethical subject in relation to an emergent social truth (what Raymond Williams calls "a structure of feeling"). If the social truth established by the revolutionary project is heroic and supports its sublimated self on a view of the socialist social contract, which appears structured *as if it were* a (voluntary, altruistic, fraternal, and therefore male) friendship, the ethical subject that seeks emancipation from the collective moral project will define herself against heroism, altruism, and occasionally even friendship to explore unexpected forms of community in nonconventional gender and ethical structures.[7]

ENA LUCÍA PORTELA'S MASOCHISM

Writing against the "straight mind," Monique Wittig, one of the founders of the *Mouvement de Libération des Femmes*, notes that the social contract is something that exists regardless of the fact that no one enters it actively. For Aristotle, says Wittig, "society was a 'combination,' an 'association,' a 'coming together,' it was not a voluntary association" (1992, 37). It happened by force, the force of being governed by those men that were more intelligent and morally superior. We are born into a social contract, Wittig claims, and it is always already male and heterosexual. This explains why Wittig sees women in general, and lesbians in particular, as able to undo the social contract exclusively through symbolic acts of marooning. She argues that women can only "achieve the social contract (that is, a new one)," if they do it "like fugitive serfs," by escaping "one by one" (45). I understand Wittig's notion of marooning from a male-dominated polis as acts of sexual and ethical disidentification. Befitting the political imaginary of the 1960s, an imaginary that was largely dominated by the Cuban revolution, Wittig advances the notion of female marooning in a 1969 utopian novel titled *Les Guérrillères*, a novel in which a group of Amazons conquer the polis and take the social order into their own hands.

Given the masculinist tendencies of the Cuban revolutionary army, it is not without a sense of irony that we can consider Ena Lucía Portela's *Cien botellas en una pared* as portraying a world of *guérrillères*. Z, the protagonist, and her woman friends form a closely knit community of social maroons. La Gofia and Mari la Roja, who frequently host lesbian parties that shock "el jefe de sector," have turned their apartment into "a permissive space where one could freely express those feelings and desires that are repressed elsewhere; a place where one can meet other women and maybe find a partner. An island within the island" (2002, 189). Z and her friends, who never condemn any type of behavior as long as it doesn't hurt anyone else, are committed to protecting the vulnerable, the weird, and the rejected. In many parts of the world, they would be considered ordinary members of what Lipovetsky calls the "after duty" (*après devoir*) generation. However, their personal ethical stance becomes political in post-Soviet Cuba. For, while refusing the Communist mandate of "being-for-the-Other," Portela's female characters do not hesitate to share their houses and usually meager resources to protect another woman or a gay friend in need. They uphold a selective yet intense sense of solidarity at the margins of the polis. Indeed, *Cien botellas* is about what happens to the revolutionary social contract when women who are bonded by what Janice G. Raymond, partly quoting Adrienne Rich, calls a "passionate friendship" (that is, an intense friendship between women, either lesbian or heterosexual, who share "a rich inner life, the bonding against male tyranny, the giving and receiving of practical and political support"[8]), live their own version of "the good life" as fugitives of the fraternal social contract undergirding revolutionary politics.

In Portela's novel, the male polis is surreptitiously conquered through one of the perversions most likely to be attributed to women: masochism. Žižek, who defines masochism as "radical self-degradation," explains that deriving a surplus of pleasure from being subjected to a sadistic form of domination "is the necessary first step toward liberation" (2003, 118). This is partly due to the fact that masochism is a privileged vehicle for empathy, as degradation affords "genuine contact" with the "suffering other." In a surprising appropriation of Frantz Fanon, Žižek speculates that, when seeing masochism "not as opposed to work, but, precisely, as the ultimate political version of the 'work of the negative,' of the Hegelian process of *Bildung*, of the educational self-formation, then violence should primarily be conceived as self-violence, as a violent reformation of the very substance of subject's being" (119). In my reading of *Cien botellas*, I will focus on masochism as a "work of the negative" which, by altering the rules of self-formation, produces the "violent reformation" of the revolutionary subject. More precisely, I will see symbolic "self-violence" as a strategy that creates a disavowed community built around female solidarity and justice. Concretely, I suggest that *Cien botellas* is a "pervert" text because it deviates from revolutionary notions of altruism, heroism, and honor, opting instead for civil and ethical corruption. Marooning as it takes place in this novel helps create a freer and fairer society, and does it, in part, by reformulating the rules of engagement of three traditional genres: the "noir" novel, the bildungsroman, and the confession.[9]

The novel follows the protagonist, Z, a heterosexual woman living alone in an old apartment in a noisy *solar* who, at the end of the novel, moves in with her best friend, Linda Roth. Linda is a former classmate who is now a famous lesbian writer of detective stories, which feed off the reality neglected by both the police and the official press. Z's gay father has emigrated to the US, leaving Z under the care of a Jesuit priest with remarkable moral flexibility and in treatment with a psychiatrist, Dr. Frumento. As far as the novel is concerned, these two men exist outside sexuality, the first due to his calling as a priest and the other by virtue of what Bersani and Adam Philips describe as the Platonic ideal of psychoanalysis—"Psychoanalysis," they note, "is about what two people can say to each other if they agree not to have sex" (2008, 1). The priest and the psychoanalyst are two characters who search for truth in ways that stand apart from, but are related to, the methods used in a detective story insofar as they operate as fictional readers whose practice gives narrative access to Z's actions and motives.

Key to my reading is the empathetic self-portrait established by the protagonist. Z, who survives thanks to her father's *remesas* (remittance) and other obscure *bisnecitos* (clandestine financial transactions) performed here and there, tries *jineterismo* (informal prostitution) but fails partly because she is white and overweight, but mostly because she likes good sex, defined unequivocally as Cuban sex, and is unable to pretend satisfaction with a tourist. Z thus establishes herself as an endearing *gordita* who loves a good laugh and is honest to a fault. Even her name, which corresponds to the last letter in the alphabet, suggests someone who always puts herself last. She also suffers physical and psychological abuse in the hands of her lover Moisés, a situation that further inspires the reader's empathy. Her image of likeability is intensified by recurrent self-denigrating comments about her lack of literary talent—a talent that Z certainly possesses but tragically wastes, according to her friend Linda—and of willpower, such as her inability to diet, to say no, and particularly, to leave her abusive lover. I believe such self-portrait is essential to her strategic "radical self-degradation," without which her marooning from social and legal responsibility would not be viable.

The reader's empathy with the female world presented by Z becomes particularly handy at the time of Moisés's death. At first sight, the text is the story of the unresolved murder of Z's sadistic lover, who is mysteriously thrown out a window in the middle of the night. Labeled an accident by the police, there is no question in the characters' or the reader's mind that the lover's death is an act of justice. When seen in the context of Wittig's *guérrillères*, the community of lesbian friends advances the plot by producing either the crime or the alibi or both. All these options are possible mostly thanks to the ghostly presence of a woman friend, Alix, who lives in Z's apartment at the time. It is suggested that Alix may have been involved in Moisés's defenestration, although her actual involvement is never fully clarified.

Portela's novel refuses to subject itself to the rules of the detective story as a genre in the same way it resists the social conventions of modern society. The novel belongs to the detective genre, albeit in an adulterated form; in her edition of the novel, Iraida H. López calls it a postmodern detective story following the guidelines set by Glen S. Close (2010; see also Close 2008). Metaphorically speaking, the text is a "perverted text" in its misuse of the mechanisms of justice in order to attain justice. In a society in which revolutionary values became adulterated in the "magical turn" brought about by the impossible demands of the Special Period, notions such as truth and justice have lost some of their original pedigree. In this context, fiction proves liberating due to its susceptibility to corruption. Such is the situation behind Portela's manipulation of the *noir* genre. The narration of Moisés's death is the latest in a series of "real" and "fictional" murders that are investigated by "real" and "fictional" detectives. While the fictional detectives (like Teniente Levi in Linda Roth's *Nocturno Sebastián*) solve their cases but are unable to put the murderer in jail, the "real" detectives prove unable to even uncover the truth. The ensuing chaos underlines the impossibility of reestablishing a certain type of social order, either because such order no longer prevails, or because it never really existed. The novel even suggests that regaining such order or illusion of order may not be desirable in the first place.

Notwithstanding, I would like to suggest that the most meaningful contractual adulteration in *Cien botellas* is the one that corrupts the confessional genre so that perversion, not confession, produces justice and solidarity. I find the key to this interpretation in the narration surrounding a prior incident, which Z calls "the soft drink war," while the police describes it as "Public scandal. Assault. Violence. Disfiguration." The situation, which involves teenage Z and her friend Yadelis, leads to the accidental injury of a waiter (Portela 2002, 59). It is memorable because it creates the conditions of possibility for three key aspects of the text: the friendship between Linda and Z, the initiation of Linda's career as a writer, and the first instance in the novel of what Peter Brooks calls "a fictional 'expedient'" or false confession (2000, 50).

The events in the café are described in the chapter "She Wanted to Be a Writer." Two adolescents, Z and Yadelis, engage in a roughhousing episode, which escalates to them throwing their sodas in each other's faces and culminates when Yadelis throws her soda along with the glass at Z, who ducks. Behind Z is Linda, the school nerd, who instinctively deflects the glass with her hand. The glass ends up hitting a waiter in the eye, disfiguring him. Because of Z's and Yadelis's unremarkable appearance, they are not conclusively identified. Instead, Linda, who is Jewish and looks "foreign," is identified by the waiter and taken into custody to force a confession. Against everyone's expectations, Linda refuses to incriminate the other girls, and offers a redeeming performance of victimhood. She uses her impeccable reputation to fend off the accusations, enlisting the school headmaster as witness to her character. She claims not to be protecting anyone else, because she has no friends—a fact everyone is able to confirm. Linda invokes the martyrdom of her race, which culminated in the Holocaust. She sets herself free without incriminating anyone. What we soon learn is that Linda lies, not out of consideration for either Z or Yadelis, but to practice how to be a writer, a profession that consists in being "a sublime liar" (Portela 2002, 72). If the police expected a speedy confession from the best student, they instead find a performance of innocence that alters the rules of the confession and, by extension, the power relations that the confession presupposes.

Adolescent Linda, explicitly described as a maroon in the novel, offers a stellar performance of citizenship through a "work of the negative," in which displacement, silence, and cunning help her take over the social order. In her testimony, Linda displaces the emphasis from acts to virtues; she invokes her reputation and extends it over the facts of the incident. She lies following the principles of what could look like the truth. Verisimilitude is in this case a discursive perversion whose legal and literary power depends on keeping its fictionality hidden. The act is sealed when the schoolmaster is summoned to attest to Linda's virtues, turning him into an involuntary accomplice who, by vouching for her character, denies her participation in the incident. After all this, the truth has become irrelevant. Linda, who was innocent from the start, establishes her innocence not by cooperating, but by producing a self-portrait of victimization. As Peter Brooks has shown, the only true aspect of a confession is the appearance of unmasking; the facts themselves cannot be corroborated (2000, 52). Here lies one of the most important aspects of the false testimony that is present in Linda's defense and which, I claim, will determine the interpretation of the novel as a whole.

The final and darkest event in *Cien botellas* is the defenestration of Moisés, Z's sadistic lover and the father of her unborn child. Moisés, a former member of the Supreme Court, is an older man with a beard, a fact that at the very least helps identify him as part of a generation that was ethically aligned with the early revolution, if not as an outright Castro-like figure. In spite of his prophet's name, he is profoundly disenchanted. So much so, in fact, that Moisés's "main goal in life was to prevent anyone at all (any of his enemies, that is to say, everyone) from deceiving him. He was always looking to catch them in the very act, to unmask their filthy masks, to squash them, annihilate them, pulverize them" (Portela 2002, 27). His attitude contrasts with Z's, who seems to trust everybody. Because Moisés despises humankind, including his two grown sons, it is not surprising that Z is afraid of telling Moisés about her pregnancy. She tries to leave Moisés at the request of her confessor, her psychiatrist, and her friends, but in the end she finds herself unable to do so. One night, Moisés falls out of a window in Z's apartment and dies, crushing to death an annoying neighbor, a loud musician called Poliéster. The police conclude that it was an accident in which Moisés had *trustingly* leaned against a window, which was covered by a thick, black curtain and supposed to be closed, and fell to his death. Neglecting the improbability of such scenario, Z confirms the accident version by adding that, indeed, the window *seemed* to be closed (250). She also invokes the testimony of her neighbors, who had seen Moisés fall and squash Poliéster, thus diverting the attention to the results (the corpses on the street) while the events inside the apartment that led to the two deaths remain unknown. For, according to her own testimony, Z had slept through the incident and only woke up when the police knocked on her door. Upon hearing the news, however, Z doesn't hide her satisfaction: "This may be the most ignoble of all confessions, the most perverse, the most horrible: I was happy . . . I got scared of myself, of my *inner beast*" (251; emphasis added). Z has no trouble confessing to an emotional satisfaction that the law cannot punish.

With its evocation of either the unconscious or the devil, Z's allusion to her "inner beast" brings us to the realm of either the confession or psychoanalysis, two methods that may be more appropriate to uncover this particular truth than the police investigation. Z suggests that the murderer is Alix, Linda's ex-lover, a potential culprit who is as dark and elusive as her own desires. Alix is a tall, taciturn, peasant girl from the countryside who is often described as "beastly" both for her unusual physical strength and her inarticulateness, and who appears in Z's life the same day she meets Moisés for the first time. Alix and Linda have a passionate love affair, but Alix's persistent jealousy upsets Linda. In a violent fight, Linda forces the girl out of her house. When Z finds Alix living in the streets, she brings her to her own house. Alix, who shows gratitude and loyalty for Z in the same passionate way that she once loved Linda, disappears without a trace the night Moisés mysteriously falls out the window. With this statement, Z suggests that it was Alix who killed the victimizer in an act of Amazon solidarity. By actualizing a form of altruism that is expected from friendship but is never meant to be actualized, Alix saves Z and her unborn baby from the bearded misanthrope, only to disappear from both the city and the text like the shadow she always was. At first sight, Alix's intervention fits a narrative of female solidarity according to which women put each other first, and which literally, in this case, rids them of male authoritarian figures. Justice is done.

In my view, Z's insistence on the weakness of her character begs another interpretation. I would like to suggest that Alix can be read as a fictional character created by Linda and Z to cover up their crime and divert the attention of the police. For months, Linda and Z speculate about ways of killing Moisés and getting rid of the body so that the police never find out the truth. Earlier in the text, because "not all women were as shy, unhappy, and patient as Z," Linda has made multiple plans to castrate and kill Moisés, displace the guilt, and create an alibi (22). Z questions Linda: "Can we do it with impunity?" Linda responds that anything can be done in and through literature. And sure enough, the police never find out what happened to Moisés thanks to the women's craftiness. Even though Linda's suggestions to liberate Z seem to belong to the symbolic realm of literature, I suggest that Linda and Z "really" resort to literature to liberate Z, by creating a fictional expedient with fictional characters to literally get away with murder. This amounts to a "magical inversion" from legal to fictional discourse: while Linda's writing formula consists of fictionalizing the truth—"You tell it as if it were *false*, you reorganize the data, invent a bit, and presto. Everyone believes it" (176; emphasis added)—her approach to the truth in legal situations is the creation of "fictional expedients," consisting of layers of lies aiming at confusing the police: "you tell it as if it were *true*, etc."

This "magical inversion" is facilitated by psychoanalysis. In his book *Troubling Confessions*, and partly quoting Freud, Peter Brooks makes a distinction between the notion of truth as it occurs through religious and legal confession and psychoanalysis: While "in Confession the sinner tells what he knows; in analysis, the neurotic has to tell more" because true knowledge is assumed to be blocked (2000, 116). Brooks explains that "much of analysis is directed to resistances, precisely to the nonconfessional or the anticonfessional, on the assumption that this is where the truth is to be sought, the place that the unconscious has marked with its power of censorship" (117). He concludes: "It is not the voluntary confession that interests the analyst, but the involuntary" (117). Even Freud in his late essays, says Brooks, puts to question the ability of the psychoanalytic transaction to reach any referential truth (117).

According to Brooks, psychoanalytic truth takes shape precisely in the anticonfessional or the nonconfessional. It resides in the resistances, the excesses, or the margins of what is usually understood as real discourse. In the context of the novel, then, we can either focus on what Z says voluntarily about the event—she slept through it, she knows nothing—or analyze her eloquent digressions. Most of the narrative space of the novel is devoted to a description of Z and her friends' underworld society, which combines postmodern ethical standards with an assortment of typically post-Soviet clandestine commercial activities. What is said about the social and moral landscape, however, matters not so much as an ethnography of that time period but as a record of Z's character so that the crime, considered necessary but undesirable, becomes not just unknowable but even unlikely, which makes her responsibility in the crime highly incredible.

I recognize in Z's testimony a cover-up mechanism that is similar to the one applied by Linda during her testimony in "the soft drink war"; a mechanism to which the reader has access not by following a reading method akin to that of the detective but rather one that is similar to that of the psychoanalyst. The reader's job is not to unveil the truth by following what the narration says, but in what it hides. Namely, to achieve justice, Z needs to appeal to radical self-degradation. Hence her insistence on the docility of her character, her lack of willpower (to diet, prostitute herself for hard currency, or leave Moisés), her natural desire to please her friends, and her incapacity to make up her mind. Laziness, warmth, and a self-deprecating sense of humor—"as Oliver Hardy would say, the fatty always loses" (Portela 2002, 30)—are all attributes or characteristics that form part of a self-portrait that emphasizes her natural docility. Z's mask of vulnerability operates like Linda's impeccable reputation during "the soft drink war." By portraying a quintessentially "good" person according to postmodern ethical standards—including a commitment to not torment one's friends (2002, 23)—Z creates confusion between her character and her acts and enlists the reader, trained to believe in Z's honesty, to vouch for her innocence. The efficiency of this mechanism is exacerbated by masochism, described by Žižek as a privileged vehicle for empathy. In Žižek's view, the assumption of a degraded subject position with full acknowledgment of the obscene pleasure in such degradation affords "genuine contact" with the "suffering other" (2003, 11). Therefore, I suggest, Z's perversion becomes her alibi.

The novel as a whole, then, can be read as what Peter Brooks calls an anticonfession. Z engages in a form of radical self-degradation so as to liberate herself from Moisés, an emblematic figure of the deteriorated revolutionary establishment. Eventually, a liberated Z will create an alternative family with Linda when she moves to Linda's penthouse to raise Moisés's child. When considering the novel as a maroon text, the reader can see the possibility of a superior postmodern ethical stance in Linda's fictional expedient. So, in fact, does Z, who, I suggest, emulates her. In other words, if in the first testimony Linda uses life as practice for literature, in the second fictional expedient Z uses the literary exercises devised by her and Linda to propagate "a sublime lie" that will bring justice in a world where traditional accountability, usually understood as a question of honor, often fails most of those involved, especially women. As Sarah Hoagland notes, "male-led revolutions—economic and military and intellectual—have not changed the essential dominance/subordination relationship at the heart of oppression" (1988, 3), whereas lesbianism, feminism, and even masochism can be defined as, precisely, "the ability to say 'no' to coercion" (284).

The possibility of starting a new life in Linda's silent and spacious penthouse suggests that literary creation will be possible for Z. Nietzsche, who demystifies lying as a sin, equates the production of lies to the production of art when he says "basically and from time immemorial we are—*accustomed to lying*. Or to put it more virtuously and hypocritically, in short, more pleasantly: one is much more of an artist than one knows" (2000, 295; emphasis in the original). True enough, Z begins her literary career with the creation of this false testimony. The novel is a self-conscious fictional expedient that purposely invents characters and manipulates empathy. Thanks to this fictional expedient, Z liberates herself from the violent lover, from the discipline power of the state, and even negotiates her way out of the noisy *solar*, which prevents literature, and into Linda's penthouse, where literature always happens. In its blatant disregard of traditional values, the novel even produces an innovative form of literature that is collectively authored: We cannot separate Z's alibi from Linda's literary experiments.

The main perversion in this text, masochism, is the agent of a political self-reformation, for it turns lying into a means for securing female "honor." Political agency is possible for women who, as Bourdieu explains, are "strong, armed with the weapons of weakness, such as devilish cunning . . . and magic" (2001, 51; emphasis in the original). The characters in *Cien botellas* have not just mastered the tricks that will allow them to survive in a world of men, but are also motivated by the desire to connect with other women in an effort to, in the words of Hoagland, "pool our resources, and to build something which makes real our dreams and what we imagine" (1988, 284). The sentimental education of the *guérrillères* consists in understanding the traps of modern ethics and learning to circumvent uniformity and loyalty to achieve plurality and solidarity instead. That perversion leads to justice reveals the vacuity to which revolutionary ideals have fallen in post-Soviet times. More importantly, the idea that female corruption leads to literary creation establishes a harsh contrast with the literary impotence of contemporary male writer/protagonists in novels like *Las palabras perdidas* by Jesús Díaz and *La novela de mi vida* by Leonardo Padura. This difference speaks of the implacable nature of the fraternal social contract, which ultimately hurts those it claims to protect.

ABILIO ESTÉVEZ'S CRUISING

In an interview bearing the somewhat misleading title of "Friendship as a Way of Life," Foucault claims that "meeting in the street, seducing each other with a look, grabbing each other's asses and getting each other off in a quarter of an hour"—protocols that define the male homosexual practice known as cruising—are acts that constitute a synecdoche for "a way of life" capable of yielding "a culture and ethics" (1981, 39). For Foucault, the notion of anonymous intimacy as a political ideal resides in the structural need to abandon "readymade formulas," such as those offered by couplehood and friendship, in order to envision unthreatening social bonds; that is, bonds that do not lend themselves to "the formation of new alliances and the tying together of unforeseen lines of force" (38). This makes homosexuality more than "a form of desire"; it makes it a desirable political model (38). Cruising, as Foucault sees it, appears as a form of advancing a homosexual *ascesis*, by which he means the subjection of the individual to a practice of transformation animated by the desire to invent oneself in "a way of being that is still improbable" (39).

The existence of individual utopias through eroticism is the promise of Abilio Estévez's *Palacios distantes*. When the house in which he lives is scheduled to be demolished, Victorio, the protagonist, abandons his decrepit room, a room that no longer shelters him, and sets off to the streets where he spends the night in various abandoned ruins. At a more abstract level, Victorio wanders the city in search of his "distant palace," an ideal place of individual happiness first promised by el Moro, a dark, handsome pilot that Victorio admired during his childhood. It is not insignificant, in this context, that el Moro should bear a nickname that can be traced back to Sir Thomas More insofar as the writer of *Utopia* is known as Tomás Moro in the Spanish literary tradition.

There is little doubt that Victorio's "palace," whose "key" originally hangs on the wall next to a photograph of the young pilot exposing his taut chest, is connected to el Moro's sex appeal. Desire is at the heart of Victorio's wanderings, during which he gladly engages in casual erotic encounters that transform his roaming around Havana into a precarious form of cruising, precarious on account of his homeless condition but also because it takes place at the heart of a society that perceives itself to be permanently at war. In fact, one of the few possessions Victorio keeps in his old room is a cannonball that, used as a paperweight, reminds him of a militarized culture. Curiously, Victorio finds his "distant palace" in the ruins of an old theater in the casual company of an old clown, Don Fuco, and *a jinetera* who uses an actress' name, Salma, as her pseudonym.

Concretely, two related types of perversion contribute to the liberating ethos of Abilio Estévez's *Palacios distantes*: cruising understood as the corruption of intimacy and sociability as a superficial form of friendship. In principle, homosexuality as an ethics is an especially seductive utopia in the eyes of the disenchanted protagonist. For this lonely, middle-aged, gay man who longs to incorporate a bit of beauty into his austere life, the creation of what Foucault describes as "polymorphic, varied, and individually modulated relationships" based on sexual pleasure implies, above all, the viability of a social ideal (1981, 39). It is somewhat paradoxical, however, that cruising offers Victorio a desirable political model only in the abstract, that is to say, in the absence of actual sex. In fact, I will argue here that Victorio's private utopia comes to being not exactly through cruising, described by Bersani as "sexual sociability," but in sociability, understood here as friendship without intimacy (2002, 9).[10]

In "Sociability and Cruising," Leo Bersani (elaborating on Georg Simmel, Foucault, and even Freud) defines sociability as a voluntary association motivated by the satisfaction to resolve individual loneliness in the union with others. Sociability is a relationship curiously similar to cruising except that "sociability is a form of relationality uncontaminated by desire" (2002, 9). Bersani discusses three structural elements shared by both forms of association: the freedom of bondage (which I will explain below), the subordination of content to "the abstract play of form," and the dissolution of the self in a totality, a process he calls "self-subtraction" (11). By virtue of its similarities with sociability, cruising can be considered, according to Bersani, as an alternative political model, given that an "identity-free" intimate contact provides the structural conditions capable of transforming social bonds into a social contract "outside power." More importantly, both cruising and sociability demand the formation of a new ethics; an *ecological* ethics, Bersani suggests, "in which the subject, having willed its own lessness, can live less invasively in the world" (22).

In what follows, I will explore the way in which the protagonists in Estévez's novel navigate both sociability and cruising in their search for a sublimated community "outside power." I will appropriate and partially revert Bersani's ideas by suggesting that sociability proves more effective at the task of imagining a political ideal than cruising in the Cuban context. The fact that social relations in the novel better approximate utopian ideals as they become desexualized responds to the structural conditions that Abel Sierra Madero has called the Cuban "nationalist, homophobic habitus" (2006, 243). I would like to suggest that *Palacios distantes* starkly distinguishes itself from revolutionary manly virtues by thematizing the search for forms of belonging outside what can be described, again paraphrasing Sierra Madero, as "social relationships understood as a permanent war" in favor of the creation of what Bersani calls an ecological ethics.[11] With the production of values and social combinations that are neither legitimized by, nor in opposition to, traditional ethics, Abilio Estévez's novel resists the bourgeois morals that, according to Guillermo Cabrera Infante, have always informed the gender culture of the Cuban revolution (see *Mauvaise conduite* 1984).

At the same time, however, by focusing on the unlikely association of a middle-aged gay intellectual, an old clown, and an ignorant *jinetera*, *Palacios* plays with the idea of uncharted voluntary relationships and the disenfranchised communities that they can produce. Most importantly, however, their friendship can be said to be ideal precisely because it exists as pure form, that is, partly void of content. At some level, at least, theirs appears as an antifriendship given that it is not built on the perpetual possibility of sacrifice for the other—a defining element of friendship—but on using shared joy to build an anticommunal community instead.

Life in the "El Pequeño Liceo de La Habana" provides a morally exhausted Victorio with a peaceful retreat from an aggressive social world. The old theater, which stages a perpetual party with costumes and games, is governed by the rules of sociability. Don Fuco, a semimagical host, invites Victorio and Salma to enjoy sensual pleasures that are often only available to them through dramatization. Upon finding Murano glasses they imagine, for instance, that, instead of water, they are drinking a refreshing orange juice. In so doing, they underline the rule of sociability according to which pleasure derives from pure form, not from the actual content. At the same time, their conversations, mostly consisting of vivid anecdotes about bohemian characters of early twentieth-century Havana, follow an idle rhythm. The characters carefully avoid personal and uncomfortable issues, following the principle that the most important aspect of social conversation is to keep the conversation alive while avoiding both confession and friction with others. With the help of Salma, the two men improvise entertaining shows in which they impersonate cultural icons. Alternatively, they play puppets or they become characters of the stories they invent. Salma is perpetually ready to play (Estévez 2002, 152). Victorio, who is truly elated to be part of an unexpected community, often "forgets himself" (103).

With this scenario in mind, I suggest that Victorio finds his "distant palace" in the pleasure of pure belonging. One could say that the experience of the protagonists in the ruins of the theater reflects the idea that, as Georg Simmel notes, "above and beyond their special content, all these associations are accompanied by a feeling for, by a satisfaction in, the very fact that one is associated with others and that the solitariness of the individual is resolved into togetherness, a union with others" (1971, 128). Free of any content, the social relation is related to the pure form of association. In this sense, sociability appears as the opposite of friendship: While friendship is defined by its content, in sociability the "pure form of interaction is its own self-sufficient content" (137).

As I already suggested, three aspects of sociability play a key role in the novel. The characters are governed by what Simmel calls "the *play-form of association*" (1971, 130; emphasis in the original) that is visible in the manner in which conversation must ensure its own continuity, avoiding conflicts and personal confessions that would impose content upon or otherwise negatively affect the tone of the conversation. It is also visible in the manner in which the three friends are joined by "the freedom of bondage," a phrase used by Simmel to describe the way in which groups of people spontaneously come together and apart during parties following the play-form of sociability (138). To illustrate this, Simmel discusses flirting, a social game that can only last as long as a decision over actual sexual intercourse can be suspended (135). Simmel notes that a woman may act and dress more seductively at a party without having to commit sexually to any man, a freedom of commitment that is considerably reduced for her when meeting alone with one or two men. This is possible because, at a party, she is not exactly herself. She can lose herself in the social game of which she is only one element. In other words, at a party each person reduces his or her social presence, subordinating him- or herself to a whole that, in turn, softens the meaning of individual actions. Sociability is only motivated by the desire to belong; that is why people must soften the extreme aspects of their personality by making their individual concerns and interests disappear. People must reduce their selves so as to be able to fit in, to be part of the whole. In the novel's case, each of the three characters reduces him- or herself in order to form a social group of what would otherwise be a collection of lonely people.

Sociability in *Palacios* can be seen as an idealized perversion of traditional friendship. Like friendship, sociability helps protect individuals against the problems of life, but it does so in the abstract. Unlike friendship, which is defined by the possibility that the friend might be called upon to sacrifice himself to help the other, the experience of life in sociability becomes lighter in view of the fact that, according to Simmel, "the whole weight of life . . . is consumed in an artistic play, in that simultaneous sublimation and dilution." Indeed, as Simmel further notes, in the pleasure of company, "the heavily freighted forces of reality are felt only as from a distance, their weight fleeting in a charm" (1971, 140). Particularly relevant to this discussion is that, in marked contrast with traditional friendship, sociability does not depend for its survival on the tests of loyalty, but on common happiness, with each person's joy depending on everyone else's. One could go so far as to say that sociability as an ethos is defined by a moderate altruism and by a self-motivated integration based on shared pleasure. Sociability, which is based on solidarity, is a utopian abstraction: "The world of sociability, the only one in which a democracy of equals is possible without friction, is an *artificial* world," one in which self-sacrifice is not only not expected, but it is undesirable (Simmel 1971, 132–133).

While self-motivated integration is the value that sustains the group formed by Salma, Victorio, and Don Fuco, each of them shows a will to selfless joy even before they converge in the ruins of the theater. Don Fuco, an amateur clown and magician, dedicates his life to bringing joy to joyless places such as the cemetery, funeral homes, and the streets of Havana in general. In the past, Salma has derived pleasure giving sexual pleasure disinterestedly, a vocation of generosity that economic need and her subsequent turn to *jineterismo* has temporarily perverted. It is interesting that *jineterismo*, which is basically a form of prostitution, usually involves the pretense and even the protocols of dating.[12] Victorio, in turn, survives in the streets thanks to the generosity of others, who give him food and systematically "forget" to charge him, and he, in turn, leaves behind a thank-you note casually; that is, as if he weren't really doing it. Even though these random acts of generosity often help satisfy someone's needs, they are performed in such a way that they divert attention from their real purpose. The reiterative celebration of casual selflessness in the novel shows a poetic deference for the forms of sociability.

The theater is the proper place to live a life of play that is formally separated from external and fundamental reality. Indeed, to leave one's identity behind is a privileged requirement in a functioning theater both for actors, who reduce their own selves to adopt the emotions, the words, and the names of imaginary beings, as well as for the audience, who are expected to suspend their disbelief, albeit temporarily, so as to share their silent fascination with unknown others. Similarly, the strange group of Salma, Victorio, and Don Fuco constantly alternate their roles as audience and actors in their games. They happily reduce their selves, even forget themselves, in the pleasure of play and togetherness. This explains in part why the word "fear" is meaningless in the ruins of "El Pequeño Liceo de La Habana" (Estévez 2002, 180).

The ethical depth of self-subtraction in pleasure can best be appreciated in what Bersani calls the asceticism of sociability. According to Bersani, the pleasure of company is possible only if it is "intransitive"; that is, only when it is geared toward an abstract form of belonging to something bigger and external to oneself (2002, 11). *Ascesis* takes place when a partly dismantled subject leaves aside his own obsessions and interests to enjoy a type of presence in the world that is related to lightness and joy. In its voluntary, ludic association with others, the self is reduced but in a nonmasochistic way; that is, it is reduced in a way that it is not related to the death drive (21). Bersani sees sociability as a "technology of the self"; that is, as a way of self-fashioning, geared toward the pleasure of being part of a harmonic whole in which the group's happiness generates individual happiness.

The novel elaborates the Foucauldian notion of pleasure as a political ideal—or as Žižek would say, of "enjoyment as a political factor." In a debate between Victorio and Don Fuco on the importance of memory over strategic forgetfulness to avoid the repetition of history, Don Fuco speaks of pleasure as a civic value:

> Victorio, listen carefully to this glorious word, pleasure . . . A man who is satisfied, joyful, free of fear, would never think of imprisoning another, robbing another, killing another . . . The reason for slavery, tyrannies, holocausts, murder, repression and war can be found in joylessness. The man who is fascinated by power, that man is an unfortunate being . . . Oh, if he could only leave the rest of us alone. (Estévez 2002, 131–132)

Don Fuco seems to be advocating for a form of hedonism or Epicureanism not so much as the "individual flight from a dominant political ideal" (Ichikawa 2001, 67), but as a political ideal on its own right. Don Fuco reminds us of Albert O. Hirschman when he claims that it is largely thanks to these moderate excesses that human life can be said to exist beyond mere survival, and that it is this surplus that guarantees a desire by humans to behave humanely. Furthermore, for the old clown the desire to perpetuate pleasure creates the need for self-regulation. Joy nurtures a commitment to tolerance.[13]

It is in its championing of the ascetic pleasure of self-subtraction that sociability can be morally superior to friendship. If friendship is defined by the need to give the other what he needs, regardless of the cost, then friendship at least in its abstract formulation includes the possibility of excessive sacrifice. In the previous chapter, I claimed that friendship among men, understood as a fraternity of equals based on absolute loyalty, constitutes an ideological trap. Sociability, in turn, offers a detour away from this trap, therefore constituting a political ideal as suggested by Foucault. By its very nature, sociability generates a form of reciprocal altruism, a form of rational social commitment according to which the promotion of one's self-interest leads to a collective well-being. If living together in harmony is in our self-interest, the primacy of the national interest in the revolutionary social contract goes against the moral values of the Cuban revolution. Even if sociability requires self-subtraction, it is a benign reduction of the self that is regulated by oneself in the search for an ideal happiness that can only result from the sum of individual instances of happiness, and which returns to the individual. What the ideal society that lives in "El Pequeño Liceo de La Habana" shows is that the ethical value of civic sacrifice does not compare to the civic value of pleasure. We could even revise Bersani's words when he defines sociability as a form of intimacy uncontaminated by desire—including, I would add, the desire to own the other, to shape his destiny, and to appropriate his convictions and complicate his possibility of happiness. When seen from this perspective, sociability is ethically superior to friendship.

Bersani even goes so far as to make cruising an existential condition of homosexuality. He ambiguously appropriates Freud and states: "The psychoanalytically defined homosexual . . . wanders in the world—cruises the world, we might almost say—in search of objects that will give him back to himself as a loved and cared for subject" (2002, 15–16). Theoretically speaking, at least, cruising participates in the ecological ethics of sociability. While sex for Victorio is always anonymous, I will discuss one episode that is particularly telling with respect to the ethics of cruising. When Victorio abandons the architectural and disciplinary structure (the communication of the demolition is delivered by the woman in charge of the CDR [Comité de Defensa de la Revolución]) to wander the city, he finds a good place to spend the night in a mental hospital that has just collapsed. The ruins of the hospital, a place that is simultaneously sheltered and open, private and public, soon become the stage for an orgiastic transformation that insinuate fantastic models of social interactions (because hyperbole is key to its utopian effect, I quote this scene almost in full):

> As soon as the sun's weak rays begin to retreat back toward the crevices through which they have managed to filter, the ruins start filling with the comings and goings of anxious shades. The collapsed building is peopled with blurred human figures—errant, desperate figures that search yearningly for one another, as if the body were the only possible cause for so great a disturbance. The voices do not matter, the gazes do not matter, it matters even less what is behind them: all that matter are the bodies.

> The nightmarish nights in the collapsed building on the street formerly known as General Lee reveal to him how versatile human tastes and needs can be. He sees fragile lads possessed by grotesque truck drivers, as well as grotesque truck drivers possessed by fragile lads; underclass mulattos together with white policemen; black athletes mated with Nordic-looking business executives; ethereal dancers articulated with rough butchers; pole-vault champions joined with playwrights in decline. The ruin is frequented by men of every social status: widowers, married men, bachelors, sterile men, revolutionary workers, varicocele sufferers, electricians, habitual vagrants, lawyers, lunatics, opera singers, pop music singers, chess players, ambassadors, transvestites, construction workers, paraplegics, sculptors, journalists, musicians, sugarcane cutters, waiters, lifeguards, composers, HIV-positives, gardeners, aviators . . . Victorio begins to infer from all this that sex may be the only form of true democracy that can exist in the world. Or perhaps he reasons that it would be best to conclude that any revolution that boasts of being democratic should begin with sex.[14]

In this fantastic sexual scene observed and celebrated by Victorio, improvised sex appears as the explicit actualization of an ideal democracy. It also participates in some of the characteristics of sociability that Bersani finds in the act of cruising. At first, the stripping of individual identity becomes obvious. Those shadow-like "blurry contours" offer minimal signs of identity. Each person is less than he is, a body without features, joined to other bodies by desire. As Bersani suggests, impersonal sex offers the opportunity for what he calls "contact 'outside power'" (2002, 22). Otherness exists but on an untouchable plane. The ruin is an interval in which eroticism touches bodies without social attributes or, more precisely, it cancels them out upon its touch. In the communion of bodies that transcend their social markers, differences complement themselves and cancel each other out, momentarily making possible the idea of equality within difference. It is in facilitating anonymous gay sex that the ruins prove most effective at deconstructing political power.[15]

Democracy in sex is possible, in part, thanks to its reciprocity. Like sociability, cruising implies a certain civic value—what the novel's narrator calls "a true democracy"—that offers a suggestive, noncannibalistic view of difference. The combination of bodies Victorio sees in the ruin shows an aesthetic and sexual appreciation of difference—difference in race, health, financial, and political power. Each body finds in the other a momentary yet perfect complement to his physical strength and social distinction, favoring moderation and social balance. Anonymous sex in the ruins of the mental hospital underlines the ecological function of cruising. In this scene differences are compensated for, extremes cancel each other out, and the individual assumes the reduction of his self to a totality. In "the freedom of bondage" of cruising, the notion of a less harmful form of social presence begins to take shape.

If Victorio believes he has found paradise in the ruins of the hospital, however, he is soon disabused. This scene, which curiously begins with military metaphors ("retreat," "infiltration"), reveals unsettling emotions like anxiety and fear. In part, these emotions can be attributed to sexual excitement, but also to an emotional negative state that can potentially preclude play. His worst fears are realized when he is seduced by a young man who looks like a U.S. Marine. This character, masculine and desirable (thanks to its size and beauty, his penis is described as "joy made flesh"), soon identifies himself as a policeman and proceeds to blackmail Victorio into giving up his mother's wedding ring. The ring, the symbol of Victorio's mother's union to his father—who Victorio nicknamed "Papá Robespierre" on account of his intransigent revolutionary values—passes from Victorio's hand to the policeman's in a wedding-like ritual. Abuse by the agent (either real or fake) of the National Police force is authorized by the revolutionary *habitus* that sees homosexuality as a national crime. Logically, the magical spell breaks the very moment the policeman identifies himself as such, and all the moving shadows become statues. For "sculptors, journalists, musicians, sugarcane cutters, waiters, lifeguards" become frozen by the fear of being excluded from an ideal masculine world.

Even though at first *Palacios* gives an idealized vision of cruising, its potential is doomed almost from the start. Cruising is not only trumped by betrayal but is itself betrayed, theoretically speaking. If we follow Bersani's view of cruising as sexual sociability, we can find here that the intercourse involving Victorio and "the Marine" is interrupted, perverted even, when two elements of sociability disappear; that is, when "the Marine" introduces interestedness and imposes his identity (either faked or real) on the interaction. The violence of these two improper elements takes over the reciprocity and joy promised at the beginning of the encounter. The militarization of the cruising scene staged by the false Marine does not speak to a fetishistic imaginary but, rather, to the opposition between being possessed and the civic imaginary of manly values.

Palacios distantes confronts the coexistence of two opposing ethical worlds: one governed by the potentially murderous rules of honor, and another contained in the ecological ethos of sexual and social pleasure. What we find in the novel, however, is that while cruising and sociability share social mechanisms and an overall spirit of selflessness, they intervene in the Cuban imagination quite differently. This is why it is not entirely unexpected that cruising fails as a democratic practice in Estévez's novel. Homosexual desire is seen as actualizing the vulnerability of a feminized citizenry in a homophobic revolutionary society, a view that still permeates the erotic imagination of some disenchanted Cuban literature. Political utopias may be found in an anticommunal community if and only if such community abstains from male homosexual desire. This is probably why Victorio moves into the utopian theater the same day he loses El Moro's photograph.

ANTONIO JOSÉ PONTE'S NECROPHILIA

In Antonio José Ponte's *Contrabando de sombras*, Vladimir, a frustrated poet, spends time in the cemetery for work. He has been hired by a European photographer to write poems to accompany images of Havana in ruins for a book that he seeks to publish. The cemetery has already been suggested by a now dead friend, Renán, as a place that exercises an extraordinary sexual pull on people. Vladimir arrives in the cemetery and finds among tomb robbers a man remarkably similar to the love of his youth, a swimmer called Miranda, who killed himself as a teenager for being gay and found out. While the novel follows in its own way the logic of triangles and betrayals present in texts analyzed in Chapter 2, the quest for love and truth in the novel is poetically resolved in necrophilia. Necrophilia is strongly suggested by the setting, insofar as sex mostly takes place in the cemetery (itself a synecdoche for the decaying city outside), and also by the ghostly presence of the dead lover. Vladimir's search culminates when he has sex with the cemetery boy, who vividly reminds him of his drowned lover, behind a dimly lit, threadbare cinema screen. The novel insists on the utopian aspect of necrophilia: "Renán was wrong . . . The cemetery is not the most impossible place . . . A truly impossible place is that in which two men get together when one of them is dead" (Ponte 2002, 109). This can be understood as a metaphysical thought, one that is expanded upon in the sex scene behind the cinema screen: "The most impossible place is not one in which a man and a spirit meet, but one in which they face each other on equal terms" (151).

The range of perverted practices designated by the term "necrophilia" can be quite broad. In *The Anatomy of Human Destructiveness* Erich Fromm lists among necrophilic tendencies: 1) acts of sexual contact with a female corpse; 2) sexual excitement produced by the sight of a woman's corpse; 3) attraction to corpses and graves and objects related to graves such as flowers or pictures; 4) acts of dismemberment of a corpse; and 5) the craving for touch or smell of anything putrid (1973, 326). Fromm includes all these instances under an umbrella definition first suggested by German criminologist H. von Hentig in 1964 of necrophilia as "*the passionate attraction to all that is dead, decayed, putrid, sickly; it is the passion to transform that which is alive into something which is unalive; to destroy for the sake of destruction . . . It is the passion 'to tear apart living structures'*" (332; emphasis in the original).

The obsessive attraction to corpses and graves is palpable in every aspect of the novel, not only in the photographer's pursuit of war-like ruins or in the obsession with graveyard cruising, but also as a pervasive theme in a novel that seeks to re-create the social texture of decaying Cuba. The work of worms (feeding off cadavers) is metonymically anticipated by that of tomb robbers and stray dogs, but also replicated outside the cemetery, where *buzos*—while the word literally means "scuba divers" in Spanish, it refers here to people searching for food in trash cans—preempt the work of trash collectors and street sweepers. The craving for that which is putrid has allegorical density, because sexual and other forms of *jineterismo*, false denunciations, and useless persecutions attend to a similar economy of survival by "tearing apart" living or moral (that is, "living by") structures; of lives refusing to be wasted by embracing indignities, by destroying the lives of others for the sake of either survival or pleasure, or both. That this economy of vampirism and substitution includes the pious recycling and reselling of candles in the cemetery chapel, preventing prayers for loved ones to complete their symbolic cycle, gives readers a sense of the deeply corrupt moral texture of revolutionary society today: Nobody is truly innocent. What is more, necrophilia has an aesthetic dimension to it, as true beauty can only be found "in its scars," according to the European photographer in the text (Ponte 2002, 36). The deterioration of Havana as a city but also as a polis—to use Ichikawa's term—lends the city a special aura. Vladimir recognizes this double dimension of the city/polis—that is, aesthetic and moral—when pressed to justify the artistic quality of the photographs: "We are all more or less dead, and there is profound beauty in the almost death we lead" (23).

In his most literal examples, Fromm privileges the female corpse not only because he operates within a heterosexual paradigm of desire, but also because one of the strongest underlying premises of necrophilia is that of the penetration of the living into dead flesh, traditionally understood to involve a male pervert penetrating a hospitable female corpse. However, the logic of permeability in the novel goes much further; it actually lends structure to a narration that follows a series of literal and metaphorical penetrations as its guiding principle. Specifically, the act of sexually forcing one's way into and through flesh attends to an obsessive search for the unthinkable and the impossible, for attaining or recuperating a world that exists before or outside present, sentient reality, and which may include a utopian world of perfect love. One could say that Vladimir summarizes the literary concept behind the novel when he explains to his friend Susan the mystery that Miranda holds for him:

> He has a scar on his chest. I touch that scar with my fingers as if it were an embossed message that I need to decipher, like a written language for blind people or an underlined passage. I hold his head and want to squeeze it until it breaks; until it emits a sound, a syllable, a yes or a no.—He lowered his voice until it was hardly audible—*When I fuck him, I just feel as if I were swimming laps in a pool in which I used to swim a long time ago.* I run into a wall that will never open to me again, if it ever did. In the last imaginable place, in that cemetery where

> Renán went with a guy because they had nowhere else to go, and where he couldn't stop going to meet others once his lover refused to return, I have seen his shoes again . . . The one who wears Renán's shoes looks just like Miranda. I don't know if it's just my imagination . . . Because sometimes I fear that I may have also sealed a tomb with soft cement, and then I forgot that the job wasn't finished and that I'd have to come back. (Ponte 2002, 108–109; emphasis added)

This confession is dense from both narrative and metanarrative points of view. Indeed, many story threads converge in this quote. Vladimir tells this story to Susan, a good friend who lives across the street from the graveyard where she has buried her son. Her son was a *buzo*, a real scuba diver who drowned trying to see "the depth of things" much like the dumpster divers, the tomb robbers, and the graveyard cruisers who seek to get to the bottom of things. In her maternal way, Susan, too, is obsessed with recuperating a lost love in the cemetery. What unites Vladimir and Susan, however, is the loss of their common friend Renán, who died in a mysterious accident after confessing his sexual attachment to the cemetery—"just seeing the cemetery walls gives me an erection," confesses Renán, a notion that Vladimir laughs off: "I had never heard of anyone getting a hard-on because of a wall" (Ponte 2002, 10–11)—and whose shoes have been stolen from his grave. Vladimir speaks of the dark passion he feels for César, a boyish man who is wearing Renán's shoes, and who tried to escape the island many times. After failing and ending up in jail several times, César has abandoned his desire to escape Havana and is now living in the cemetery; he has traded the city of the living for the city of the dead. As mentioned earlier, part of the appeal of César is that he reminds Vladimir of his first love, a boy whose last name was Miranda. Miranda committed suicide in the school swimming pool after he was discovered having sex with the school bully. Vladimir's swimming coach knew about the setup and saved Vladimir, who was going to meet with Miranda that afternoon: "It is either you or him" (139). Instead, the coach invites Vladimir to swim with him in what becomes a deeply sensual act of coordinated movement and breathing between coach and pupil in the water heated by the afternoon sun (eventually, the coach will shave Vladimir's pubis so he will look like the child he was when they first met and then have sex with him). More important, however, is that the key to César's identity seems to be contained in the scar on his torso. Vladimir is obsessed with the idea that César's scar can unravel the truth about his connection with Miranda: Is he a reincarnation of the former lover or an illusion? Is the scar a sign for what Brad Epps has called the indelible mark that identifies the homosexual as weak, subordinate, dishonorable? Vladimir, who is a poet, is consumed by the desire to read César's scar like a book in the dark. If César is a double of Miranda, his scar has, in turn, two doubles: one is the mended patch on the cinema screen, which can only be seen with the reflection of very light objects such as the projection of the Pacific Ocean. The other one is on the leg of a corrupt woman who betrayed and destroyed César's family long ago, and who will save him now from jail at considerable personal risk for the pleasure of claiming as her own the beauty of Vladimir's words—corrupting herself for poetry, as it were.

The metanarrative weight of this quote, in turn, rests in the phrase "*When I fuck him, I just feel as if I were swimming laps in a pool in which I used to swim a long time ago.*" The act of sexual penetration leads not only to pleasure, but also, or primarily, to a past that contains the first love, the loss of innocence, and the guilt of betrayal and survival, all feelings associated with the pool where Miranda drowned. More importantly, this penetration is replicated in other forms of permeability. For instance, someone who is not from this world enters Vladimir's apartment to write "faggot" on the wall and to steal pages from a book. The book in question is Fernando Ortiz's *Historia de una pelea cubana contra los demonios* (A Cuban Fight Against Demons), about the burning of the city of Remedios in the seventeenth century, but which alludes to a specific scene in which eighteen "amujerados"—effeminate men—were burned to death by the Inquisition on an island called Cayo Puto. The scene of men with feathers stuck to their skin (*pájaros* is a colloquial word for homosexuals) burning on a raft in the ocean appears in Vladimir's dreams, and many of the tomb robbers as well as the graveyard cruisers, including Renán, seem to have recurrent dreams about the same episode, suggesting that they are in fact the present or past victims of a foundational act of murderous homophobia in Cuba. The past is not exactly past, the dead are not exactly dead, and love is a mystery related to death and contained in César's scar. The scar is itself the mark of a past wound, of skin that has been punctured, pricked, penetrated; a grapheme that contains a story and a wound, the trace of which can be found on César's skin and, metaphorically, in Vladimir's soul. When he penetrates César, however, Vladimir encounters a wall ("I run into a wall that will never open again to me, if it ever did"), a metaphorical wall that, like skin, prevents the carnal act from truly becoming the absolute union with the other; that is, the absolute knowledge of the other that Vladimir seeks, either a truth about love in general or about Miranda in particular, a truth that cannot be grasped, and therefore remains in another world, the realm of utopia.

Necrophilia, the sexual encounter with or in close proximity to the dead, is identified as the rite of passage that unveils such truth. The culmination of the protagonist's quest for love, and of Ponte's book, is an episode that unites the living and the dead "on equal terms" through a series of operations whose key can be found in photography. Consider the following scene: César, now banned from the cemetery, is obsessively searching for something, either something to replace the cemetery as an object of desire, or something for which he was searching in the cemetery in the first place. The cemetery, in this context, becomes a means to transcendental knowledge.

Suggesting that he has found that something, he leads Vladimir through a dark, narrow tunnel inside a broken public bathroom that opens up to a narrow strip of space between the back of the dimly lit cinema screen and a wall. César takes off his shirt and the projection of the Pacific Ocean, an image so slow as to suggest a film still, casts a bluish light on his torso. Vladimir has the impression that César, who had tried to swim his way out of the island many times and failed, is now swimming in waves of pale blue light and shadows. At that moment, Vladimir caresses a ghost, finds a wall—both real and metaphorical—and traverses it in an act of sexual penetration that is also an entrance into sublime knowledge and love:

> he got closer to the wall. He touched the grayish light on it and felt a faint breeze on the tips of his fingers, like short puffs that came to him and quickly withdrew, like someone having difficulty breathing.
>
> He tried to lift his hands from the wall but wasn't able to. From behind, a pair of arms, the arms attached to the chest that was gently being cradled by the waves, undressed him . . . Vladimir closed his eyes and was again alone with the breathing on the wall.
>
> He placed his mouth on it and pushed the wall with his forehead. The wall opened up to him. His forehead, his nose, his chin went through it and in to the other side. He was now capable of going through walls and talking with ghosts. On the other side, he moved his lips and talked to someone . . . And, as if it were not coming from his own body, he watched the trajectory his shot of sperm made behind the screen. (Ponte 2002, 150)

The narrow strip of space behind the screen is like a pantheon, a tomb of light, a metaphysical *camera lucida*. The space can only be accessed through a dark, narrow, humid tunnel in a public bathroom in a ceremony that could evoke the act of birth. Yet, it is not an exit related to creation, reproduction, and beginnings—homosexuality has been condemned by César's mother as "a love that begets nothing" (Ponte 2002, 125)—but it is rather an entrance into a tomb-like place in which love and knowledge, the utopian encounter of the dead and the living "on equal terms" happens materially and metaphysically at the same time.

The tunnel that marks the passage between the city and the realm of the dead is evocative of three semantic sites in which penetration becomes a practice of cognition: the scar, the photographic shutter, and the rectum. First, the scar is explicitly charged with metaphorical signification in the text insofar as it encapsulates both the notion of beauty for the photographer and of love for Vladimir. But the scar also functions as a mark of identity that undergoes endless substitutions. Indeed, the text suggests that the mended patch on the screen and the scar of Miranda in Vladimir's heart are associated with César's real scar. It is the coincidence of metaphor and referent that makes the connection between living flesh and material ghost magically take place.

Second, the tunnel evokes a camera shutter. In photography, a shutter is a device that allows light to pass for a determined period of time so as to expose film or a light-sensitive surface to light, capturing a permanent image. Through the shutter, light creates material meaning, making possible the co-presence of subject and object, a co-presence that is the medium's most basic and distinctive statement. According to Roland Barthes in *Camera Lucida*, a capacity intrinsic to photography is to cancel itself as a medium. The photograph becomes not a sign, but the thing itself (1981, 83). In *Contrabando de sombras*, light becomes a "carnal medium," as Barthes calls it, allowing for "a co-presence of a metaphysical order" (84). Light becomes skin, a skin that Vladimir can feel and touch, taking what Laura Marks calls "haptic visuality" (vision that becomes a tactile experience) to another level (2000, xi). César becomes someone made of light, a specter. Sex with an image, with light, is the deepest form of interaction between fiction and the real. The scar on both the screen and on César's skin can also be thought of as representing what Barthes calls a *punctum*, that detail on the signified that pricks the viewer (Vladimir, but also the reader) emotionally and gives the image a special significance.

Third, the penetration of a tunnel in a bathroom that culminates in ejaculation suggests anal sex. The tunnel viewed as a rectum brings the sexual discussion into a political arena. In his essay "Is the Rectum a Grave?" Bersani discusses how passivity in gay sex has, since the AIDS epidemic, recuperated the connotation of uninterrupted sex, of an unquenchable appetite for destruction once associated with prostitution and syphilis in the nineteenth century. Evoking Epps and partly quoting Foucault, Bersani states: "There is legal and moral incompatibility between sexual passivity and civic authority. The only 'honorable' sexual behavior 'consists in being active, in dominating, in penetrating, and in thereby exercising one's authority' . . . *To be penetrated is to abdicate power*" (1988, 212; emphasis in the original). Bersani furthers Epps's statement (discussed above) regarding the intimate connection between sex, politics, and honor when he suggests: "That judgment [*To be penetrated is to abdicate power*] is grounded in the sacrosanct value of selfhood, a value that accounts for human beings' extraordinary willingness to kill in order to protect the seriousness of their statements." This leads Bersani to conclude: "The self is a practical convenience; promoted to the status of an ethical ideal, it is a sanction for violence" (222). *Contrabando* can be interpreted as promoting an ethics *against* honor in which honor is understood as both the key to membership in an exclusive masculine fraternity and a sublimated justification for murder. This is the same form of ethics that informs the ghostly story of Cayo Puto that permeates the lives of the novel's characters through their dreams, in tombs, and through the walls.

One can conclude that the truth in *Contrabando de sombras* is the murderous desire implicit in revolutionary notions of masculine honor, of which Miranda is but one victim. In a text that operates within several rhetorical levels, however, the figure of speech that most consistently reveals and contests this truth is anastomosis, the permeation of one word into another, or, in this case, of one world into another: the city in the cemetery, one dead lover and an alive one, the skin and the screen, dream and consciousness. Indeed, the novel starts with an image of permeability—"the ceiling between wakefulness and dreams had leaks" (Ponte 2002, 7–8)—and continues to be structured by the same logic of substitution in which the permeation of one world into another calls on the ethical ideals of the revolution as a simulacrum of ethical truth. One can read in this movement of invasion and inversion a condemnation of the revolution's sanction of homosocial violence. By staging narrative worlds in which a new conception of ethics, one that shuns the revolutionary imperative of loyalty and honor in favor of individual commitments and private loyalties, the novel offers an effective resistance against friendship as "a political crime."

What is more, the scar and its doubles—the mended patch, the wound, the rectum, and so on—can be seen to function as what Lacan calls a "*point de capiton*," that is, an "upholstery button" or "quilting point," insofar as these scars tend to fix meaning by stopping the endless *glissement* of signification if only momentarily. It is on the basis of this Lacanian concept that Žižek speaks of a "magical inversion"—an operation through which a former negative becomes a new positive (1991, 29). In the seminar *Les Psychoses*, Lacan discusses the transformation of all fears into courage in light of "the fear of God." Žižek explains that a kind of "transubstantiation" takes place by "presenting their very opposite—God—as a thing more frightening than all earthly fears. And—that is the 'miracle' of *le point de capiton*—this supplemental fear, fear of God, retroactively changes the character of all other fears" (1991, 17). In Ponte's novel, the scar acts as a "*point de capiton*" that turns perversion, a former negative, into solidarity, love, and beauty. Through various forms of permeation, homosexuality in this text can be said to short-circuit institutional codes by introducing love where there is supposed to be only law, rule, or habit, to paraphrase the quote by Foucault that I used as an epigraph to this chapter. As interruption, irruption, piercing, and puncturing, but also as sharpness, clarity, sensitivity, and profundity, penetration in *Contrabando* cancels out the rhetorical conflation by the revolutionary project of a masculinist ideology with an ethical ideal.

PERVERSION AS TROPE

Žižek notes that *le point de capiton* is an optical illusion; it always produces a misreading (1991, 19). One could even go so far as to say that it produces an apparent perversion of meaning that better illuminates the truth underneath. In *Ethics of Reading* J. Hillis Miller asks "how does the non-linguistic become language?" and proposes that it permeates the narrative through the spread of certain tropes, thus seeing the relationship between literature and ethics in terms of infection, because rhetorical figures operate like "the entry of a parasitical virus within the host cell, interfering with the working of that cell and reprogramming it in unforeseen ways" (1987, 8). In other words, he sees rhetorical figures as a perversion of meaning capable of producing an ethical interpellation. Hillis Miller defines an "ethical moment" as that particular point in which the reading experience calls for an immediate and unequivocal response: "There is a necessary ethical moment in the act of reading as such, a moment neither cognitive, nor political, nor social, nor interpersonal, but properly and independently ethical" (1).

As I have argued, perversion produces an ethical interpellation through a prick, a *point de capiton* that can help explain the ethical weight of the other "optical illusions" I discussed above—a scar, a mended patch, a tricky window, or a stage door to a more benevolent world. These *points de capiton* produce a magical inversion by which something that has been traditionally considered unproductive or even negative becomes an unexpected good. Here perversion produces civility and solidarity. These perversions, I suggest, best illuminate the ideological force of (revolutionary) ethics and Hillis Miller's identification of ideology as a case of anamorphosis. He defines both as "the transformation of one form into another which is recognizable as being a distortion of its original only when viewed from a certain angle" (1987, 7).

As I have argued in this chapter, perversion in the post-Soviet Cuban novel provides an ethical call not only because it subverts values but rather in its capacity to produce discomfort. Like physical discomfort, which makes us change positions frequently, moral discomfort forces us to change subject positions frequently. We therefore find ourselves testing new vantage points, so as to better tell apart ideals, ideology, and simulacra. The corpse as a distorted projection of the living human; the love for the corpse as a substitute for an impossible living human connection; the lie that uncannily resembles truth and, like truth, creates justice; the ethical superiority of a friendship that is not one, that only reproduces its form but not its defining ideals—all these forms of perversion act as prisms that shed light on the ideological nature of revolutionary morals. Perhaps unexpectedly, they also shed light on the mechanics of coming of age, a theme that is constitutive of the masculine novels on social and political aging that I discussed in the previous chapter. For, in biological terms, anamorphosis, an instance of metamorphosis, refers to a gradual progression into a higher type in certain species. It therefore suggests the transformation of the original creature into a new type of subject, a subject of a different truth-process, which comes to being as a result of learning (evolution) not of violent change (revolution). Anamorphosis, which in biology means "to reach adulthood by the acquisition of additional body segments," questions what it means to be in the present but always in relation to the lessons of the past. What better rhetorical figure, I wonder, for understanding perversion as an enlightened form of coming of age.

4 The Poetics of Evil

> Throughout the century, cruelty has been less a moral question than an aesthetic one (yet another debt to Nietzsche).
>
> —Alain Badiou (2007, 115)

We may locate post-Soviet Cuba in what Jean Baudrillard calls an "after-the-orgy" moment. Strictly speaking, Baudrillard calls "orgy" that intense moment in the twentieth century when "modernity exploded upon us," prompting liberation at all levels (sexual and political liberation, liberation of the forces of production and of destruction, liberation of art, etc.), and which, even in its successes, failed to bring about the ethical, political, and aesthetic utopias that they were expected to produce. Baudrillard ponders, "What do we do now the orgy is over?" His answer? Simulation:

> Now all we can do is simulate the orgy, simulate liberation. We may pretend to carry on in the same direction, accelerating, but in reality we are accelerating in a void, because all the goals of liberation are already behind us . . . This is the state of simulation, a state in which we are obliged to replay all scenarios precisely because they have all taken place, whether actually or potentially. The state of utopia realized, of all utopias realized, wherein paradoxically we must continue to live as though they had not been. But since they have, and since we can no longer, therefore, nourish the hope of realizing them, we can only "hyper-realize" them through interminable simulation. We live amid the interminable reproduction of ideals, phantasies, images and dreams which are now behind us, yet which we must continue to reproduce in a sort of inescapable indifference. (1993, 3–4)

In Cuba, and Latin America in general, that moment of hopeful liberation described by Baudrillard was epitomized by the 1959 revolution.It was a great political, social, and ethical event, in the sense that Alain Badiou gives to the word "event"; that is, as a truth-process that gives meaning to the actions, values, and words of an epoch. Its failure, which became apparent in the 1990s, can be explained in terms of reasons both internal to Cuba, such as the authoritarian style of the revolution and the failings of a dependent economy, and external to it: not only the dissolution of the Soviet Union, which implied the loss of economic support and of key trade partners, but also perhaps a generalized disenchantment by a younger generation uninterested in the sacrificial nature of any such political project. This attitude defines what Gilles Lipovetsky calls the "after-duty generation," which I explored in the previous chapter.

Contemporary thinkers such as Slavoj Žižek and Badiou seem to hold views consistent with Baudrillard's. Žižek declares in *Virtue and Terror* that the end of communism in 1989 finished a whole era that had begun with the French revolution, an era in which it was accepted that there was no limit to the sacrifices and violence that were required for revolutions to take place and survive. In other words, virtue required terror. What comes after 1989, according to Žižek, is at most the desire for a "decaffeinated" revolution, equal to "1789 without 1793," that is, a revolution without "the 'divine violence' of terror." Žižek wonders what we may possibly want in a post-1989 culture of "freedom of opinion," "market competition," and "pluralist interaction" (2007, vii–viii). He concludes that today we want neither virtue nor terror. Accepting Žižek's premise implies a contemporary ethos of disaffection from any regime that, like the Cuban one, officially pays heed to both virtue *and* terror, and can therefore only be seen as doubly anachronistic.

In his efforts to delimit the twentieth century so as to better "meditate philosophically on all this," Alain Badiou defines it in terms of two possible and partly coextensive "centuries": the Soviet century, which begins with the First World War and "comes to a close with the collapse of the USSR" in 1989; and "the totalitarian century," a little shorter than the Soviet century, but not very different:

> It begins in 1917 with Lenin (some would happily have it begin in 1793, with Robespierre, but then it would grow far too long), reaches its apex in 1937 with Stalin and 1942–5 with Hitler, and to all intents and purposes comes to an end with Mao Tsetung's death in 1976. It lasts about sixty years—provided one ignores exotic survivors like Fidel Castro, or certain marginal and diabolical resurgences, such as Islamic "extremism." (2007, 2)

What Badiou calls "the totalitarian century" is a period that, having come to an end for all intents and purposes in the 1970s, justified terror in the name of virtue. However, revolutionary Cuba still belongs to this period, mostly as a relic of an outmoded totalitarian conscience, and, at least officially, Cuba has not entered into the next historical stage. According to Badiou, a new era begins everywhere else "after the seventies (with the end of revolutionary fervour)." This era is characterized by "the victory of the economy, in all senses of the term: the victory of Capital, [as well as] economizing on the unreasonable passions of thought." Badiou concludes his description of recent times by calling this unimaginative, thirty-year-long period "the liberal century" (2007, 3). The liberal century can be said to exclude post-Soviet revolutionary Cuba as a political project, although it does not necessarily exclude its citizens, who are aware of inhabiting a space of what Baudrillard calls simulation.

There are important similarities among the thinkers I have been discussing so far. Badiou, like Baudrillard, identifies the conclusion of a political era with the end of "revolutionary fervour," and deems Fidel Castro's survival an exotic anachronism (the ethical implications of which I try to elucidate throughout this book). Badiou also echoes Žižek in his suggestion that the revolutions of the twentieth century belong to a similar impulse of liberation and terror that started with the French revolution.Given how Žižek, Badiou, and Baudrillard conceptualize the ideological patterns of the last century, one can extend their analysis to conclude that the prolonged eventlessness that characterized Cuba in the years between 1991 and 2008 has in fact been little more than "the interminable reproduction of ideals, phantasies, images and dreams" of an idealistic revolution that has long been "behind us," in the words of Baudrillard. Particularly significant under this head is these authors' identification of a radical rupture in the way revolutionary faith is experienced and interpreted. In fact, when foreigners ask Cubans, as they often do, what will happen next, they seem to be asking, "What is going to happen now that the revolutionary orgy is over?"

In 2001, Iván de la Nuez, a young Cuban intellectual, asked twelve of his peers to imagine a post-post-Soviet future for a volume entitled *Cuba y el día después* (Cuba and the Day After). Ena Lucía Portela titled her contribution using a citation from Paul Auster's *City of Glass*, "Tan oscuro como muy oscuro" (as dark as very dark; 2001b). Without using quite the same words as Baudrillard, Portela situates herself *after* several "orgies." One such "orgy" is nationalism: By calling herself "*the nowhere girl*," in English in the original, Portela is suggesting that she doesn't write from the perspective of someone who belongs to a nation (2001b, 186; emphasis in original). Another "orgy" is that of feminist liberation, which Portela describes rather cynically as an attempt to let men know that "they were not the only idiots [writing] in town" (2001b; 185). As a further indication that Portela consciously inhabits an "after-the-orgy" world, she replies to the question posed by de la Nuez with another question: "What? Did anything happen?" (2001b, 183).

It is clear to Portela that, if the Cuban revolution epitomizes the modernist lust for liberation, the period that started in 1991 is an artificially slow process of awareness that the orgy is over. The political changes are so conspicuously slow that Portela can only show an "inescapable indifference." It is revealing that when Portela reminisces about 1989–1991, she does so in terms of age rather than history:

> The news from Moscow gave us unlimited happiness . . . The communist regimes dissolved one after another like bubbles and we ("we": the adolescent as a tribal subject dissolved in the group, in the plural voice of attenuated responsibility) were elated. Mostly, for the love of

> anarchy; for the youthful, Jacobin passion of dismantling everything in one strike, or at least of cheering those who did. But also, for the pure pleasure of erasing all the names invented by our elders . . . in order to rename the objects around us and the processes within which we all lived. For the simple desire to *rewrite* the story. (2001b, 188–189; emphasis in original)

The dramatic events that marked the dissolution of the Soviet bloc constitute the cultural landmark of her generation, the adolescents of Portela's "tribe." Portela paints the love of liberation as part of a youthful exercise, one that requires celebration: "The best news, the best parties: when Gorbachev dissolved the Party after a coup attempt; when Ceausescu was squashed . . . and, of course, the fall of the [Berlin] Wall" (2001b, 189). It is no doubt ironic that the events celebrated by Portela's generation marked the irreversible end of an era for everyone in the Soviet socialist camp and elsewhere, *except* for Cuba. Furthermore, Portela's parties, we are led to understand, celebrated not so much the end of a regime, but rather "the end of revolutionary fervour" *in the name of* revolutionary fervor. For what are Portela's parties if not a youthful, ritualistic, aesthetic *simulation* of what once was a legitimate "Jacobin passion"?

I take it that when Jorge Fornet suggests that Ena Lucía Portela and other "novísimos" (young, innovative writers of the early 1990s) "were born in another country, as it were" (2001, 45), he means that they can more accurately be portrayed as citizens of Baudrillard's postmodern world than of revolutionary Cuba even in its post-Soviet incarnation. It is true that Portela, along with a significant sector of the younger Cuban population, belongs to a different "century," that is, to a different worldview than the one upheld by the generation before her. Her "tribal" celebration of the end of an era that, while very pertinent to Cuba, failed to alter the Cuban political landscape, squarely locates *the nowhere girl* in the paradoxical situation that revolutionary Cuba occupies in the "after-the-orgy" moment. Portela's sarcastic question "What? Did anything happen?" brings those paradoxes to the fore. The persistence of Cuba's pursuit of an unsustainable political project—its *eventlessness*—belongs to the realm of simulation, what Baudrillard describes as "accelerating in a void." It is not surprising that the Cuban film that best illustrates the condition of simulation that I have been describing is the allegorically fuzzy yet memorable film *Juan de los muertos* (*Juan of the Dead*) in which a group of (dissident) zombies are fought and defeated by an equally corpselike army of non-zombies. The after-the-orgy moment I have been describing consists of a paradox: an official Cuba that for decades perseveres in a political program of virtue and terror and demands faith from a citizenry that believes in neither. This situation largely explains the state of paralysis and the overall affect of absurdity that characterizes post-Soviet Cuba. And, as Baudrillard points out, "where there is stasis, there is metastasis" (1993, 15).

TERROR WITHOUT VIRTUE

Metastasis refers to a widespread disorder that compromises a living organism such that it critically endangers its survival: "When a living form becomes disordered, when (as in cancer) a genetically determined set of rules ceases to function, the cells begin to proliferate chaotically" (1993, 15).[1] Baudrillard uses this medical metaphor to name the generalized affect that pervades artistic codes when a modern (presumably capitalist) society can no longer believe in utopia. I, in turn, will borrow Baudrillard's metaphor to describe in post-Soviet Cuban terms the notion of a break in the genetic code of the revolutionary ethos, as well as the affect and aesthetics such structural situation yields.

Socialist legality, which was reduced to simulation in the period that followed 1991, continued, even in the early 2000s, to drastically curtail the mechanisms of repair usually available to citizens in democratic systems, such as the right to voice and exit, but which have been relinquished to protect the sovereignty of Cuba and the survival of a purportedly ethically superior political system. However, the long inoperativeness of the Cuban socialist social contract, and the incapacity or unwillingness of the government to adapt and change, makes it a structurally damaging condition.[2] The gratuitous dehumanization of the citizenry, as well as their persistent lack of faith in a better future, creates a political situation in which terror survives without, or even at the expense of, virtue. This predicament, in my opinion, can best be described as a structural evil. Traditionally, evil is defined as the infliction of unnecessary pain on someone so that his humanity is put into question. I call it structural not only because political evil is experienced as though it were an instance of natural evil (earthquakes, illnesses, hurricanes, etc.), but also because it puts its victims, the regular citizens, in a situation in which they have no other choice than to become accomplices to the crime. This structural problem more intensely affects intellectuals who, by the fact of having partial access to voice, are more susceptible to simultaneously becoming victims and accomplices of an unsustainable situation.

What I have been calling "stasis" is best illustrated by the work of the Stasi. In two related articles, Antonio José Ponte (2011) and Jorge Luis García Vázquez (2007) comment on an exhibition on "diversionismo ideológico" (ideological deviationism) held in Havana in 1974, which was organized by the Ministry of the Interior and the office of "Seguridad del Estado," and whose program was discovered by García Vázquez in the archive of the German Stasi. The exhibition showcased—among other "evident proofs of ideological deviationism" such as "personal letters, recording of radio broadcasts, and literary awards"—the material collected during the systematic persecution of two writers, Heberto Padilla (Operation "Iluso") and José Lezama Lima (Operation "Órbita").[3] According to Ponte, the publishing houses run by the state—and all of them were—refused to publish

Lezama's manuscripts but used them to fuel his status as enemy of the state. The exhibition catalogue shows that the government displayed Lezama's unpublished manuscripts as well as his "work in progress," which were presumably taken from his house. The writer who wants to get published either legally in Cuba or illegally in foreign markets (as was the case in the 1970s), or who simply writes in his own house, feeds, in spite of himself, the very machine that terrorizes him. That the state had no conflict in "curating" an exhibit based on this material speaks of the need for spectacle that terror requires in its attempt to create an efficient, generalized affect of fear.

Much of the literature of the post-Soviet period is devoted to addressing the experience of fear, its convoluted mechanisms, and morally maiming effects. Eliseo Alberto's memoir *Informe contra mí mismo* (A Report against Myself) is an emblematic text of this trend, which takes as its point of departure the request that was put to him during his military service to spy and report on his own family members and friends. As the son of national poet Eliseo Diego, Eliseo Alberto, also known as Lichi, grew up surrounded by artists, foreign visitors, and members of the local bourgeoisie that stayed in Cuba. This betrayal, however, takes the form of a hybrid text. *Informe* is a memoir that celebrates the bohemian circles Lichi was supposed to have denounced. In another text, Wendy Guerra, a former children's television entertainer turned writer and artist, describes in her fictional journal *Todos se van* (Everyone Leaves), a landscape of oppression and, what is worse, its internalization and perpetual reenactment in private relations. Like Reinaldo Arenas's *Antes que anochezca* (Before Night Falls), Jesús Díaz's *Las palabras perdidas*, and Ponte's *Contrabando de sombras*, Guillermo Rosales's *Boarding Home* (The Halfway House) also alludes to the mysterious disappearance of manuscripts, the blacklisting of writers, and their doomed relegation to civil nonexistence.

The atmosphere of oppression is succinctly described in Ena Lucía Portela's essay "As Dark as Very Dark." In spite of her avowed attempt not to discuss politics, Portela takes stock of the affective toll of the cultural politics of the Revolution: "The balance? A couple of traumatized generations, a few sad books, an overwhelming backwardness in critical models; and, worst of all, a profound, visceral fear that still preys on writers, theorists, university professors, etc, who lived in that preamble to paradise" (2001b, 186). Addressing the powerful combination of fear and faith reigning over intellectual circles, she wonders in her distinctive cynicism: "What stuff were those beliefs made on? The nowhere girl didn't know; probably a strange, distorting, faith-inducing material" (2001b, 191). Portela unveils the impossible nature of the social contract by comparing it with a hallucinatory, "faith-inducing" drug, thus depreciating as delusional the utopian ideals of the revolution.The intellectual landscape she describes is the impossible situation in which artists operate as if they had full access to voice and exit in a social contract that structurally denies them both. It is hardly surprising, then, that contemporary Cuban literature shows a deep anxiety not just toward the prolonged survival of a failed political project but also toward the violence that comes from insisting on the promise, understood as impossible, of reaching the ideals of community, justice, loyalty, and fraternity through unlimited self-sacrifice.

In this chapter, I read a type of fiction that can be described as "a poetics of evil," a poetics that takes literature as a radical vocation of perpetual antagonism. I will contend that the poetics of evil is productively destructive of the convergence of ethics, aesthetics, and politics as established in the socialist social contract. Within the framework established by several theorists of evil, particularly Badiou, Nietzsche, and Baudrillard, I will read Guillermo Rosales's *Boarding Home* (The Halfway House), Wendy Guerra's *Todos se van* (Everyone Leaves), Ena Lucía Portela's *La sombra del caminante* (The Wanderer's Shadow) and "El viejo, el asesino y yo" (The Old Man, the Murderer and I), and Pedro Juan Gutiérrez's *El Rey de La Habana* (The King of Havana) as taking part in an anticommunal aesthetics that breaks away from the socialist social contract, declaring it as pure simulation. Specifically, I aim to do three things: I bring to a conclusion the argumentative arc that I opened in Chapter 2 regarding the conflation of ethics and politics as a foundational confusion in the socialist social contract; I begin to explore more explicitly the connection between ethics and aesthetics that I develop more fully in the next chapters; and, ultimately, I try to understand the role evil plays in contemporary philosophy in order to elaborate upon the structural problem that arises from the Cuban revolution as an exhausted truth-process.

THEORIZING EVIL

Originally, the Cuban revolution constituted itself as a good in opposition to a specific evil; namely, American imperialism and the concentration of political control in the hands of a foreign-oriented oligarchy. Early on, it proclaimed itself as a Marxist endeavor. In the light of the dialectical materialism it embraced, the revolution saw itself as the final stage in a dynamic process of revolutionary attempts and failures since the wars of independence that would help free Cubans from imperial bonds once and for all.[4] However, by rejecting concepts like "criticism from within," the revolution also failed to view itself critically, therefore preventing the possibility of enabling further qualitative change. Eventually, the permanent war against imperialism became an excuse for the perpetuation of the political class, creating an artificial state of affairs that pays lip service to the values of 1959 but no longer sustains them. One could say that the revolutionary state no longer invokes the truth in whose name it operates. Now an inoperative situation, the institutionalized revolution is a Simulation, in Baudrillard's words, or perhaps a Simulacrum, one of the forms of evil recognized by Badiou.

In his *Ethics: An Essay on the Understanding of Evil*, Badiou analyzes ethics as a generalized social mechanism put in motion by a game-changing event. Drawing on the work of Foucault, Lacan, and Althusser, Badiou argues that no values exist outside the situation created by an event; therefore, it is the fidelity to the situation that determines the codes according to which we participate and interpret historical and social situations, as well as the general rules that govern our being together. In the Cuban case, fidelity to the revolution as a truth-process is apparently in place. Politically, at least, the ideal of the revolution still functions as a virtual point of reference. Remarkably, the situation that began in 1959 did not come to a recognizable end in 1989, nor did it undergo any significant modification. The post-Soviet socialist social contract not only failed to correct the imbalances of the original Soviet-style revolutionary contract, but actually rendered it unsustainable. This is how an ethically superior political endeavor became a simulacrum of truth. In the Special Period, the combination of a lack of freedoms and of basic goods could be experienced by a single individual as belonging to an order of things comparable to that of natural disasters. Unrestrained austerity put most of the population in a situation of intolerable, subhuman living conditions in the name of a collective faith that was scarce in practice. The fact that this situation could have been avoided by applying consistent political and economic changes that were expressly forbidden by an inoperative socialist social contract makes this dehumanization both artificial and unnecessary. Post-Soviet socialist Cuba is a truth that has been pushed too far. Alan Badiou would call the current state of the revolution "a simulacrum of truth," for it is a truth-process that "convokes not the void [that it really is] but the full 'particularity' or presumed substance of the situation" it no longer is (2001, 73). No doubt due to its all-too-real effects, "a simulacrum of truth" is, essentially, "terror directed at everyone" (77).

In what follows, I interpret Badiou as advancing a (Nietzschean) notion of evil as potentially productive and even good. It is important to remember that, for Badiou, ethics only exists in relation to a situation, not in categorical terms. So, following this logic, evil constitutes less a betrayal to the ideals defining the situation than a naming of the betrayal and a subsequent call for change. This is particularly relevant in the structurally impossible association of communism and community, which lies at the heart of the schema of betrayal. For Badiou, "the community and the collective are the unnameables of political truth: every attempt 'politically' to name a community induces a disastrous Evil" (2001, 86). In contrast, he argues, "not only does Evil destroy the situation . . . but it also interrupts the truth-process in whose name it proceeds, since it fails to preserve, within the composition of its subject, the duality [*duplicité*] of interests (disinterested-interest and interest pure and simple)" (85). By this I understand, building on Badiou's original formulation, that the assumption of consensus required for the identification of a political community has disastrous consequences. A community that has been "named" includes in its very definition the origin of either the potential disintegration of the community or the repression of singularities required to avoid its fragmentation. It follows, then, that a community can only truly exist as a desire. For Badiou, the political community that has been named, and in whose name actions are decided upon and implemented, is already a beyond-community. Thus, if I am right, the union of politics and ethics (of politics and truth) only resides in its foundation. Once it is named, the Cuban revolution is justified in resorting to terror to defend its truth (like the revolution's "right to exist" defended by Fidel Castro in his "Palabras a los intelectuales"), a truth that cannot in any way encompass the specific complexities that divide a community in whose name it speaks as if it were an absolute. The idea that evil may destroy a truth-process that is no longer viewed as legitimate suggests a scenario in which any emergent ideologies with the potential to convoke a new event appear at first as a form of evil. Badiou himself suggests as much when he states that consensus is always conservative, and that every emancipatory project can be seen as the will to put an end to consensus (2001, 32).

If, as I mentioned earlier, one of the forms of evil recognized by Badiou is the naming of a community as a unified political entity on the basis of an assumed consensus and at the expense of singularities, evil's capacity to destroy a situation and to preserve the duality of interests can be an emancipatory tool. In this context, Badiou's evil is potentially positive, as it allows for the ideal pursuit of a "destiny of *truths*, in the plural" (2001, 3; emphasis in the original). In this radical understanding of ethics, Badiou seems to echo Nietzsche, whom he calls "a prophet of the century" (2007, 31)—although it would be more accurate, in my view, to call him the prophet of the "after-orgy."

In *Human, All Too Human*, Nietzsche points out that "morality is primarily a means of preserving the community and saving it from destruction. Next it is a means of maintaining the community on a certain plane and in a certain degree of benevolence. Its motives are fear and hope" (2009, 303). As morals are essential both to the survival of the community and to the preservation of its defining characteristics, various degrees of conscious and unconscious intimidation are required to maintain the absolute sense of duty toward the community.[5] The importance of the Good for the survival of the community at the expense of individual interests leads Georges Bataille to conclude in his book *On Nietzsche* that, in fact, the "good would be the interest of *others*."[6] A similar vision is underlying the structure of the post-Soviet revolutionary social contract, which demands extreme personal sacrifices in the name of sovereignty and an ideology that justifies itself as a superior ethics.

The post-Soviet situation is dominated by the large human cost of the perpetuation of two "goods" that originally defined revolutionary Cuba, the union of politics and ethics, on the one hand, and the promise of community, on the other. In this context, it is doubly productive to entertain

Nietzsche's thoughts on a good that may not be so good and an evil that may be liberating. In his elaboration of evil, Nietzsche "takes to court" the value of values that, I argue in the context of Cuba, sustain the faith, or at least the simulation of faith, in the revolutionary social contract. For Nietzsche, values such as the expectation of self-sacrifice for a common cause, on the one hand, and the notion of a disinterested aesthetics, on the other, constitute ethical subterfuges:

> There is no other way: the feelings of devotion, self-sacrifice for one's neighbor, the whole morality of self-denial must be questioned mercilessly and taken to court—no less than the aesthetics of "contemplation devoid of all interest" which is used today as a seductive guise for the emasculation of art, to give it a good conscience. There is too much charm and sugar in these feelings of "for others," "*not* for myself," for us not to need to become doubly suspicious at this point and to ask: "are these not perhaps—*seductions*?" (2000, 235; emphases in the original)

The word "seductions" is very suggestive of both the allure of the promise of community and of its impossibly dual nature. For instance, solidarity, a value that is at the heart of both friendship and community, can easily become a trap. Solidarity only works when it is reciprocated; when it is not it feels a lot like subjection. Such insight is revealed when one sees virtues not in their abstract definition, which appear in their ideal, unimpeachable form, but rather in the imperfect, contradictory role they play in social practice.

The seductive language of revolutionary altruism, I argue, has largely paralyzed revolutionary intellectuals. As I have discussed in previous chapters, the state promoted a revolutionary social contract as if it were an ideal friendship, that is, as a commitment to a fraternal community of equals based on altruism, solidarity, and justice. It ignored, however, that these social formations are not only different by nature (one is political, the other is moral), but that the definition of friendship itself is purely abstract. The ethical magnificence of friendship, defined by unfailing solidarity and altruism—living for the other—is impracticable in real life. Friendship has this in common with the revolution, as they are both defined in terms of their principles, regardless of how these ideals fare when put into practice. The difference is that friendship is a voluntary and reciprocal bond, and therefore has built-in tools, namely voice and exit, that help provide limits to its extreme nature. However, this is not the case of the socialist social contract, which, while also defined by altruism, solidarity, and loyalty, precludes any mechanism of control to either ensure the reciprocity of the contract or, in its failure, to regain social and political control. As I have been arguing, the nationalization of virtues is central to the foundation of the revolutionary project. These values, which are also the values of traditional friendship between men, are not only associated with heightened notions of masculinity but are also affectively and culturally sublimated by mostly male intellectuals and mostly male politicians. As such, these virtues have a political force that can replace, or at least supplement, coercion. The appropriation of the values of friendship is what I have called, following Derrida, the "political crime" of the Revolution.

Pursuing my reading of Badiou further, I would like to suggest that an aesthetics of social and emotional destruction is invested in the fracture and the fragmentation of an established truth. It forces the naming of the simulacrum. Two hypotheses can be advanced: 1) as an aesthetic device, evil can be said to effectively take to court the values on which an illusory community was built and thereby unveils its human cost; 2) at a political level, evil breaks the consensus. It puts an end to the duplicitous nature of the revolutionary social contract as well as to the illusory union of communism and community.

Evil is productive thanks to its intransigence. Indeed, the most radical view of evil is the one offered by Baudrillard, who argues that evil exists beyond promises, and beyond social contracts. Baudrillard stresses this characteristic of evil in his book *The Transparency of Evil*:

> The Good consists in a dialectic of Good and Evil. Evil consists in the negation of this dialectic, a radical dissociation of Good and Evil, and by extension in the autonomy of the principle of Evil. Whereas the Good presupposes a dialectical involvement of Evil, Evil is founded on itself alone, in pure incompatibility. Evil is thus master of the game, and it is the principle of Evil, the reign of eternal antagonism, that must eventually carry off the victory. (1993, 139)

This is what Baudrillard calls the "irreconcilability" of evil: While the good is always within good and evil, evil is always already outside the dichotomy, negating the validity of its terms. As I said earlier, the revolution constituted itself as a good in opposition to a specific evil—American imperialism. In practice, however, the permanent war against imperialism has long been seen more as an excuse for the perpetuation of a leading class in power, creating an artificial state of affairs that pays lip service to its founding values but no longer sustains them. It is poetic justice that the forces of post-Soviet stasis can best be "taken to court" by a poetics of evil.

What I am calling a (post-Soviet Cuban) poetics of evil revisits the same themes as those that occupied the previously discussed texts, such as community and betrayal, voice and exit, the new man, the social contract, and a utopian faith in the future. However, contrary to the case of ethical dilemmas that unfold in the course of a narrative and are, therefore, mostly analyzed through the discussion of plot, evil does not always require a story, but rather resides on the unsettling power of a certain scene, in instances of unexpected or relentless cruelty, or in a particularly disturbing metaphor. It is important to note that the distinction between traditional and Nietzschean notions of evil (the evil that harms and the evil that liberates) occupy complementary yet antagonistic positions.

Three principles of moral philosophy will guide my analyses. First, I believe, like both Foucault and Badiou, that "ethics is the principle that" not only judges but also enables "the practice of the Subject, be it individual or collective" (Badiou 2001, 2). Second, I believe, following Nietzsche and Badiou, that the categorical imperative can in fact be a cruel proposition. Not only does it crush singularities, but it also assumes a consensual, ahistorical, and *a priori* notion of what constitutes evil. Third, I believe, following Maurice Blanchot and Jean-Luc Nancy, that the communitarian imperative of communism is its inherent structural impossibility (more on this later). With these principles in mind, I will argue that the poetics of evil can be read as an exploration of the formation and deformation of the revolutionary subject. Through an analysis of the social and moral mechanisms of evil, and partly based on Nietzsche and poststructuralist philosophers Žižek, Badiou, and Baudrillard, I will argue that evil disrupts the revolution as a truth-process because it fails to preserve the duality of interests that defines the revolutionary subject, thus unmasking the post-Soviet social contract as simulation.

WENDY GUERRA'S VOICELESSNESS

In a striking scene in Guerra's fictional journal *Todos se van*, Osvaldo, a handsome artist that seventeen-year-old Nieve has been following for some time, brings her to his house. Osvaldo leads Nieve to his black-painted bedroom and then to a bed covered in black satin sheets, where he proceeds to deflower her. Nieve writes in her journal:

> Osvaldo touched my small round breasts. A glass bead fell from his neck and into my mouth, choking me. I swallowed it with terrible difficulty and chewed the rest without realizing I was bleeding. My tongue was purple and swollen. He thought of desire. I thought of pain. (2006, 182)[7]

The scene is brutal and stunning. The imagery of the glass beads choking and hurting the seventeen-year-old virgin girl's lips and tongue conjure the fragility of her emotions, the intensity of her desire, and its closeness to pain. The presence of blood in her mouth foreshadows the bleeding that follows the moment "his sex made its way against the graceful resistance of my tiny but firm innermost shield" (2006, 184). The blood operates also as a warning, suggesting that love may also be a form of poison (she claims her generation has embraced a "No Love" philosophy). Between the intense ecstasy of sexual pleasure and the tenderness of a soothing bath, Nieve reflects on her emotions. In contrast to Osvaldo's worldliness, her vulnerability makes her feel like "a minuscule pearl drowning in his oyster, trapped by lust and pain" (184).

Chewing glass beads, the pain, the blood, the water in the soothing bath, and the allusion to both the feeling of drowning and a pearl all echo a past initiation of sorts. During her childhood, Nieve's father had neglected to feed her for days and had thrown away the food sent to Nieve by the neighbors and by her stepfather. In turn, Nieve's revenge was to refuse to eat. When her father forced her to drink milk, Nieve vomited the milk until she saw blood, which signaled to her that there was absolutely nothing left in her body (2006, 61). She then flushed the toilet only to be soothed by the sight of the water draining out in a whirlpool, which reminded her of the lagoon of her early childhood where, surrounded by love and warm seawater, she had been happy. The repeated abuse inflicted on her by her father culminated the day when he hit the eight-year-old girl so fiercely that her earlobe was torn letting loose a pearl earring. Her father forced Nieve to swallow the pearl, a present from her stepfather, and she was advised to keep an eye on her bowel movement to recover the pearl. After this event, she partially lost her hearing. Nieve then promised she would leave her father even if she had to lie.

Both experiences, the one with the pearl and the one with the bead, suggest a coming of age of sorts. On the one hand, the glass bead of her adolescence suggests a more traditional initiation ritual including a loss—the loss of her virginity and her childhood—and a gain—love and her entrance into an exclusive, bohemian circle. On the other, the pearl of her childhood suggests her loss of trust in the world, in the adults, and in the bureaucracies that are failing to keep her safe. From the moment she swallows the pearl, she will only trust herself. She follows through on her promise by hurting herself on purpose in order to put in motion her release from her abusive father's custody. Both the pearl and the bead bring pain and liberation to her.

Part of what fascinates me about these two ceremonies is their intense corporeality; the idea that initiation requires not only pain, but a violation of different holes throughout her body by alien objects, however beautiful, which pass through her mouth and entrails only to be expelled in the form of vomit, stool, and blood. I find the orality in these two ceremonies to act as a metaphor for the complex relationship between voice and exit.

The title *Todos se van* alludes to the fact that everyone leaves the island, which is largely explained by the fact that the protagonist is surrounded by artists and, particularly, visual artists, who "have run away one by one after the witch-hunt that followed their exhibitions" (2006, 235). The situation in the fictional diary alludes to the actual exodus of visual artists in Cuba in the 1980s (see Mosquera 2001). Everyone else leaves but Nieve doesn't. The girl can leave with her mother for Sweden, following her adoring stepfather, however Nieve's father refuses to sign her exit permit because he is afraid of losing the favor of the Communist Party. But then, when he manages to leave through El Mariel, and is, therefore, free from official pressure, he is no longer able to sign because he is away. In an unreasonable structure of bureaucratized fear, the girl, a minor, simply cannot leave, thus preventing her mother from joining her foreign partner. This story also repeats itself with Octavio, who spends over a year in Paris and has "requested" her as his spouse. However, by the time she is of age and owns a passport, Octavio has officially defected from Cuba with a highly publicized speech. With not one word to her, he leaves Nieve behind. By leaving, both men thwart her exit in a world where everyone else leaves.

More important, both her father and Octavio forbid Nieve to speak or to write in her diary. This replicates the censorship in the world at large, rendered visible in Nieve's mother's radio program. Radio is an interesting medium to consider in this context: It is ephemeral, it allows for immediate connection with a large public, and it may creatively channel a plurality of voices through their music programming. However, shows that incorporate opinions, and are therefore supposed to be spontaneous, are always recorded to ensure no criticism is aired by chance. Songs, like Carlos Varela's, are interrupted because they include the word "freedom." Her mother periodically pushes the limits of expression in an effort to widen the margins of freedom. She uses the radio to send messages through songs to Nieve while the girl is in military training. The songs, fashionable at the time, also allude to silence: Luis Alberto Spinetta's "Ojos de papel" begins by saying "No hables más, muchacha" (Stop talking, girl), whereas Joaquín Sabina's and Luis Eduardo Aute's "Eclipse de mar" lists a number of truths that never appear on newspapers. Nieve's listening to the radio, her friend Lucía's reading her grandfather's banned novel, and their friend Alan's graffiti put the three kids in front of a disciplinary commission. Censorship also touches Osvaldo's friend Cloe, who cannot publish her novel because "it is not possible to vomit so many truths and remain in Cuba. Her novel can't be published here" (Guerra 2006, 234). Cleo eventually publishes her novel abroad and leaves the country. As a general rule, Nieve is always reminded that one should speak as little as possible in an authoritarian state.

Guerra's novel is, at least in part, about the untranslatability of structural evil. There are no appropriate or at least effective ways to describe evil. Evil is unintelligible, ineffable, impenetrable, it cannot be consumed, and it cannot be co-opted. Aesthetically, what I have been calling structural evil is a sensation that cannot be organized into words (in fact, structural evil can only be defined through a catachresis—there is no way to define it; it requires a violent misuse of language). This is why adolescent Nieve, who is an art student, designs art projects that speak through her body, by making installations including a photograph of her bald self surrounded by the hair she cut off, and by dreaming about covering the school walls with enlarged, illuminated versions of her diary pages (which of course she can't do). This trend culminates in her graduation project, which consists of burning sculptures made of books. In the entry "My Graduation," she explains

> I have prepared a piece based on my friend Juan Carlos García's work "How to Organize the Library Now?" I have put together large

> structures of books. I have covered some of the books but not others. The structures look like giants that will be burnt in the schoolyard during the opening ceremony. I have covered about one thousand books but some are exposed. Marxism, science fiction, esotericism, History, math, political science, scientific communism, romantic novels, contemporary novels, Kant, Aristotle, and several philosophers and thinkers. (2006, 239)

While Nieve's mother suffers with the idea of burning books, and Nieve wonders about the meaning of burning Milan Kundera along with Marx (2006, 243), her art teachers like the concept and the scale of the work. It is not clear whether they are aware of the ironic statement on censorship contained in the gesture (the antecedent: upon discovering Lucía reading her grandfather's banned novel, teachers in the military camp burn the book in front of everyone). For Nieve, this performance piece is about voice: "This is a way to say all those words that are choking us" (245)—and her words echo the bead scene. Perhaps one of the most effective performances by Nieve is an unintended one:

> What a strange sensation crying on a motorcycle. Tears disseminate over the city. Your face feels like a piece of cellophane deformed by the wind. Always on the brink of death, you feel grateful for the fragility of your life. (216)

This scene combines heartfelt pain with the ephemerality of performance art. It also alludes to stasis in the circularity of moving around on an island you cannot leave. More important, it brings to the fore the most primitive, nonverbal expression of pain, which has always been a good adolescent cry. For Nieve claims that she is "exhausted of trying to understand the strange combination of ideology, ethics, and aesthetics and the infinite whole that makes up her boyfriend's [Octavio's] private club" (234). This comment can be extended to Cuba. It is really her diary, the labor of a life told in a perpetual present tense, that tells the structural impossibility of revolutionary Cuba. That her diary comes to full meaning only when read by a militant (a photographer and her second lover) who "gets her" (so she feels) but totally misunderstands her (why did she focus her diary on herself and not on the dates and the battles of the Soviet empire?) and who is there to fight but then disappears, is an irony only matched by being named Nieve in a city like Havana.

PEDRO JUAN GUTIÉRREZ'S LONELINESS

The protagonist of Gutiérrez's novel *El Rey de La Habana* leads a life suspended in a social void. Rey (Reynaldo), freshly escaped from prison, is a sixteen-year-old homeless loner who roams through the streets of Havana trying to find something to eat, often in garbage cans, and a woman to have sex with. Occasionally, Rey's sexual partners—an array of older women, young prostitutes, and a charismatic transvestite—briefly shelter and feed him. The Havana of Pedro Juan Gutiérrez is a stateless land. The socialist state is rarely present and then only in the form of policemen and prison guards, who usually see nothing since everyone takes their business elsewhere upon their arrival. Social bonds are temporary, improvised, and mostly cruel. Rey has toughened up in order to survive in an inhospitable world. In spite of Rey's solitary ways, there is a woman he keeps coming back to. Magda, who lives in an uninhabitable building in Centro Habana, is almost as filthy and destitute as he is, and certainly as tough. Though underplayed, there is a recognizable glimmer of love between them. Love, however, is a structural impossibility in a place devoid of trust and ruled by urgent needs.

Particularly telling about the moral texture of Gutiérrez's Havana is Rey's inability to hold on to his feelings. This is particularly evident in a scene in which he has expressly gone out to the streets in order to find Magda after a long absence:

> "But where can that woman be? And who with?" he asked himself a couple of times and then erased her. He [Rey] kept walking on the Malecón for a couple more blocks. Hungry and penniless, he didn't know where he was going. To live in the most immediate present was both his luck and his misfortune. He would unfailingly forget what had happened the minute before, and he would never anticipate what the next minute would bring. Others would take one day at a time; Rey would take one minute at a time. He needed to focus exclusively on breathing in order to survive, but that need prevented him from projecting himself into the future. His life was like contaminated, stagnated water that evaporated amid an abominable putridity, only to disappear. (1999, 159–160)[8]

In spite of the fact that Rey is expressly searching for Magda, his sexual and affective anchor, he can't hold on to the purpose of his actions. For no reason, he erases the thought of her. That incapacity to transcend the basic present is part of the structural evil that conditions all his actions and his entire existence, which proves to be quite brief. For, just a few pages later, after a hurricane demolishes the house where Magda lives, they both move to a junkyard where he improvises a little house for them, kills the woman he loves (who is pregnant), rapes her corpse, is gnawed on from head to toe by garbage dump rats while burying her rotten corpse in the trash, and dies a slow horrible death in his own putrefaction. As if that life and that death weren't enough, Rey rots quickly and nobody ever finds his corpse.

It takes the protagonist of *El Rey de La Habana* 176 pages to feel "like a person for the first time in his life," but the feeling does not last. In this world of exaggerated animality, vulnerability, degradation, and the impossibility of love, the main theme is the absence of a future. Rey's dehumanization is most palpable in his incapacity to project himself into the future. He doesn't feel any hope and he never makes plans. Furthermore, he thwarts the future by killing his pregnant lover. After that horrible end, his body is never found and never missed. Rey's stagnant life and premature death amid "an abominable putridity," is, in my reading, a philosophical stance.[9]

I interpret Rey's roaming throughout the city looking for Magda and then forgetting about her against the light of Alejo Carpentier's definition of humanity. A modern, secular theodicy, *The Kingdom of This World* elaborates on the moral smallness of man, who will fight tirelessly to free men from bondage only to enslave them again. While this circle is bound to endless repetition, it becomes clear in Carpentier's novel that evil needs to exist. Carpentier's contention is that it is only in man's projecting himself into the future, in his desire for a portion of happiness beyond that which was allotted to him, that the true greatness of man may take place (1967, 143).

By contrast, for Gutiérrez, the pursuit of a better society through political struggle is the kind of utopian hope that justifies terror. The promise of a better future at the expense of the present becomes the ethical justification of a social contract that Gutiérrez's protagonist, who embraces stagnation and putridity, won't buy. Rey is revolutionary, or antirevolutionary (depending on where you speak from or against), in his incapacity to live in the future, and Nietzschean in his primitive understanding that faith in the future at the expense of the present is a seduction. Although I will develop Nietzsche's idea further in the next section, I would like to provisionally conclude that while Gutiérrez's chaotic world speaks to the cruelty of the post-Soviet "truth-process," Rey's lack of investment in the future "takes to court" the notion of faith in a better, more just revolutionary society yet to come. Interestingly, the lack of futurity is also a commentary on the overall argument of this book, because *El Rey de La Habana* is essentially an antifriendship novel.

Rey's futureless philosophy makes the ending of the novel somewhat inevitable. He dies a few days after turning seventeen, having thwarted his chance of a future in killing the woman he loves and her child (who may or may not be his) out of pride, and his body decomposes in the same trash where he lived. His death refuses all possibility of transcendence. "Nobody ever knew," the last words of the novel, denies ultimate survival after death—which friendship is meant to ensure according to a philosophical tradition that goes from Cicero to Blanchot and Derrida—and has led Simon Critchley to equate *philia* with *necro-philia* (1999, 257–258). No hope in the future is, in Gutiérrez's novel, an act of contempt for the human condition *tout court*, a Nietzschean response to what the novel portrays as a dehumanizing simulation.

ENA LUCÍA PORTELA'S UNSOCIABILITY

In Ena Lucía Portela's novel *La sombra del caminante* (The Wanderer's Shadow; an explicit Nietzschean title echoing the third part of *Human, All Too Human*) the protagonist, alternatively called Gabriela and Lorenzo

(GL), is the author of a gratuitously cruel scene. GL arrives at a shooting range and just because it seems possible, she kills the instructor and several other students, whom she doesn't even know. GL spends the rest of the novel waiting for the police to find her but there is never a sign that they are even searching for her. This constitutes another Nietzschean gesture in that the conscience of the subject takes shape through punishment, punishment that, in this case, never arrives. GL goes to the movies and sees a French film, *Joan of Arc*. The film has no subtitles, and a good-willed spectator mistranslates the film for the audience. Eventually GL wanders around the streets of Havana, searching for either recognition or punishment. There she meets a girl named Aimée and they kill themselves in a suicide pact.

I suggest that this unsettling text dismantles three notions that have been co-opted by revolutionary rhetoric: the current validity of the social contract; the official appropriation of the language of friendship; and the ethical conscience of the subject. Consider the text's opening scene in the shooting range where "shooting is a sport": GL is a university student taking a shooting class in order to avoid Physical Education classes. As a rule, survival in the shooting range depends on the existence of an implicit social contract that enables an armed group of perfect strangers to focus in the simulacrum of an enemy offered by the target, instead of killing one another. GL, the protagonist, rebels against the precariousness of such contract and kills just because it is possible:

> What a lovely idea to respect the social contract. What a nice idea to behave decently and honorably. Very nice indeed. Although God's finger is above all contracts—ponders our hero while carelessly stroking the bullet box. But if you really think about it, each act is in itself an accident . . . (2001a, 16)

In her representation of immorality, Portela points toward the inoperability of the social contract in place and thereby denounces the absence of a new behavioral code that could replace the older one so as to lend meaning and give ethical sense to a Cuban subject today. Her characters seem to embody what Vaclav Havel describes in his essay "Politics, Morality, and Civility," namely the "enormous and dazzling explosion of every imaginable human vice" that took place in a post-Communist society that had become "morally unhinged." Havel explains such situation in these terms:

> The authoritarian regime imposed a certain order—if that is the right expression for it—on these vices . . . This order has now been shattered, but a new order that would limit rather than exploit these vices, an order based on freely accepted responsibility to and for the whole of society, has not yet been built—nor could it have been for such an order takes years to develop and cultivate. (2002, 391)

Havel's words comment on the fact that while the rise of communism was a truth-process that produced a subject with specific moral values, its end lacked momentum as an event. This can be attributed to the fact, pointed out by Baudrillard, that we now live in the era of simulation. This situation is aggravated in Cuba, where no new order has been established (like in Eastern Europe) and no event has visibly taken place (unlike in Eastern Europe). What we find in Portela's texts as well as in her post-modern cohorts, then, is a society that has become aware of a void in which the Cuban communist community is no longer valid at economic, political, or ethical levels. What is more, they seem to be reacting to the moral entitlement of a series of "manly" virtues that were inherent to the revolutionary social contract and that have proved to be both morally and politically inoperative.

In this regard, the ethical comment made by the presence of Joan of Arc, banalized by the atrocious translation, is powerful. With such an emblematic figure decontextualized and parodied, Portela ridicules the age of personal sacrifice, now justified neither by religion nor by ideology. She suggests that trust in a political formation is always already breached, and it is only within private relations that it fulfills a legitimate social function. In the novel, GL and her friend Aimée die in a suicide pact, a pact that rests on mutual trust (trust defined as the belief in someone's good intentions in spite of uncertainty). Joint suicide has been seen by Jean-Luc Nancy as "a mythico-literary figure" of "infinite reciprocity" (1991, 12). Nancy explains that, in the joint-suicide framework, "death accomplishes the infinite reciprocity of two agencies: impassioned love conceived on the basis of Christian communion, and community thought according to the principle of love" (12). So, in its rather tortuous way, GL achieves in the moment of her death a community of love perfected by evil.[10]

If, as I argue, unconscious faith in a project that is both political and ethical was built on the basis of the nationalization of certain personal values, it may be appropriate then to see virtues such as loyalty and honor, and even, perhaps, solidarity and generosity, in the more critical light shed by Nietzsche's questioning of virtue in *The Genealogy of Morals*:

> The *value* of these "values" was accepted as a given, as fact, as beyond all question. Previously, no one had expressed even the remotest doubt or shown the slightest hesitation in assuming the "good man" to be of greater worth than the "evil man," of greater worth in the sense of his usefulness in promoting the progress of human *existence* (including the future of man). What? And if the opposite were the case? What? What if there existed a symptom of regression in the "good man," likewise a danger, a temptation, a poison, a narcotic, by means of which the present were living *at the expense of the future*? . . . So that morality would constitute the danger of dangers? . . . (1996, 8; emphasis in the original)

On the Genealogy of Morals—a book that Badiou considers "Nietzsche's most systematic book, the one that sums up his 'vital' critique of values" (2001, 87n1)—proposes a radical reconfiguration of a dominant ethical imaginary. Nietzsche suggests an upside-down moral cosmology, one in which the "good man" may be more evil than the "evil man." He argues that in our investment in some simple notions of what is good we are compromising the future in favor of a more virtuous present, and compromising knowledge and change by protecting moral customs or habits. Nietzsche suggests that morality acts like a narcotic that, not unlike Portela's "faith-inducing material," confuses our understanding of how the human animal operates, thinks, and feels. This mental or moral obscurity is why the good may in fact be "the danger of dangers."

With this provocation, the *Genealogy* offers an invitation to rethink the history of morality as a set of accepted lies. In keeping with Nietzsche's argument, one might advance Judith Butler's claim, presented in *Giving an Account of Oneself*, that the only way to be ethical is to become one's own social theorist, that is, to put one's life history in narrative form so as to explore the conditions of one's own emergence as a subject. From this perspective, one can read Portela's protagonist, who, like those of Gutiérrez and Guerra, analyzes herself as an ethical subject both within and against revolutionary society. One might describe Butler's proposal as a Nietzschean invitation to become an archaeologist of morals. This process is motivated by the need to understand morality as mere moral custom, thus stripping it of its supernatural aura. It is only through the knowledge that can be gained by means of this archaeological process that one can embody the idea of a supra-ethical being, defined precisely as the one who goes beyond custom.

ENA LUCÍA PORTELA'S MURDEROUS TRIANGLES

At first sight, "El viejo, el asesino y yo" (The Old Man, the Murderer and I), one of Portela's first short stories, follows the logic of triangular desire that I analyzed in Chapter 2. The story follows the flirtations between a young woman writer (the "I" of the title) and an older famous gay playwright ("the old man"), as zealously observed by the playwright's young lover ("the murderer") during a party in the latter's apartment. The story unfolds in a familiar pattern: The young man is getting more and more jealous as the night progresses; drunk with rum and emotions, he threatens to kill the narrator. At the end of the night, the narrator and the young man argue at the top of the stairs outside the party, and, in a violent episode in which neither is completely innocent, she falls to her death.

This short story replicates the narrative model based on male-male-female erotic triangle inherent to male homosocial desire that helps provide the glue holding the revolutionary community together. As I argued in Chapter 2, a shared male desire provides the cohesion sustaining the collective identity of revolutionary Cuba. I suggest here that Portela's story takes the triangular structure of the friendship plot a step further. In contrast to the importance of loyalty and honor in the friendship plot, Portela's short story suggests that betrayal is inherent to human nature; that love only exists as an impossibility; and that evil is the only way to reach human greatness, or, at the very least, to transcend mediocrity. It doesn't exactly hurt my point that by unveiling the truths about the fraternity of writers in her own novels, Portela's narrator provides a stinging critique of the male intellectual community in socialist Cuba.

But this seemingly simple structure has more to it than meets the eye. Although in appearance the murderous triangle is the one suggested by the title—the female narrator, the old man, and his young lover—several other possible triangles are suggested in the text. For example: the narrator, her female lover, and the old man; the narrator, the murderer, and the murderer's mother; the narrator, her female lover, and Paris. I argue, however, that the most important triangle is the one that joins the narrator, the old man, and a dead writer with whom the old man is forever infatuated. She has arrived too late in the old man's life and can only go so far into his heart, before "she hits a wall" (2000, 325). The pull of the dead writer is such that no one can measure up to him.

For her to compete with the dead writer, she must die in order to become a dead writer herself. She manipulates the situation by indulging the young man in his jealousy—playing Iago to his Othello. Once the young man's jealousy is set in motion, she can trust him to become violent. As I mentioned earlier, the narrator leaves the house to follow the old man who seems to have summoned her to come with him. The young man follows her and they get into a violent argument during which he seems to push her down the stairs. However, when analyzed in detail, the episode seems to suggest that he actually grabs her by the arms and then, scared of his own fury, lets go of her. She then falls to her death. As the mediator in the primary triangle, the young man is from the beginning a mere instrument, although he doesn't realize that he is being used. The narrator knows from the start that she has to be killed in order to achieve true greatness. The narrator, whose malice is repeatedly praised by the old man, is evil of the worst kind, for she is the type of manipulator that makes her victim an accomplice to her own crime.

I have two reasons for discussing this short story. The first is the repetition and augmentation of the triangulation of desire present in the first group of texts that I analyzed, but taken here to a metanarrative level. The second is that evil provides more clarity than the good. Let me begin with the first. Contrary to the common reaction to this text, which consists in trying to identify the cast of writers alluded to by the characters, it is, I believe, the metanarrative power of the story that makes the strongest statement about Cuban intellectuals. The metanarrative level can be seen in the title of the story and main characters' names, all of which allude to types, not individual people. The characters do not have any names other than the role they play in a triangular plot, and even the two minor characters who seem to have names really lack names (one of the two named characters is "Norma," the murderer's mother, who stands for the norm; and the narrator's lover, a painter named Amelia, stands in for all female painters because her name reminds us of the famous Cuban painter Amelia Peláez). The narrator, who describes herself as a snake that brings temptation and misfortune, is more interested in species than in specimens (2000, 314). It is emblematic of this that she cultivates cacti, a hardy, unfriendly species from which she learns how to behave in society.

By rewriting this archetypical story on the basis of types, not individuals, the protagonist comments on the friendship plot. She seems to be talking about the male writers I discussed in Chapter 2 of this book when she claims, "like in a group portrait, they all want to look good" (2000, 312). Their discussion is a competition for who has remained more loyal to his original ideas of art, to revolutionary commitment, and to friendship. She, on the other hand, states her belief that dishonor is a higher virtue than honor, a maxim she lives (and dies) by. From her point of view, writers are a species called forth to tell the truth about human nature. To accomplish her mission, to actualize her being as a writer, she must forgo all loyalties, because loyalty compromises the truth.

The principle that guides the narrator's actions, her ethical makeup, is stated in the epigraph, which was taken from Thomas Mann's *The Magic Mountain*:

> "I hope that you have nothing against malice, my good engineer. In my eyes it is the brightest sword that reason has against the powers of darkness and ugliness. Malice, sir, is the spirit of criticism, and criticism marks the origin of progress and enlightenment."[11]

A temptress who cherishes her bad reputation, she sees malice as the only weapon against stupidity and mediocrity. Like the old man, she admires rudeness and deliberate brutality as an expression of independence of thought. And this is how it best unravels the false notions that sustain the friendship plot. In a move that recalls Nietzsche, the narrator suggests that to not know evil is to live blindfolded. This is why Portela's narrator, who inhabits an after-the-orgy world, is not exactly pained by the betrayal. She is simply astonished at the fact that the others had not seen it coming.

COMMUNITY AND COMMUNISM (VIA GUILLERMO ROSALES)

All the novels I analyze in this chapter take place, at least in part, in bureaucratized communities: the orphanage, the asylum, and the hospital, as well as the art school, the agricultural school, and the military service training camp. Institutional and bureaucratized communities present an involuntary and hyperregimented form of togetherness in which rules are not only often inhumane but also have an unspoken code of behavior that is usually more corrupt and cruel than the official one. In Rosales's work, it is the "boarding home" (a privately run asylum) and the psychiatric hospital; in Wendy Guerra's work, we see a succession of places including the orphanage, various schools, and the military training camp, but also the art school; in Gutiérrez's, the juvenile prison and the *solares*; and in Portela's, the military training camp and the psychiatric hospital, as well as improvised and ephemeral communities such as those that occur at parties and movie theaters and which present unexpected, cruel behaviors. The importance of the bureaucratized settings is that the human dimension is already degraded by a fixed chain of command, which invites abuse; by a highly regimented access to voice and exit, which increases vulnerability; and by a strict discipline. In these novels, however, there is a remarkable continuity between disciplinary institutions and those communities founded by the young revolutionary state for the purpose of fostering art and creativity. The failure of these institutions helps allegorize the failure of community in revolutionary Cuba. Specifically, I want to suggest that the failure to deliver community is one of the ultimate betrayals of the socialist social contract. I conclude this chapter by tracing the structural evil I have been discussing back to what I believe is its philosophical origin. To that end, I analyze the community/communism conflict inherent to the revolution through the lens of Guillermo Rosales's *Boarding Home* as seen by its protagonist, William Figueras.

In his introduction to the English translation of the novel, José Manuel Prieto describes William Figueras, a post-Mariel Cuban exiled poet, as "a dejected man . . . defeated by history," and the boarding home where he was dumped by his Miami family as "a sort of sewer where misfits end up and are preyed upon by Curbelo, the manager" (2009, 2). Rosales's world is unfit for human habitation. Mentally unstable, severely neglected, and covered in filth, the population of the boarding home, most of them Cubans, are underfed and constantly taken advantage of by the "manager" Arsenio who robs and hits the men and rapes the women. The manager is not afraid of being fired by his boss, Mr. Curbelo, and the secret of his job security lies in the combination of three determining factors: First, Curbelo doesn't really care about the fate of the people in his care. His only desire is to accumulate economic and social capital in ways that remind of Adolf Eichmann, whose involvement in the Holocaust inspired Arendt's term "the banality of evil". Second, the manager, Arsenio (a name that shares its etymology with arsenic), is too cheap to fire. Third, and most important, the patients, having been labeled as "crazy" for all practical purposes, have no credibility whatsoever. Their voice is useless by the very fact of being where they are. This, however, doesn't preclude them from "expressing themselves" by peeing in every corner of the house, clogging toilets with towels and pieces of clothing so they overflow, and other forms of incontinence that contribute to the general filth and chaos of the house.[12]

With its petty, undiscerning population of lunatics led by a manager who profits from ignoring their real suffering, the halfway house invites comparison to Cuba. I should clarify that the novel was published in 1987, and therefore before the fall of the Berlin Wall. The fact that it was published in Spain by an émigré who was an outsider to the Cuban-exile community, however, explains why it presents a discussion of disenchantment more aligned with the Special Period than those texts that were published in either Cuba or Miami at this time.[13] Indeed, this home in which people are underfed, lack basic hygiene, and try to take advantage of one another can easily be compared to Pedro Juan Gutiérrez's Centro Habana. The difference here is that Curbelo is present and fully aware of the abusive environment of the home he runs, whereas an authority figure is usually absent in the stateless Havana of Pedro Juan Gutiérrez. In a place in which everyone is dehumanized, Curbelo is understood as the worst animal of the pack. Ida, one of the patients, calls him "the old fox," insisting that "Curbelo (the old fox) is the most repulsive thing there" (2009, 77), to which Figueras adds "you have to be made of the same stuff as hyenas or vultures to own this halfway house" (2009, 78). Like Gutiérrez's novels, Rosales's unveils the socialist utopia as an organism metastasized by the principle of "terror without virtue," in which the crazy inhabitants are socialized into becoming accomplices of one another's victimization. Their strength and their powerlessness reside in the fact that they exist outside contracts. The promise of a better society governed by solidarity, fraternity, and justice for all has betrayed them: They are there because "nothing else can be done."

A telling scene is one in which Figueras is watching TV in the company of his fellow patients. On the screen, a star called El Puma (another animal) suggestively gyrates his hips while singing "*Viva, viva, viva la liberación*" to the delight of those Miami women who reject Figueras as an outcast. The poet sees his own negative in El Puma, who has never "read Coleridge and doesn't need to, [who] will never study Marx's *Eighteenth Brumaire*." It is in this distorted mirror image of El Puma that Figueras offers a glimpse on his own madness. For, unlike Figueras,

> He [El Puma] will never desperately embrace an ideology only to feel betrayed by it. He'll never feel his heart go "*crack*" in the face of an idea in which he firmly and desperately believed . . . He'll never feel the joy of taking part in a revolution or the subsequent anguish of being devoured by it. He'll never know what the machinery is. He'll never know. (2009, 35; emphasis in the original)

By discussing all the ways in which El Puma is different from him, Figueras reveals the profound disenchantment behind his mental breakdown. He has known the joy of faith and the anguish of betrayal. The magnitude of his disenchantment is captured most immediately in the notion of his heart going "*crack*," the devastating sensation rendered more vivid by the onomatopoeia, and by the self-evident horror of his present life. That El Puma sings "Viva la liberación" points to that moment, around 1979 for Rosales (1976 for Rafael Rojas), in which the revolution became its own simulacrum.[14] We are in the simulation of liberation, a situation that makes the betrayal sound like a bad joke. I suggest here that this realization lies at the source of Figueras's madness. The same can be said about a woman called Frances, who is Figueras's lover and victim in the home (he sometimes likes to choke her to near-death while she calls him "my angel" encouragingly). She had participated in literacy campaigns in Sierra Maestra like Figueras, and, like him, had also become disenchanted with the revolution. But, as Frances says, "nobody understands." When she tries to explain her sense of betrayal to her psychiatrist, he just prescribes stronger pills (2009, 85).

It is suggestive that Figueras describes the revolutionary process as a *machinery* that has *devoured* those who truly believed in its ideals, including him. It is also suggestive that he speaks of the project in terms of faith in the previous quote, but then switches to the language of crime when composing what seems to be his own epitaph: "This [the boarding home] is the end of me. I, William Figueras, who read all of Proust when I was fifteen years old, Joyce, Miller, Sartre, Hemingway, F. Scott Fitzgerald, Albee, Ionesco, Becket. I who lived twenty years within the revolution, as its victimizer, witness, victim. Great" (2009, 65). In what follows, I suggest that the machine that first devoured and then corrupted Figueras alludes to the failure of the foundational promise of the socialist revolution. I believe that while the promise of community was a question of faith, its impossibility, rendered self-evident with time, put into motion a machine of simulation. Pretending to believe in it, and to operate according to its rules, resulted in a number of crimes of intolerance, humiliation, and injustice (*actos de repudio* and silence in critical moments among them). To know better and still pretend to believe is to become the revolution's victimizer, witness, and victim. But who can blame him? How not to fall for one of the most powerful seductions of history?

In his *Socialismo y el hombre en Cuba*, Che Guevara suggests that participating in "this strange and fascinating drama" that is "the construction of socialism" was precisely the "double existence" implied in simultaneously "being unique and a member of a community" (2007, 8). The viability of this view, which reflects the idealist nature of the modernist orgy, has since been challenged. Community is a structural error inherent to communism for Jean-Luc Nancy and Maurice Blanchot. In his book *The Inoperative Community*, Jean-Luc Nancy states that "the gravest and most painful testimony of the modern world . . . is the testimony of the dissolution, the dislocation, or the conflagration of community" (1991, 1). The word "communism," according to Nancy, responds to "the desire to discover or rediscover a place of community" even at the expense "of liberty, of speech, or of simple happiness" (1991, 1). If communism as an emblem of community is out of circulation today, this is due not so much to the fact that the states that extolled its virtues have betrayed its principles. Rather, "it was the very basis of the communist ideal that ended up appearing most problematic: namely, human beings defined as producers . . . of their own essence in the form of their labor or their work" (1991, 1–2). Nancy calls the "schema of betrayal" the impossible demand from communism that man can appear as the producer of his own essence (a task traditionally reserved to the gods) on the basis of his work (the human *oeuvre*).

Taking Nancy's "schema of betrayal" as his point of departure, Maurice Blanchot explains the communist doctrine and its failures on the basis of the nostalgia for a lost sense of community. With the understanding that "dishonored or betrayed concepts do not exist, but concepts that are not 'appropriate'," Blanchot locates the original betrayal in the very definition of communism, in the impossibility of communism to produce and demand community. He suggests that the similarity between the words "communism" and "community" is at the center of one the most "grandiose miscalculations of history" (1988, 1–2). Blanchot speaks of an essential flaw of communism; that is, its incapacity to create the community their common etymology suggests:

> Communism, by saying that equality is its foundation and that there can be no community until the needs of all men are *equally* fulfilled (this in itself but a minimal requirement), presupposes not a perfect society but the principle of a transparent humanity essentially produced by itself alone, an "immanent" humanity (says Jean-Luc Nancy) . . . Here lies the seemingly healthy origin of the sickest totalitarianism. (1988, 2)

Considering the similarity between the words "community" and "communism" as illusory, Blanchot cannot help but wonder, "What about this possibility which, one way or another, is always caught in its own impossibility?" (1988, 2). Community is an ethical disaster because it contains in its own definition the certainty of its own impossibility.

Nancy's and Blanchot's views on community and communism help explain the institutionalized revolution as an ethical disaster. In post-Soviet Cuba, the ideals of communism are upheld, however lethargically, and its inoperativeness—which is better acknowledged in international circles and, even then, mostly in economic rather than philosophical terms—is far from being openly accepted by the local intelligentsia at the time considered in this discussion. This fact is even more striking when considering that the world political order that framed it, namely the Cold War, only exists today, albeit phantasmatically, in Cuba. The inoperative community left behind in Cuba by Figueras reproduces itself in the boarding home first, and then in the psychiatric hospital. I will finish this chapter by alluding to a scene in Rosales's novel that advances and questions some of the philosophical stakes in the poetics of evil.

After his failed attempt to leave the boarding home, William Figueras is temporarily taken to a state psychiatric hospital where he persuades a doctor who shares his love of Hemingway to help him gain control of his future. Feeling hope again after his interview with the friendly doctor, Rosales witnesses the following:

> I go back to the room with the other nuts. I arrive at the exact moment that the man who was reciting Zarathustra has trapped a black woman in a corner and has begun to lift her dress forcefully. The woman tries to slap him away. The Zarathustra guy throws the woman to the floor and starts to touch her thighs and sex. While he is doing it, he says with a voice from beyond the grave:
>
> *I have walked through valleys and mountains.*
> *And I have had the world at my feet.*
> *O man who atoneth: suffer!*
> *O man [who] believeth: have faith!*
> *O rebellious man: attack and kill!* (2009, 114)

After witnessing this scene, Figueras goes back to his room and reminisces about Frances hugging him and asking: "My angel . . . were you ever a communist?"

> "Yes"
> "Me too. In the beginning. In the beginning. In the beginning . . ." (2009, 114)

I would like to address this phrase "In the beginning," which is repeated three times as an incantation, and the fact that it follows, and is perhaps inspired by, the Zarathustra reader raping a fellow patient. Nietzsche's Zarathustra is a godless figure who preaches in parable style to fellow thinkers about a being superior to man, the Übermensch—MacIntyre translates the term as "the man who transcends" (2007, 257) and Kaufmann as Overman—who releases himself from herd morality. Finding no objective source of values outside himself, he decides his own values. With the Zarathustra invocation, we witness the destruction of community. Liberated from morality, the Übermensch lives in a society of one.

I read this rape scene by the aspiring Übermensch through the lens of a section in the third part of Zarathustra entitled "On Virtue that Makes Small." After spending some time in solitude, Zarathustra tries to figure out if man has become greater or smaller during his absence. He finds that human beings have become smaller due to their belief in virtue (Nietzsche 1995, 167). Zarathustra believes that true liberation comes from liberation from herd morality: "I walk among these people and I keep my eyes open: they do not forgive me that I do not envy their virtues. They bite at me because I say to them: small people need small virtues—and because I find it hard to accept that small people are needed." He also believes that small people are bad actors, unconscious and involuntary actors, who claim to share that doctrine of small virtues, but their faith is not genuine (168–169). For Zarathustra, egoism is natural to a noble soul: "honor says: One should steal only if one cannot rob" (169). The inversion of honor and dishonor, and the causal relation between mediocrity and virtues, invites an implicit comparison between the New Man—who would shun material advancement and embrace, instead, the glory of virtue—and the Overman.[15]

However, it is difficult to tie all the loose ends of this scene, and not just because I was unable to find anything that resembled that quote in either of two different English editions of *Thus Spoke Zarathustra*, but also, and more to the point, of the unpalatable idea that someone is being raped by said Overman. This cruel act in the name of liberation reminds us of the fragile balance between the evil that harms and the evil that liberates, both of which I have intertwined throughout my discussion. I now return to the quote by Badiou that I used as an epigraph to this chapter—the idea that cruelty has become more an aesthetic question than a moral one, which Badiou traces back to Nietzsche—and the certainty that, as a literary character, the strength of this Overman may not rely so much in his accountability as in his suggestiveness.

NIETZSCHE OR ARISTOTLE?

Literature is a perfect laboratory for the testing of alternative worlds. Throughout my analysis, I have tried to discuss the way in which literature maintains a certain degree of correlation with a given historical reality, with the ethos it produced, and then the way such ethos changed so that the genetic code of a highly moralistic political project became a simulation of its own self. If it is "moral solipsism which constitutes Nietzschean greatness" (MacIntyre 2007, 258), a question begs to be asked: What forms of engagement would a Cuban emergent civil society based on evil bring? Once you have taken to court the false morality of a political project, what is left? Or, as MacIntyre succinctly asks: "Nietzsche or Aristotle?" (2007, 256).

In the second chapter of this book, I concluded that the revolutionary social contract failed because it falsely pretends that it enables the pursuit of the good life, when in reality it does not. This view is further revealed by the fact that perversion, as explored in the third chapter, creates spaces of solidarity and fraternity better than traditional virtues. In this chapter, I discussed the power of evil as an aesthetics of "radical antagonism" and "pure incompatibility." By placing itself outside all social contracts, evil is productive in its destruction. Not only does evil preclude the possibility of the good life, it even presents it as undesirable. A Nietzschean ethics destroys the social in the name of the human, leaving virtually no room for new societies and new values. It is fair to say that a (post-Soviet Cuban) poetics of evil obliges us to reflect on "the century" with eyes wide open. However, what good may such radical antagonism bring to the value of values that seem to be, at least in the abstract, indisputable? What is in store for an after-the-orgy humanity? Can we afford to lose Marxism as a point of reference, even if every practical enactment of it has led to disaster? I believe the question "Nietzsche or Aristotle?" just by the mere fact of being posed today, demands a divided answer. There needs to be an Aristotelian good life somewhere out there, either in local communities (as MacIntyre suggests) or in that moment in which a community is desired and put into motion as a "structure of feeling." However, we also need aesthetic forms of evil for their capacity to limit the devouring power of any idealized society. A poetics of evil redraws our affective maps, pushing the boundaries of an ethical imaginary that, for better and for worse, defined a whole era. Or, perhaps, a postsimulation generation needs to come of age, like Nieve, the protagonist of Wendy Guerra's *Todos se van*, by burning Nietzsche alongside Aristotle.

5 Ethics Is the New Aesthetics

> It looks like the socialist nation no longer needs us. It has developed a sacred capacity to create a People without people.
>
> —Ernesto Leal, *Diglosia*

In *Revolution Not Televised*, an exhibition held at the Bronx Museum of the Arts in New York City in 2012, two installations compete for the spectators' attention. José A. Toirac's *Opus* (2005) is a looped, 4:49-minute-long audiovisual piece consisting of a projection of numbers on a wall. The numbers, which go from a hundred to millions, have been extracted from various speeches by Fidel Castro, whose intense voice speaks the succession of projected numbers one after another, overwhelming the spectator. Extricated from any possible context, the numbers make no sense. The critical dimension of the piece, however, is unequivocal: An adept orator comfortably manipulates an array of tones, hammering down "data" into the spectator's brain until her physical discomfort and inability to think become unbearable. The sensation is the message.

In a small room within hearing distance of Castro's voice is *Diglosia: una solución práctica* (Diglossia: a Practical Solution; 2010), a video installation by Ernesto Leal that is part of the collective *Video cubano*.[1] Leal's *Diglosia* is a twelve-minute-long video installation conceptualized as addressing the problem of a society living in two languages, or, rather, with a double discourse. Except for occasional street sounds, the piece is silent. With considerable speed, the camera focuses successively on words isolated from the revolutionary slogans and José Martí quotes that pervade the streets and billboards of Cuba, making a collage of words that are essentially *objet trouvés*. Presented in a quick and apparently random succession, the isolated words form unexpected sentences. Words like altruism, socialism, and patriotism become part of phrases such as "malicious patriotism," "it has been some time since socialism is not popular here," and "not because of altruism but because of fear." The piece, which has been described as "a lengthy address to the Cuban government, constructed entirely from individual words taken from signs and wall slogans,"[2]addresses the key question faced by Cuban intellectuals: how to speak the truth to power effectively in a place where the language of ethics and liberation has been co-opted. The "practical solution" proposed by Ernesto Leal is to reappropriate the co-opted words from the perspective of someone who knows better, who doesn't fool herself. The fact that the piece is silent, that the authors of those words are anonymous, that the true "author" of the new sentences is the spectator, reinforces the idea that no one is truly saying what is clearly being said.

Figures 5.1–5.5 Ernesto Leal. *Diglosia: una solución práctica*. Video, 2010. Stills courtesy of the artist.

The most powerful statement in Leal's piece is the one that appears as the epigraph of this chapter: "Parece que la patria socialista ya no nos necesita. Ella sola ha desarrollado la sagrada capacidad de construir un pueblo sin personas" (It looks like the Socialist nation no longer needs us. It has developed a sacred capacity to create a People without people; see Figures 5.1 to 5.5). With this apparently anonymous and random utterance, Leal captures the moral paradox at the heart of the communism/community illusion: By pitting concrete human multiplicities—*personas*—against one abstract "People," the affirmation brings to the fore the intolerable sacrifices demanded from real human beings in the name of a rhetorical figure, the metaphorical "People" of Socialist discourse, the incommensurable referent, the *prosopopoeia* of every political speech. In an effort to reclaim the human experience of the communism/community assumptions underlying the revolutionary social contract, *Diglosia* exploits the materiality of slogans while emptying them of their original meaning. This is how Leal's piece, like Toirac's, is as much about politics as about an ethics of representation.

Leal's and Toirac's ethical response to a double discourse, in one case, and to official rhetorical excess, in the other, combines authorial effacement with an unmediated sensorial impact. Each piece in its own way can be said to continue an aesthetic trend that became popular in the art and the literature of disenchantment of the 1990s, and which I will analyze here in the context of trauma. Indeed, the deterioration of the quality of life in revolutionary Cuba reached almost intolerable degrees in the 1990s. Scarcity of essential products was so acute and generalized that, under the name "Special Period in Times of Peace," a war economy was declared even in the absence of a real war. Ariana Hernández-Reguant describes the Special Period with unique sharpness:

> Across the board, its invocation brings up memories of deprivation and hopelessness; of hunger and heat; of wheeling and dealing; of dreams of a life elsewhere. Raising pigs in bathtubs, making omelets without eggs and pizzas with melted condoms, getting married for the state-allocated free case of beer, and other epic tales of survival, seldom void of black humor, form the lore of the time. (2009, 1–2)

It is not surprising that the affect of the time was one of unimaginable hopelessness. More succinctly, Antoni Kapcia describes the Special Period as an economic crisis "beyond anyone's worst nightmare" that created "deep psychological trauma and fears" (Kapcia et al. 2012, 15).

The combination of material deprivation and the affect of irretrievable loss during the Special Period was like "sustaining a violent blow on the national body," a metaphor used by Eric Rosenberg to describe the Great Depression in his analysis of Walker Evans's photography (2006, 37). Like in the 1930s, the blow in the 1990s in Cuba was felt in the real lives and bodies of a citizenship that was economically and politically vulnerable. The Great Depression seems comparable to that of the Special Period in many ways: While neither is explicitly related to massive injustice and death—like the horrors of the middle passage or the Holocaust undoubtedly are—they are both defined by the moral and physical maiming that results from living in subhuman conditions. Like Rosenberg says about the Great Depression, the Special Period "was obscene and the result of an arguable obscenity of historical condition" (2006, 38), although I believe the Special Period reached deeper levels of obscenity than the Great Depression. I suggest that the experience of the 1990s shares three characteristics constitutive of trauma identified by Rosenberg: dehumanization, persistent indignity, and speechlessness.

In *Cuban Palimpsests*, José Quiroga argues that there is no "stable grammar" suitable for explaining today's Cuba (2005, 2). Art and literature are usually called upon to produce the language needed to comprehend, and even sublimate, the conditions of human life. Art and literature are not only subject to numerous rules of engagement that are in alignment with a paradoxical post-Soviet social contract, but also have the mission of explaining an unbelievable and unflattering reality. The incapacity of language to name the unnamable under these conditions helps explain why the art and literature charged with bringing clarity to the current state of affairs has often assumed a combination of the following: a raw factuality, an emphasis on materiality, and a sensorial overload. I see the intensely sensorial and material quality of Cuban art as capable of producing an ethical interpellation, one that can be described in J. Hillis Miller's words as that moment in the aesthetic experience that calls for an immediate and unequivocal response (1987, 1). I suggest here that by appealing to a synesthetic materialism, this aesthetic trend, which I call hyperrealism, is not only more effective at promoting "truth" than what we normally call realism, but also more ethical because it forces upon the reader/spectator an instinctive, prelinguistic form of ethical judgment.

Hyperrealism is usually understood as a tendency in contemporary painting that aggressively incorporates the visual likeness and technical effects of photography. Although the term refers to a technical imitation of photographic mimetic representation, it also encapsulates an ontological, sociological, and ethical emulation of photography as a medium. I take this definition further by considering it in the light of Eric Rosenberg's notion of photography in the context of trauma. For Rosenberg, photography in its traumatic moment is pure materiality. In his view, the representation of trauma requires the abdication of metaphor. An "art without metaphor," adds Rosenberg, "would seem to speak to a mode of representation fundamentally *damaged* vis-à-vis our normal expectations of a *language* of representation" (2006, 38; emphasis in the original). Rosenberg seems to agree with Roland Barthes, who not only speaks of trauma as the "suspension of language, a blocking of meaning" in his essay, "The Photographic Message," but also insists on the fact that photographs function semantically *un*like language (Barthes 1977, 30).[3] These are two complementary premises that lay the ground for the argument I make in this chapter. In what follows, I suggest that, if the trauma of the Special Period is incommensurate with the use of metaphorical language, than the materiality of contemporary literature and visual culture constitutes an ethics of truth akin to that produced by the apparent sensorial directness of photography. For, in obvious and not so obvious ways, photography's presumption of veracity not only helps circumvent the limitations of language to describe impotence and pain, but may also be seen as a privileged form of expression in a place where official rhetoric has fundamentally compromised the meaning of idealistic words and values. Following Rosenberg's notion of photography as "the abdication of metaphor," I suggest that a large part of post-Soviet literature and art can be described as hyperrealist inasmuch as it too can be seen to experiment with the conventions of photography as a genre, particularly of the documentary photography that was cultivated in the first years of the revolution, so as to produce an alternative form of representation that facilitates both moral and political interpellation. What I call hyperrealism, then, is a referential aesthetics that seeks to abolish critical distance by establishing an immediate physical connection with the reader/viewer. So defined, hyperrealism, I argue, helps unveil the insurmountable obscenity of living for almost two decades under the material conditions of a war that exists only in words.

Susan Sontag alludes to the inevitable participation of photography in "the usually shady commerce between art and truth" (1973, 6). With this phrase, Sontag simultaneously addresses and dismisses the uncomfortable place that photography occupies in the modern social pact, a pact that demands a strict separation between reality and representation. Unwittingly, Sontag's phrase "shady commerce" seems a good description of several obscure transactions that keep revolutionary Cuba in place. For instance, it accurately describes the intolerable terms of the socialist social contract in its post-Soviet reformulation. In a revolutionary imaginary that remains attached to an obsolete Cold War logic, the loss of the political and military protection of the Soviet Union jeopardizes a hard-earned sovereignty, thus leaving the island more vulnerable to American imperialism. This vision has contributed to the tacit acceptance on the part of the Cuban people of an unfavorable exchange according to which the state abandons its obligation to provide basic services in exchange for loyalty, an intensified form of loyalty given the disproportionate nature of the threat. It is not surprising that silence is the affective response to what neither language nor logic can explain. To the three elements of trauma identified by Rosenberg (indignity, dehumanization, and speechlessness), one should also add the consolidation of political impotence.

The phrase "shady commerce" alludes as well to the precarious balance between voice and silence that artists in the socialist sphere need to maintain in order to guarantee their protection by government cultural institutions. Contrary to all expectations, the disappearance of state subsidies for the arts during the Special Period opened, for artists and intellectuals, new channels of publications and opportunities to disseminate their work in international circuits. As a result, the partial exception of the intellectual within the revolutionary social pact was somewhat modified, as it put in motion the decoupling of the social persona of the artist or intellectual living on the island from their public voice, which could now circulate freely abroad, mostly in Europe, and which demands a support system of talks, book presentations, and invitations to foreign universities. However, in order to participate in these activities, which usually represent his or her main source of income, the artist has to be careful not to offend the government because he or she needs institutional support for a travel permit.[4] Such precarious situation of being and not being subject to official censorship has produced some of the most original narrative experiments of the last decades, not the least of which is hyperrealism.

In all the cases mentioned above, the phrase "shady commerce" refers to a cultural pact that, though mutually binding, is governed by implicit rules that are never as stable and symmetrical as they profess to be. In a sense, "shady commerce" can also be seen to describe the role played by the indexicality of photography within the specificities of ethical analyses. I believe that ethical criticism necessarily requires the acceptance of two apparently contradictory views of photography: on the one hand, it needs to contextualize the modes of production and exhibition of a photograph—which amounts to unveiling its constructed nature—while, on the other, it derives irreplaceable benefits from acknowledging the documentary value of a photograph. It follows that a responsible ethical analysis needs to embrace the paradoxical nature of photography and accept it as both a constructed representation and as a distinctive discourse of truth, distinctive in the sense that it can speak of a reality in a way that no other medium is able to do. Accepting the paradox of photography as an enabling premise, I focus on contemporary cultural forms that seek to emulate the materiality and sensorial impact of photography as "an abdication of metaphor," and propose that such hyperrealism is the art form that provides a stable grammar to describe today's Cuba. I suggest this with the understanding that hyperrealism is itself a form of "shady commerce" (i.e., a cunning strategy of representation that simulates authorial silence as a form of voicing resistance).

In this chapter, I analyze various forms of representation that promote an intense material experience: the installation *Atados de memorias* (Bundles of Memories) by José Manuel Fors; the photographic series *Ojos desnudos*

(Naked Eyes) by Abigail González and *Man Made Materials* by René Peña; the novels *Contrabando de sombras* (Smuggling Shadows) by Antonio José Ponte, *Trilogía sucia de La Habana* (Dirty Havana Trilogy) by Pedro Juan Gutiérrez, and *Los palacios distantes* (Distant Palaces) by Abilio Estévez; and the film *Suite Habana* by Fernando Pérez. I attempt to do two things: to argue that these works share a certain aesthetic language in spite of their differences and to explore the ethical value they may hold as an aesthetic trend. In other words, I try to unravel what W. J. T. Mitchell calls "the secret of their vitality" (2005, 352). Then I bring the discussion to the larger argument guiding this book, which is the substitution of ideology for ethics in government rhetoric, a gesture that, I suggest, has enabled the extraordinary duration of the revolutionary social contract. Within this framework, I seek to demonstrate that the materiality of postmodern Cuban realism—what I have been calling hyperrealism—is a strategy of reappropriation of ethical language, one that turns a crude aesthetics into an unconscious form of ethics. Ultimately, I suggest that Cuban hyperrealism transforms the tastes of the senses into the tastes of reflection so as to unveil the depleted moral structure of the revolutionary project, thus deconstructing the notion of civic identity that was mystified by official rhetoric.

As suggested previously, three concepts of "truth" animate this discussion: political, ethical, and factual or referential. First, the political concept of truth is inseparable from the role of the intellectual. Edward Said defines the intellectual as the one who speaks the truth to power. He is unambiguous about this definition, even though he wonders how to say it (i.e., by appealing to which discursive strategies), and what particular form of "truth" is ultimately at stake (1994, 88). The answers to the questions "what" and "how" are directly related to two other concepts of truth that I discuss here. The question "what truth" corresponds to Alain Badiou's notion of an evental truth, which guides the general conversation in this book. As I have claimed earlier, the Cuban intellectual is suspended in an ethical void between an outmoded original revolutionary truth consisting in freedom of imperial domination at any personal cost, and which has now become the language of what Said calls "the power," on the one hand, and the lack of a new event that would hint at a viable new society with a new vocabulary and new values, on the other. Trapped in the paradox of an aged official discourse about radical change, many artists have opted for the elaboration of a language "without language." I claim that the vitality of Cuban hyperrealism resides in this gesture. The "how," then, is a sensorial directness that can be understood, metaphorically speaking, as the emulation in various media of the inherently photographic.

PHOTOGRAPHY AND TRUTH

"Theoretically speaking, photography is nothing other than a process of recording, a technique of *inscribing*, in an emulsion of silver salts, a stable image generated by a ray of light," summarizes Hubert Damisch

(1980, 287). The abstraction that characterizes photography as a medium has often led many theorists and historians to revisit two key questions: What is photography? And, to what extent can it be considered a reliable instrument of knowledge? In the second half of the twentieth century, critical discussion has put two successive and opposing views into motion: the first focuses on the close connection between the medium and its referent, whereas the second argues that a photographic representation is an object that exists independently of phenomenological reality. In a detailed historical account of artistic photography, Sabine T. Kriebel marks the beginning of the first moment with the publication of *The Photographer's Eye* by John Szarkowski in 1966 and closes it with the publication of *La Chambre Claire* (Camera Lucida) by Roland Barthes in 1980 (2007, 16). In his efforts to justify a more central place for photography in modern art, Szarkowski describes five formal aspects proper of photography as an aesthetic language: factuality, detail, frame, time, and vantage point. Contrary to frequent claims by art critics in the '80s and '90s, Szarkowski didn't really promote the notion of absolute transparency in the photographic image, but rather defended the idea that referentiality was always to some extent illusory.[5] In turn, in the essay "The Photographic Message" included in *Image-Music-Text*, Roland Barthes goes as far as to define photography as "a message without a code." He clarifies that, whereas a photograph is an analogical representation of the object and not the object itself, what "defines the photograph" is precisely its perfect analogical capacity (1977, 17). In the chapter "Rhetoric of the Image" that appears in the same book, Barthes insists on the analogical capacity of the medium by stating that "of all the kinds of image only the photograph is able to transmit the (literal) information without forming it by means of discontinuous signs and rules of transformation." Whereas photography "can choose its subject, its point of view and its angle, [it] cannot intervene *within* the object (except by trick effects)." Barthes concludes that it is in its relationship of continuity with reality that resides the distinctive "ethics" of photography (43; emphasis in the original).

With the advent of poststructuralism, critics left behind the definition of photography as a medium to concentrate, instead, in the experience and the use of photography. For poststructuralist critics, photography as a language is an unstable means of signification. Most theorists who reject the indexicality of the medium stress the potential for distortion that exists at every instance in the process of producing a photograph, ranging from the moment of capturing and developing an image (framing, selecting, focusing) to the variety and quality of the technical equipment (lens, camera, film) to the elements of chance, such as natural light. With this in mind, Anne McCauley wonders:

> Where do we locate the "inherently" photographic? Every physical feature that draws Barthes to particular photographs (from the studium to

> the punctum to the "that which has been") is one that has been made visible through the labors of a chain of human engineers, chemists, and camera operators who worked to get it there . . . all elements that result from human intervention and are historically determined. (2007, 419)

At a more philosophical level, critics like Joel Snyder question the gaze itself, arguing that the natural appearance of the photographic gaze is historically constructed: For Snyder, photography doesn't replicate natural vision, but rather reproduces visual habits constructed since the Renaissance. In turn, John Tagg argues that the complexity of photography resides not so much in the effort to replicate human vision, but in representing space in two dimensions. According to Tagg, one should never assume the apparent naturalness of the photographic image as if it were a faithful representation of pre-photographic reality.

Cultural criticism in photography has been based on the notion that photographers, photographs, and the photographed exist in webs of discourses that make signification possible, but can only do so within systems of power. This Foucauldian notion inspires feminist views such as Abigail Solomon-Godeau's, who finds that the apparent transparency of the medium makes it a more powerful instrument of patriarchal ideology. Similarly, Tagg's expressed Foucauldianism justifies his vision of photography as an instrument of power frequently used against marginal groups such as the sick, the criminal, and the poor.

I believe it would be productive to reevaluate both poststructuralist and culturalist tendencies from the critical perspective offered by Geoffrey Batchen in *Burning with Desire: The Conception of Photography* (1999). In the first place, Batchen attributes the view of photography as a vehicle of discourses of power to a misreading of Foucault. Batchen notes that critics like Tagg and Solomon forget that the main effect of the panopticon, for Foucault, is not oppressive surveillance, but rather self-discipline. Also, Batchen criticizes the infelicitous appropriation of poststructural methods by critics who frame their arguments within the same binary structures that poststructuralism sought to undermine (1999, 190). More important, Batchen considers that, by speaking about photography in terms of discourses that are alien to it, the antiformalist approach has become too partial and incomplete: "Indeed, the assumption here is that, as a thing with no fixed identity or historical unity, photography potentially belongs to every institution and discipline *but its own*" (1999, 7; emphasis in the original). While Batchen recognizes the limitations of formalistic essentialism, he also understands that there are critics who are so blinded by cultural essentialism that they have forgotten that photography has its own way of relating with both the artist and the world. In other words, he questions the conception of photography as a discourse of power insofar as this position is based on the critical denial of the particularities of photography. I believe Batchen is right when he advocates for a view of photography that is more attuned to the complexities of the medium.

Methodologically speaking, one could say that while cultural studies demand the suspension of the traditional distinction between written text and visual image—a distinction that exists, according to Mieke Bal, and that cannot simply be abolished (2005, 148)—a comparative discussion demands that such suspension be suspended. This is justified, first, by the fact that any serious comparison between literature and photography as media must necessarily begin by accepting the differences between the two. Only by appreciating the distinctive representational mechanisms of each medium is one truly capable of imagining the political and ethical dimension implicit in their strategic fusion and crossings. Second, as I have already mentioned, an ethical analysis demands the exploration of such double vision given that both conceptions of photography, the cultural and the ontological, are equally relevant their own way. On the one hand, it would be impossible to discuss the ethical value of a photograph without considering the material circumstances and ideological values of its production (who the photographer is and what purpose the photograph serves may explain the difference between the journalist, the blackmailer, the scientist, and the pedophile). On the other hand, to deny photography its documentary potential is to negate its capacity to increase awareness, to imagine the unimaginable, and to identify both victims and perpetrators (like in the case of wars and genocide, for instance).

By stating that "the photograph is an idea as much as a thing," Anne McCauley simultaneously justifies and brings closure to the ontological debate on photography (2007, 420). McCauley accepts ambiguity as an inherent aspect of the medium, and resolves the conflict by distinguishing two categories that often overlap. Whereas photography as a *thing* (i.e., as a specific image) is in itself a historically determined product that participates in a series of cultural discourses, photography as a medium is fundamentally an *idea*. In this way, photography as an abstract concept is defined by the rules and principles that make sense within its own discipline. The distinction between the photograph as a thing and as an idea will be maintained throughout my discussion on ethics. Before moving on with my argument about representation and trauma, it is appropriate to note that McCauley finishes her essay with an appeal to stop debating the ontology of the photograph and to think, instead, of its ethical function.

Photography is neither representation, nor trajectory or metaphor—photography, "in its traumatic moment," is pure materiality, says Eric Rosenberg about Walker Evans's work on the Great Depression (2006, 35). By stressing materiality, Rosenberg seeks to describe the failure of language (including much of visual language) to fully comprehend the pain of trauma. The materiality of photography creates a language that disavows metaphor. As I have mentioned previously, Rosenberg and Barthes understand photography, at least in certain instances, as a language of almost pure denotation.

They do so not so much because photography is constructed on the basis of certain conventions, but rather because no language of representation is sufficient to capture the intensity of trauma. When seen from this perspective, photography alludes to the material connectivity that takes place when the represented object imposes itself as a presence, re-creating the personal and direct experience of a specific object, and therefore alluding to an existence prior to and independent from any symbolization process. This is how Rosenberg argues for a type of "straight" or "transparent" photography that explores the capacity of the medium to oppose language and to conjure, instead, a strategically essentialized factuality. As Eric Hobsbawm has noted, however, transparency in a photograph depends mostly on how "hidden its ideological codes are behind a rhetoric of neutrality and description" (1994, 192).

I believe it would be productive to understand "the abdication of metaphor" as an instance of what Charles Sanders Peirce calls "Firstness." In his *Theory of Signs*, Peirce groups human understanding in three forms or qualities. Firstness is the category that refers to what the human body perceives spontaneously, the "raw experience." In Peirce's words, "Firstness is the mode of being of that which is such as it is, positively and without reference to anything else" (qtd. in Short 2007, 75). Although all description is a form of conceptualization, "some demand that we attend to our experience in a certain way," clarifies T. L. Short, so that we can successfully approximate the raw experience (2007, 76). In my view, hyperrealism can be said to approximate the raw experience by demanding that the reader participate in the aesthetic experience at a physical, unmediated level. This takes place through detailed descriptions and sensorial stimuli that expose the reader to a selected material reality in an instinctual, often violent way. The reader's visceral reaction preempts an ethical or aesthetic processing of the material as the experience remains outside preestablished cultural codes. In contrast, Peirce defines Thirdness as what we perceive "to be intelligible, that is, to be subject to law, or capable of being represented by a general sign or Symbol" (qtd. in Short 2007, 85). In other words, Thirdness refers to the moment in which consciousness makes the leap from raw experience to understanding, thought, and interpretation.

I would like to suggest, on the basis of Peirce's distinction, that Firstness (material connectivity) in Cuban hyperrealism supersedes Thirdness (ethical judgment) by imposing itself in a blunt interpellation process that bypasses critical thinking but which nonetheless demands an intense and almost instinctive moral response. I consider Firstness here as assuming three specific forms: the eloquence of the photographic document as opposed to the failure of artistic language; a sensorial immediacy that includes but is not limited to vision; and the materiality of the collage. The Firstness of photography can be seen in terms of the "idea of photography" that I discuss in this chapter, that is, as an ethics of representation that closely resembles the distinctive capacity of the medium, according to Barthes, of *transmitting* without *transforming*. In turn, when considering photography as an object, it is not only the cultural circulation of an image that counts, but also its synesthetic quality, explored by cultural critics Mieke Bal (2005, 146) and Laura Marks (2002). Marks suggests that the evocation in film and photography of senses like touch and smell, which constitute privileged vehicles for what Pierce calls Firstness, can offer access to Thirdness when the critic accepts "to maintain a robust flow between sensuous closeness and symbolic distance" (2002, xiii). In what follows, I explore Firstness in various works produced since 1991 in Cuba. I contend that each of these works explores the inherently photographic by following the compulsion, at times obscene, of showing it all and of producing a corporeal experience. I suggest that the works I analyze below explore in Firstness the illusory experience of an "art without metaphor."

FRONTALITY IN ABIGAIL GONZÁLEZ AND RENÉ PEÑA

There is little doubt about the importance of photography in the process of constructing the Cuban revolution as an "event." In the early days, the government avidly became the exclusive client of photographers who had had successful careers in advertising in the 1950s. The original spirit of the revolution created an aesthetic language of its own, thanks to images by Raúl Corrales, Korda (Alberto Díaz Gutiérrez), and Osvaldo Salas, who combined documentary photography and advertising techniques to better grasp the profoundly ethical mission of the revolution. As Cristina Vives has noted, "the greater reproductive capacity of photography and its utility as propaganda were its karma" (2001, 96). Korda's photography is particularly emblematic of the prolific propagandistic apparatus of the film and photography of the early days, which established a successful language to show everyone that the world, in Ambrosio Fornet's words, "had finally become sane" (2008, 252). A case in point is Korda's *El Quijote de la farola* (Quixote on the Lamppost), in which a man wearing a white hat and peasant clothes smokes nonchalantly while sitting atop a lamppost (see Figure 5.6). Below him, a sea of similar white hats under the sun indicates an exulted crowd waiting for a speech by Fidel Castro. It is 1959, and each of the members of the crowd is synecdochically contained in the figure of the dreamer perched on the lamppost. The man above the crowd is also a mirror of the awaited speaker, the visionary leader thanks to whom the impossible is now possible. Korda is also the author of some of the most iconic photographs of all times, including *Guerrillero heroico* (Heroic Guerrilla), in which a bereted Che Guevara looks solemnly at a point far and above the spectator (see Figure 5.7). This 1960 image, however, is slightly out of focus, which explains why it didn't circulate until much later (Hernández-Reguant 2004, 5).[6]

Figure 5.6 Alberto Korda. *El Quijote de la farola*. Gelatin silver print, 1959. Courtesy of Alberto Korda's estate.

Figure 5.7 Alberto Korda. *Guerrillero heroico*. Gelatin silver print, 1960. Courtesy of Alberto Korda's estate.

These and other photographs by Korda show that the aesthetic language of the revolution was highly iconic (which comes from the photographer's experience in advertising) while also being concerned with the immediate representation of the surrounding reality (a technique borrowed from documentary photography and film). As José Quiroga notes about revolutionary photography, "it circulated at the threshold, it moved back and forth within the circuit of the professional look and the artistic gaze" (2005, 95). This combination of art and propaganda was in a way programmatic. In its early days the revolution created a variety of institutions dedicated to the promotion of culture and revolutionary values. Among these, the new government founded ICAIC (Cuban Institute of Film Art and Industry) in March 1959, less than three months after the entry of Fidel Castro into Havana, in order to produce documentaries and newsreels that "would serve as a permanent record of the revolution." The young film directors adopted an Italian Neo-Realistic style for their incipient film production, one that used nonprofessional actors in its search for a more authentic representation of popular masses. Filmmaker Joris Ivens, who had experience documenting the Spanish Civil War, gave the new directors a striking piece of advice "so that they would not become bureaucrats of the camera": "Film rapidly and as directly as possible whatever is taking place. *To accumulate direct red-hot material can be considered the best way of achieving a cinema with national characteristics*" (King 1990, 148–149; emphasis added). The reasoning informing this practice is that the urgency of the material justifies the grainy or slightly out-of-focus quality of a given image. Graininess, a sign of being caught in the middle of things, of being an artist-activist, could be thought of as what Barthes called an "effect of the real." The rushed texture of some of the images was a small price to pay in the process of documenting the grandeur of revolutionary history as it appeared in simple, everyday details.

The iconography of the revolution has been a major source of political and aesthetic influence. This is, in part, the vision that Iliana Cepero Amador presents in her essay "Myths and Realities: Cuban Photography of the 1960s and 1970s," in which she reviews the exhibit "Cuba: 10 years of Revolution" that took place in London in 1964. According to Cepero Amador, the propagandistic effect that can be appreciated in the images immediately following 1959, and which can be attributed to the genuine euphoria shared by most photographers at the time, also responds to the fact that these photographers abandoned prosperous careers in advertising, like Korda, to accompany the revolutionary forces. This leads Cepero Amador to conclude "these photographers (unconsciously, or perhaps unknowingly) participated in one of the most effective propagandistic programs of the postwar period" (2008, 232). The euphoric gaze of the first years of the revolution has profoundly influenced contemporary artists regardless of changes in the perception of Cuban reality. According to Tim B. Wride, curator of the exhibition *Shifting Tides: Cuban Photography after the Revolution*—which was held at Los Angeles County Museum of Art in 2001, and was one of the first exhibitions to explore the conceptual changes that took place in Cuban photography since 1959—the epic themes and personality cult that the first generation of photographers promoted "continue to function as the defining style of Cuban photography" (2001, 30). It is in direct contrast with the documentary photography of the first years of the revolution that one should consider the idea of photography as a new aesthetic language in post-Soviet Cuba. This is particularly evident in the work of photographer Abigail González.

Some critics claim that the series *Ojos desnudos*, made by Abigail González during the hardest years of the 1990s, expressly "quote" the mechanisms of the documentary photography of the first years of the revolution. However, the same cannot be said about his themes. González's series presents trivial scenes of young people in various states of undress, which lends an erotic tone to these images. In fact, Abigail González would produce very explicit sexual images only a decade later. In *Ojos desnudos*, however, the sordid decor dominates the scene in what looks like candid pictures taken by one of the protagonists, or, at any rate, by somebody invisible to them. In *Shifting Tides*, Tim Wride comments on the spontaneous allure produced by "the artist's use of vertiginous perspectives, apparently random cropping, and grainy print quality, all of which contribute to a sense that the images were taken without the knowledge of their subjects" (2001, 68). Nevertheless, Wride insists that these shots have been carefully put together by González, because he emulates the language of the documentary photography of the first years of the revolution. Wride calls this phenomenon visual conditioning.

Partly based on Wride's criticism, I suggest that the series *Ojos desnudos* appropriates the techniques of documentary photography as an ethics of representation distinct from (and now ironically used against) the revolution as an event of truth. If the topic of revolutionary photography consisted in celebrating the worker and his values of heroism, solidarity, and dignity, González's project, however, consists in revising the obsoleteness of those values from the perspective of a simulated candidness. With an aesthetics that approximates and combines the techniques and effects of both documentary photography and pornography, Abigail González uses the aesthetic assumptions cultivated during the collective euphoria of the 1960s so as to better portray the profound moral disenchantment of the 1990s.

The series *Ojos desnudos* shows images of young people in apparently spontaneous situations. They appear in domestic scenes in which dirt, chaos, and the precariousness of the infrastructure produce discomfort (see Figure 5.8). In part, however, the sordidness of living conditions is understated by the naturalness with which the naked protagonists interact; a fact that has been understood as a sign of the sexual openness of Cuban society in general, and which I'd rather explain in terms of the experience of trauma. In his elaboration of Walker Evans's photography during the Great Depression, Rosenberg makes an interesting distinction between trauma as we define it and the emotional field generated around it. Whereas, according to Rosenberg, trauma is "obscene, terrifying, intimate, undefended, appalling, [and] damaged," the emotion that surrounds it is usually subtler. The photograph of trauma, then, is not so much the record of horror itself, but of "the manufacture of dignity in the face of obscenity" (2006, 38), or, at least in this case, the manufacture of joy. Abigail González himself has discussed sociability and sexuality as awarding a space of freedom among vigilance and chaos.[7] He does it, however, by forcing the gaze of the spectator, who would rather not look, but can't help looking.

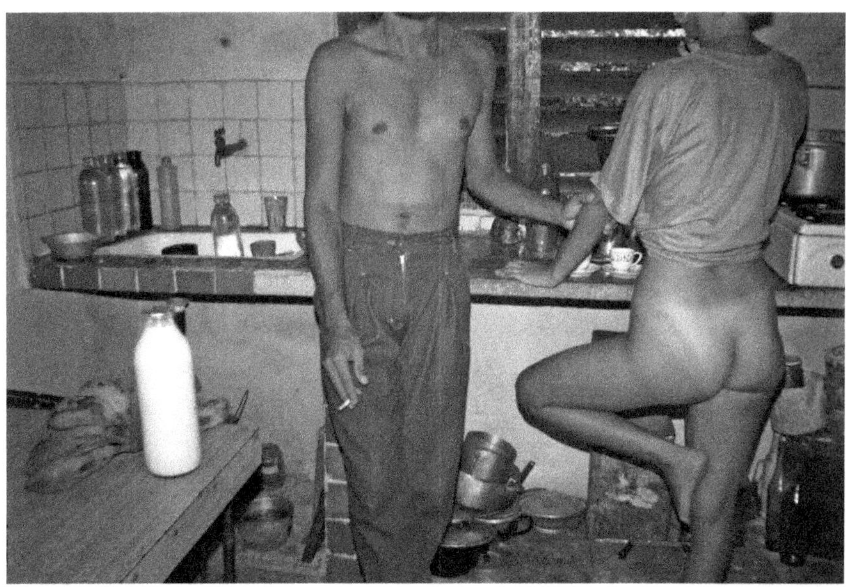

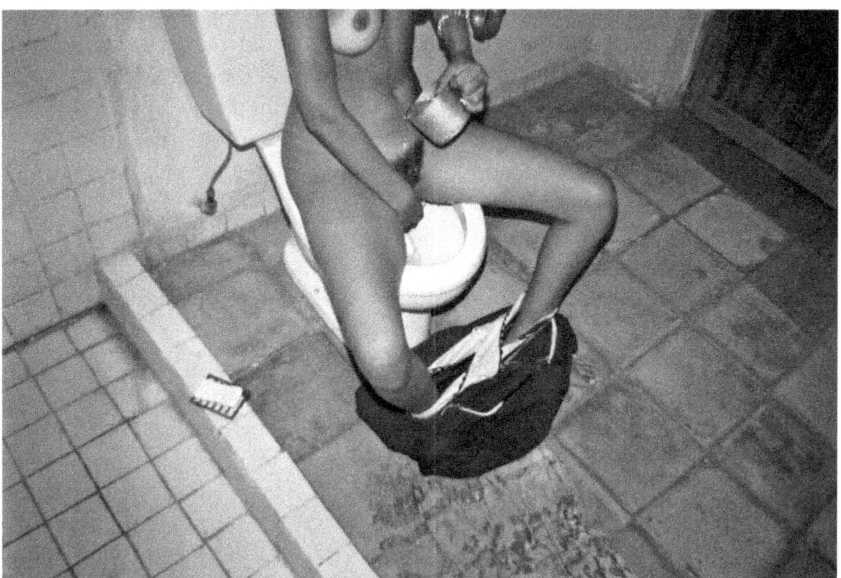

Figures 5.8–5.9 Abigail González. *Ojos desnudos*. Gelatin silver print, 1992. Courtesy of the artist.

One of the most interesting images of the series shows a scene of personal hygiene. In a photograph that is both intimate and alienating, a headless female body ("decapitated" by the frame) appears sitting on a toilet in a bathroom (see Figure 5.9). In spite of the grime, the straight lines of floor and wall tiles create a sense of order and give texture to the background. They also direct the spectator's eyes to the female body, which looks strong yet vulnerable. The lines create a grid-like design that is elegantly interrupted by a few circular shapes: a rusty mark on one of the tiles; the curve of the cold, white toilet that has no seat; and the curvy female body. Whereas the first two, rusty and broken, speak of decay and the passing of time, the body looks fragmented but young, healthy, and beautiful. In fact, all the straight lines strategically converge in the double circle of the breast and the areola, and in the pubic triangle; that is, in figures of femininity that are geometrical yet organic, and softer to the eye than the cold porcelain and tiles. The softness of the body is underlined by its gracefulness, its openness, and, what is perhaps more disconcerting, by the lack of face. Indeed, the faceless body allows the spectator to look at it without feeling interpellated in turn, a detail to which I will return later.

Perhaps what is most striking about the photograph, however, is its aura of decay: Both what is broken (the shower without running water and the toilet without seat), as well as the patina of time (the rust and the ingrained dirt in a supposedly civilized space), have an ideological effect. An inoperative bathroom reminds us of the failure of the promises of modernity (Esty 1999, 32; see also Anderson 2010; De Ferrari 2007). Decay reminds the spectator about one of the conditions that became evident during the Special Period: the failure of domestic technology to simplify and even hide certain daily operations, to domesticate the human animal and to give her more space to live humanely, and to enjoy her civilization and reaffirm her civility. While undoubtedly sordid, the decay in this photograph helps create an auratic effect in the sense that Walter Benjamin gives to the term and that Laura Marks reinvents when speaking of decay as the sensorial and emotional marks of "a long-gone, *living* presence" (2002, 132; emphasis in the original).

Thematically, the economy of organization and interruption, hard and soft, old and young, helps underline two unexpected elements. The first is the water pitcher that turns the toilet into an improvised shower in a way that is both vulgar and baptismal. The lack of modesty of the female subject, together with the cleansing water that flows generously from a cheap metal pitcher, suggests the possibility of a purity that is still attainable. Or, as Eric Rosenberg would say, they speak of dignity despite squalor. The second element is the lack of a face for a body whose warm presence is so commanding. In principle, as I mentioned earlier, the lack of face liberates the spectator from a possible interpellation in a situation that is openly voyeuristic. Also, it hides an identity, and with it, the possibility of an expression or a gesture. This allows us to universalize the object of our gaze, to turn a human body into landscape. The spectators find themselves confronted with the living conditions of an anonymous individual that is doubly objectified by the camera and by the material conditions of a life that consists in barely surviving. The need for creativity with which this faceless body approaches daily tasks stresses the failures of modern utopias. Furthermore, the lack of response to the spectators' gaze increases the sense of hopelessness. The spectators are left alone with their own discomfort produced by the violence of the camera's gaze. The explicitness of the image, the evident poverty, and the improvised manufacture—the poor lighting, the abrupt frames—help present a world that is both attractive and repulsive. The images in *Ojos desnudos* are aggressive in the sense that the immediacy of the image forces the spectators to confront the shame not just of looking at that which they should not, but also the shame of having saved themselves from such destiny. In my view, the title of the series, *Ojos desnudos*, refers not just to a displacement of the nakedness of the object to the pretended simplicity of the camera, but rather alludes to an ethics of representation in which, ultimately, the humanity of the spectator is questioned.

According to Tim Wride, González's work "provides a complexly layered commentary on public space (in this case, forbidden and subversive space), the revolution, and photographic tradition and function" (2001, 68). Following Wride's commentary, I would suggest that the series *Ojos desnudos* thematizes the idea of photography as avant-garde art inasmuch as it lets the medium do its own theoretical work. One could say that the nakedness of the title suggests a way of looking that is based on "the abdication of metaphor." The alleged transparency of photography as a medium promises the spectator a direct access to the truth, a truth that is as constructed as it is undeniable. González's work seeks to intensify the referentiality of photography understood as analogical to the human gaze by turning the image into a bodily experience. In fact, I see *Ojos desnudos* as combining the principles of documentary photography with those of pornography, two uses that are, in their own way, opposed to that of artistic photography. Interestingly, the convergence of those subgenres in this image helps make an ethical and political commentary. I suggest, in fact, that the revision of the mechanisms of photography as a medium in *Ojos desnudos* exploits the structural Firstness of both a documentary and a pornographic aesthetics: On the one hand, we find the naturalized visualization of a scene that pretends to ignore the spectator (the spectator is irrelevant in the *mise-en-scène*); while on the other, we perceive the explicit desire to create a predictable, material reaction in the spectator's body that, beyond the spectator's will, manages "to resonate within our bodies," a phrase that Laura Marks uses precisely to describe pornographic film (2002, 69).

The blurry images, the unexpected angles, and the inadequate lighting all conform to a technology of improvisation of sorts. Not only do they contribute to the creation of an aura of authenticity, but they also allow for the activation of various senses beyond the purely visual. In fact, when Wride describes the "vertiginous perspectives" and the "grainy print quality," he suggests a type of visual image that can be felt and touched. For, underlining the texture of González's image is what Laura Marks calls a "haptic visuality," a form of synesthetic visuality that, by alluding to the sense of touch, evokes an unmediated bodily connection with what is represented. By resisting—at least partially—the control of vision, says Marks, the spectator consumes the image as a more vivid bodily experience, "get[ting] closer and explor[ing] it through all the senses" (2002, 118). The more imperfect the image, the more direct and complete is the spectator's experience. This is why I suggest that it is through the convergence of different instances of Firstness (i.e., by re-creating the emotional field that is created by the senses and the aura of lived experience) that González establishes an ethics of representation akin to the trauma of the Special Period.

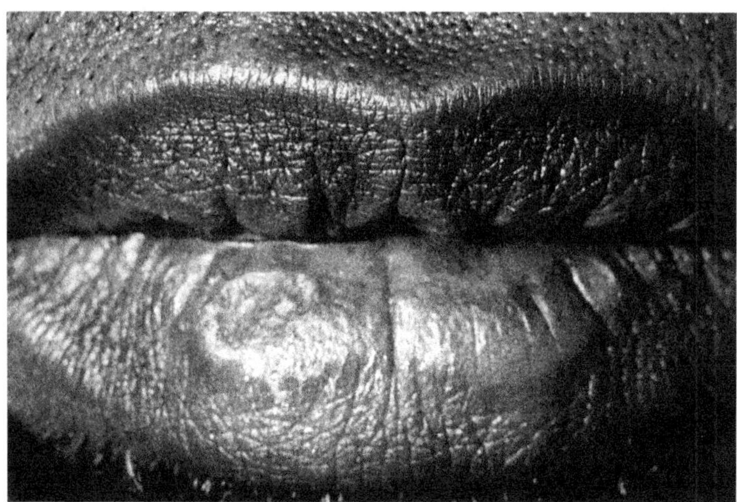

Figure 5.10 René Peña. *Man Made Materials*. Gelatin silver print, 1998. Courtesy of the artist.

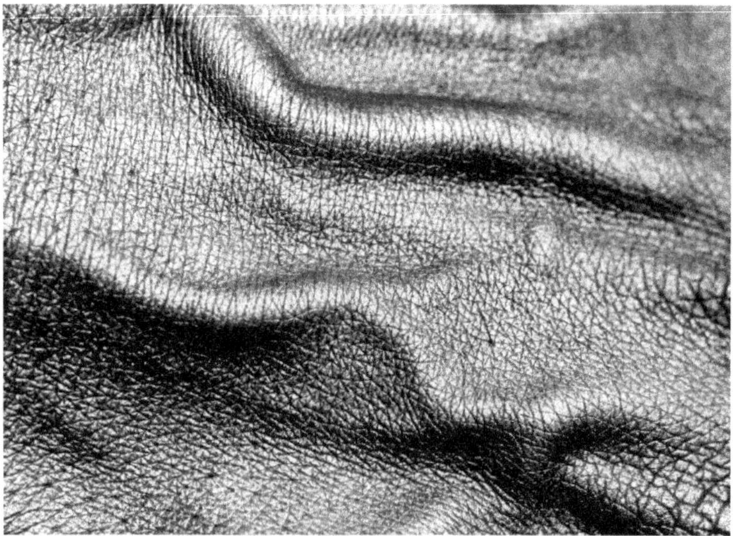

Figure 5.11 René Peña. *Man Made Materials*. Gelatin silver print, 2000. Courtesy of the artist.

A similar instance of Firstness can be found in René Peña's photographic series *Man Made Materials* (the original title is in English), with two significant differences: The series shows a much more careful composition and conceptualization than González's, making them stunningly beautiful, and they introduce the topic of race. The emphasis is no longer on the sordid surroundings, but rather on the capacity of photography to produce an intense emotional reaction simply by reducing the human body to pure materiality. In *Man Made Materials*, René Peña presents his own fragmented body in extreme close-up (see Figures 5.10 and 5.11). The spectator sees enlarged fragments of skin, face, and pubic hair, showcasing them as either pure form (as in the outline of the mouth) or texture (as with skin or hair). Peña's images thwart recognition. The extremely close shot of a body "mutilated by the violence of the photographic frame," as critic Israel Castellanos León notes, confuses the spectator (2005, 146). By depriving the body of the marks of social identity, Peña shows us a black body in its pure or unmitigated state, that is, free of all the metaphors, prejudices, and euphemisms that have been naturalized around the question of race and that have not been produced from and by the body itself.

These beautifully composed images become disturbing upon seeing them for a second time. This is due to the presentation of race, one of the silenced topics of the revolution, as it appears in its most basic traits (the color of the skin, the fleshy mouth, the texture of hair), which leaves the task of either reconstructing or rejecting the social narratives of racism they imply entirely to the spectator. In other words, what the spectator sees and understands in Peña's work is entirely her own responsibility. The interpretation of *Man Made Materials* demands that the spectator either consent to or stand up against a humanistic, modernist, revolutionary project that was violently unequal. According to Castellanos León, Peña uses his own body as the material support for an idea (2005, 146–147). This idea consists in the return of the ethical gaze right back to the spectator. I agree with Odette Casamayor when she asks:

> Where is the violence, exactly? Does it lie in the fact that we are seeing a black "human" body? Peña's most effective weapon against racism consists, precisely, of simply placing the black person within the human project—beyond any social, political, ideological or cultural discourse. The black man emerges from a concept, a form and an image that fail to explain him; he becomes that visitation or Lévinasian epiphany that attacks the unconscious by surprise. (2007)

The "violence" in Peña's photography originates in the way in which he exposes a given racial conscience while deactivating the sociocultural mechanisms that construct the idea of race. It thereby restores a certain presymbolic purity or innocence to the body: a human essence that is not yet essentialized for, from the strictly material point of view, what we call race is a question of melanin, not of morality. By focusing on the Firstness of the black body, *Man Made Materials* is an ethical gesture that compensates for the failed notion of revolutionary equality. Casamayor discusses the capacity of interpellation in Peña's work in terms of a reversal of roles:

> When, aesthetically speaking, we move from confrontation to contestation, we see that critical language detaches itself from the object to become the spectator's. Peña's photography neither says nor suggests anything. Only the spectator can provide the critical language to describe it. One could even go as far as to say that the object becomes the spectator in the sense that it "witnesses" the performance of its public. (2007)

I agree with Casamayor that what is unsettling in Peña originates in the extremely close angle, which works as a double lens: The spectator watches this fragmented body while she herself is looked at and implicitly judged. This is possible thanks to an ethics of representation that offers a truth that is fragmented and incomplete, and therefore "raw" in terms of conceptualization and interpretation. Like Abigail González's work, René Peña's *Man Made Materials* lets the medium do its own conceptual work. By this I refer to the capacity of interpellation that originates in a fragmentation, which is, ultimately, inherent of the medium, and which the artist has taken to a provoking degree by pushing the decontextualization that is natural to the framing of the photographic image to uncomfortable degrees.

As I have been suggesting, a defining aspect of Peña's photographs is the frame. As the formalist John Szarkowski noted, framing is a key aspect of photography that comes from selection, not conception. According to Szarkowski, the process of selecting and eliminating that goes in the act of framing forces attention to the margins of the image, as well as to the fissures within, and the shapes they suggest. This effect is based, no doubt, on Walter Benjamin's idea that photography is "the art of citation without quotation marks" (Cadava 1997, 113). One could then say that the power of interpellation mentioned by Odette Casamayor originates in the capacity of the image to isolate certain elements out of a narrative that is both alienating and familiar. Following the law of continuity with the photographic frame, the spectator is forced to continue the interrupted images, placing them within an imaginary context. However, the context provided by the spectator belongs to her entirely, not to the represented object. As Sabine Kriebel notes, "photography, like the talking cure, reveals associations and presences not immediately available to the conscious mind" (2007, 13). The ethical interpellation operates here in the intuitive process of reconstruction that is demanded by the laws of continuity between the within and the without of the photographic image, and then by the complicity with discourses of power that such reconstruction reveals about the spectator. The spectator is forced to reconsider her instinctive participation in how she sees what she sees, and to make herself responsible for what she believes she sees.

SILENCE IN ANTONIO JOSÉ PONTE AND FERNANDO PÉREZ

In contemporary Cuban art, disenchantment is often articulated through the metaphor of death. Several critics liken the silent ruins of Havana to the decadence of the national body. Esther Whitfield suggests that "peeling, crumbling, and fading become forms of inscription, to be deciphered and parsed in an attempt to read the times" (2008, 128), whereas José Quiroga comments on the ruins' "extraordinary aesthetic effects—collapse somehow allows the city to levitate in pictures" (2005, 81).[8] Ruins expose layers of metaphorical density, and artists like self-appointed "ruinologist" Antonio José Ponte and filmmaker Fernando Pérez appropriate the poetic texture of ruins and turn it into artistic language. It is in this intimate connection between ruins and death that authors like Miguel Mejides and critics like Whitfield have explored in the notion of Havana as a city ravaged by war, a "Caribbean Beirut" (Whitfield 2008, 127). "New ruins," the ruins that are created over a short period of time, are usually the result of modern war (Whitfield 2008, 123). This is (Whitfield) and is not (Quiroga) the case of Havana, a paradox that can be explained by the fact that although war exists only at a rhetorical level, it has in fact had material effects on the physical constitution of the city. Part of the appeal of the ruins of Havana stems from the tension between their metaphorical density, their nostalgic patina, their political connotations, and their vitality; for these ruins are, for the most part, inhabited, as Vicky Unruh notes, "by the laboring bodies of a quotidian present" (2009, 197).[9]

Theoretically speaking, the visual obsession with post-Soviet Havana can be attributed to its implicit connection with the sublime. Like war photography, part of the beauty of post-Soviet photographs of Havana stems from the anxiety they produce, from the fear of losing oneself in the implicit violence and death of the ruined city. Charles Merewhether, who views photographs as "the tomb of history" (1997, 28) and cameras like "portable tombs" (31), understands that photographs, like ruins, show death in the present tense. Most famously, the relationship between photography and death was discussed by Roland Barthes, who speaks of each photograph as a microdeath, and argues that, by turning the subject into an object, the photographic process produces a specter (1981, 14). According to Barthes in *Camera Lucida*—a book that Barthes devotes to the process of mourning his mother—photography has something to do with resurrection. Susan Sontag, in turn, attributes the affective impact of photography to its capacity "to seize death in the making" (2003, 24). Building on Walter Benjamin's idea that knowledge reveals truth by "flaming up the veil" and producing a "high point of luminosity" in our understanding process,

Eduardo Cadava further develops the association between truth, light, and death that is at work in photographic knowledge: "That there can be neither truth nor photography without ashes means that, like allegory, both take place only in a state of decay, in a state that moves away from itself in order to be what it is" (1997, 22).

I would like to suggest that the aesthetics of death at play in the theory of photography, and which is cultivated in Ponte's novel and Pérez's film, not only evokes the death of illusions (proper of aging in both people and utopian projects) but also turns a lack of voice into sensuous flesh. Silence, defined as the absence of words, is immaterial, even ghostly. However, silence in these works can be felt in the fetishized vision of a decadent Havana (i.e., in the sensual photographic obsession with the city in ruins). Silence speaks to the incapacity of language to deal with the pain of trauma with insistent eloquence. This is perhaps why, as Quiroga notes, "by the Special Period, photography was mourning something the text still sought to celebrate" (2005, 97). Focusing on the capacity of photography to produce a strong affective field while negating language, I will analyze the motifs of silence and death in the novel *Contrabando de sombras* by Antonio José Ponte and the film *Suite Habana* by Fernando Pérez as propitiating through the Firstness of photography a complex allegory of the deterioration of a political project.

Ponte's *Contrabando de sombras*, a novel with a strong preference toward the metaphysical, begins when a German photographer hires the protagonist, a Cuban poet named Vladimir who falls in love with a ghost, to compose poems to accompany his images of Havana in a future book. In order to complete his task, the protagonist finds himself in Colón cemetery face to face with the sculpture of an angel with a finger on his lips signifying silence. The statue, which is prominent in the photographer's oeuvre, is part of a Christian iconography suggesting that the dead are sleeping and waiting for resurrection. It is also a not-so-veiled allusion to Benjamin's "angel of history." The photograph of the statue of the angel, a twice-mediated representation of history, death, and silence, can be seen as holding the secret to Ponte's novel's vitality. In this sense, it may be useful to compare Ponte's angel of disenchantment with the words of Eduardo Cadava:

> Like an angel of history whose wings register the traces of his disappearance, the image bears witness to an experience that cannot come to light. This experience is the experience of the shock of experience, of experience as bereavement. This bereavement acknowledges what takes place in any photograph—the return of the departed. (1997, 11)

As I suggested in Chapter 3, the allegorical power of the novel takes shape by presenting photography as a wordless medium in which pain is mystical, and truth becomes flesh. Cadava's notion of experience as "the experience of the shock of experience, of experience as bereavement" helps us understand the warlike trauma of loss (of dignity, of health, of humanity) that is the trademark of the Special Period, but also, at a more anecdotal level, as the mourning of the irretrievable (the loss of love, of youth, of dreams) that the characters "contraband" with in the shadows of Ponte's cemetery.

In his own project, the foreign photographer in *Contrabando* combines images from Havana with a series of photos from Beirut, thus positing the notion of post-Soviet Havana as a city destroyed by war. The value of these images explicitly resides in the fact that they show the citizens of Havana as "more or less dead," and that "there is beauty in leading one's life in such proximity to death" (2002, 23). The lawyer/translator that manages the commercial transaction between poet and photographer, as well as between word and image, brings the discussion on artistic value to a close by "translating" the photographer's words: The beauty of a ravaged Havana is inseparable from truth, and death from resurrection (24). It is particularly relevant to my argument, however, that while the images in the novel undeniably represent "a quantum of truth"—to quote John Berger (1980, 293)—this is not always the case with words: the "translator" often fails to translate; Vladimir's "out-of-stock" books, whose existence is supposed to accredit him as a poet, were never published; the poems that Vladimir writes for the photographs never appear in the novel; and the guilt that tortures the protagonist originates in his failure to speak up to avoid the death of his gay lover, whose ghost he finds and loves behind an image projected on an old cinema screen. Truth, which seems so self-evident in the writing of light on either paper or cloth, proves to be impossible to grasp in and through language. In fact, the scuba diver that drowned, an adolescent with so few words that he was called "el mudito" (the mute), who was the only one able "to get to the bottom of things" (2002, 29). If we consider that the sensorial perceptions of a scuba diver are filtered by the profound silence of the water, we find in this image alone a powerful attack on the rhetorical excesses of the revolution. The magical possibility of finding truth in and through water is further re-created at the end of the text, when the protagonist has an erotic encounter with his lost lover behind an old movie screen. As I suggested in Chapter 3, the screen has a mended patch that not only reminds the poet of the scar on the dead lover (who drowned like "el mudito") but it is revealed to him only against the extended projection of the Pacific Ocean. In fact, it is relevant that the text suggests a connection between light and truth that is significantly mediated by the presence of water (in the luminous projection of the Pacific Ocean, "scuba diving," or even "drowning"). Only light can write, to use Cadava's metaphor, the tragic truth of homosexual love in revolutionary Cuba, but its meaning only becomes real through salty water. This makes the act of swimming analogous to developing film, a process that is, precisely, called "revelar" (to reveal) in Spanish. In Ponte's novel, a poetic tribute to both lost loves and political disenchantment, truth finds no words, rather, it is resurrected in the materiality of the photographic image.

Disenchantment is pure affect. In Fernando Pérez's film *Suite Habana*, the death of dreams becomes flesh in the pale colors and the texture of the decaying city. Using a tone of solemnity, the film follows the lives of twelve people, many of them very old and all of them nonactors, in the city of Havana from sunrise to midnight. The careful editing turns the film, which has neither dialogue nor music (except for what is occasionally produced by the actors), into a sad visual poem. The film offers a slow succession of images depicting repetitive, everyday actions to the monotonous rhythm of a life without words. A certain degree of dehumanization occurs in the absence of dialogue. The silence fosters a profound sentiment of melancholy and loneliness. In the succession of scenes that has no narrative thread except the one offered by time and the trajectory of the sun, the tactility of the decaying city stands out. Layers of peeled paint and exposed concrete suggest the aura of the lived experience, the experience of a war without war, without epic. That the only signs of joy in the film come from Francisquito, a small child with Down syndrome, underlines the notion that disenchantment results from a deeper historical conscience. Likewise, the realistic contract with the spectator plays a key role: Typical of the Cuban "docudrama" production, Pérez uses people with no acting experience who are there to simply represent themselves. Reality thus imposes its own political value, a proposition that is reinforced by the characters' statements about their dreams, which can be read during the credit sequence.[10]

Much like it does in *Contrabando de sombras*, the photographic object helps tell the story in *Suite Habana*. A photograph of a smiling young bride in a 1960s dress and hairdo underlines the passing of time, promises made and broken, illusions lost. This image, which hangs on a wall of Amanda Gautier's house, is a young version of the old lady we see on the screen roasting peanuts to sell in the street. The contrast between the young and the old Amanda helps expose the failed narrative of the revolution. The meticulous repetitiveness involved in the cleaning of peanuts, the roasting process, and the making of paper cones, all activities carried out with a solemn face, makes her seem like a machine.[11] Old Amanda, who stands as evidence of the stoicism required from a single fragile human being in the name of the collective good, blends in with the daily life of the city. She would be invisible in the city if the camera had not stopped on her. Her demeanor shows that she has been drained of her feelings and her illusions, and, when her turn comes to describe her dreams during the credit sequence, she declares to have no dreams. When put in the context of my broader discussion, it seems that the sadness that emanates from her, rendered all the more obvious by the contrast established by the wedding photograph, posits her as a fossil of a long-forgotten dream. In the photograph on the wall, which gains focus as old Amanda loses hers (see Figure 5.12), we see her as a young, happy bride in 1960s fashion. The contrast that the camera so eagerly seeks to establish places old Amanda as evidence of the dreams that the revolution left behind.

Figures 5.12–5.13 *Suite Habana*, 2003.

Pérez's camera, which focuses for minutes on a character's facial expressions and most minute gestures, is intrinsically voyeuristic. This is particularly obvious in the case of Jorge Luis, a character who spends most of the film packing his things to move to Miami. He has married a Cuban American and is leaving his family and country to live with her. He, his family, and the spectators know that he will never again live in his house, with his family, in Cuba. While this apocalyptic feeling is felt throughout the film, it reaches its highest intensity partly off camera. When he is just about to board the plane after effusive farewells by family members, the young man stops for a moment at the top of the stairs. The plane hides his face, but not all of his body. He might believe that the spectators think he has already boarded the plane. The truth, however, is that we can see part of his clothes. We know he is there, and we believe he is taking one long last look, taking the city in for the last time. That he steals this moment of anticipated nostalgia underlines the voyeuristic operation undergirding the documentary. The intrusion of the camera, made obvious by Jorge Luis's stolen moment, works as an act of authenticity.

As several critics have noted, *Suite Habana* is not a typical documentary. In her book *Experimental Latin American Cinema*, Cynthia Tompkins calls Pérez's film an experimental pseudodocumentary (2013, 219). Not only does Pérez force occasional interactions between characters whose paths would not normally cross, but, as Ana Serra has pointed out, the use of certain dramatic techniques regarding illumination, framing, and editing help highlight the fictional aspects of *Suite Habana* (2006, 97). Cuban art critic Rufo Caballero has described the film as an exercise in "subjective manipulation" aimed at moving the spectator through the constructed illusion of a transparent reality, following no doubt Fernando Pérez's own explicit desire to create through artificial means a reality more real than reality itself (Caballero, n.p.; see also Serra 2006, 97). Indeed, Rufo Caballero defines the aesthetic of *Suite Habana* as "a stimulating intellectual exercise" that emanates from the paradoxical terms of the mimetic contract: "Aesthetically speaking, *Suite Habana* requires the deactivation of the ingenuousness of representation at the very moment in which you have, at the same time, appreciated true realism" (Caballero 2003, n.p.).

In part following Caballero, I would like to suggest that we see this film not so much as a documentary piece, but rather within the unique complexity afforded by the photographic social contract, in which poetry, realism, and constructedness may harmonically coexist. It is true that the lack of either first-person testimonies or a narrating voice makes it an intensely visual experience closer to photography than to film. The camera work is so slow, the composition so stylized, the shots so long, that each image has the feel of a photographic still life. Each shot is carefully constructed and produces meaning on its own. For instance, one long-lasting shot, focused on a sign that reads "revolución," shows rusty red letters against an old building and a twilit sky (Figure 5.13). The letters are illuminated unevenly, and the letters *r* and *e* are almost gone. By concentrating all this decay on such a word, a word emblematic of dreams and progress and change, this image bluntly materializes the established allegory that sees in the decadence of the city the aging of the revolutionary project.

Even though Fernando Pérez's storytelling is eminently visual, the eloquence of his film comes from an intense emotional field created in part by the rich tactility of his images, and particularly by the bare (and baring) simplicity of human silence. Regardless of whether we see *Suite Habana* as a lyrical documentary, a visual poem, or a visual homage to disenchantment, the true *punctum* of Pérez's film, to use Barthes's term, is the absence of words. The extended speechlessness underlines the facial expressions, the slowness that comes with old age, and the decrepit city. The overwhelming sense is that people have nothing else to say. Instead, the textured silence of the dilapidated city is in charge of telling an untellable story. Profound disenchantment is pure affect. This is probably why actual words—the statements containing the protagonists' unlikely dreams—appear as a mere postscript. Or rather, as a *coup de grâce.*

POST-PHOTOGRAPHY IN JOSÉ MANUEL FORS AND ABILIO ESTÉVEZ

In *The Nature of Photographs* Stephen Shore defines photography as "in most instances, a base of paper, plastic or metal that has been coated with an emulsion of light-sensitive metallic salts" (2007, 15). If the most basic definition of photography as an object does not mention a reference to the camera it is because, as the philosopher Hubert Damisch suggests, the magic of photography resides in its capacity to forget, at least in part, the very existence of the camera (1980, 287). Once the technology that made a photograph possible is forgotten, what is left is a concrete, physical image subject to cultural and political interpretations. According to John Berger, "we think of photographs as works of art, as evidence of a particular truth, as likenesses, as new items. Every photograph is in fact a means of testing, confirming and constructing a total view of reality" (1980, 294). It is precisely the understanding of the image as a metonymy of reality that lends the medium its ideological capacity. For, as Berger notes, every image is "a weapon which we can use and which can be used against us" (294). The effectiveness of a given image depends on its social life. Shore reminds us:

> As an object, a photograph has its own life in the world. It can be saved in a shoebox or a museum. It can be reproduced as information or as an advertisement. It can be bought and sold. It may be regarded as a utilitarian object or as a work of art. The context in which a photograph is seen effects the meanings a viewer draws from it. (2007, 26)

Thinking of the photograph as an object—that is, not as an idea or a practice—allows us to better reflect on its political function. The meaning of a photograph is largely determined by the logic of its presentation, the associations suggested by contiguous images as well as by the way in which a given group of photographs is organized as a whole. As Rosalind Krauss points out, a photograph changes its function and meaning according to the discursive space it occupies. Be it casual, intuitive, or conceptual, the contextualization generated by and from their discursive space attributes each image a genre (family photo, war image, etc.) and greatly determines their proper use and establishes a specific "grammar" of signification. Keeping in mind the capacity of a given photograph to produce meaning more effectively than language, I next analyze the installation *Atados de memorias* by José Manuel Fors and the novel *Los palacios distantes* by Abilio Estévez. I explore the eloquence of bare materiality as it operates within what Leal calls "diglossia"; that is, as a language constructed through objects that, by creating its own syntax, is both alternative to and more revealing than official rhetoric.

José Manuel Fors's *Atados de memorias* (1999) takes the notion of the photographic object to an allegorical level. In his installations, Fors, a graduate from both the Academia de Arte San Alejandro and the Instituto de Museología, offers a vision of photography from the perspective of the collector or the curator. For Fors, the photograph is an object whose true meaning is always about to be decoded. He explores the capacity of the family album—the one that you own and don't exactly need to open to know what it contains—to produce affective associations. In *Atados de memorias*, Fors piles up old photographs of the same size in mysterious and attractive bundles (see Figure 5.14). Only the top one is visible: usually a sepia image of Cuba in the early 1900s that is blurry and scratched. Paradoxically, the old patina helps create a distance between the image and our present reality, while at the same time it forces an emotional connection. Both in what it shows and in what it hides, the piece speaks of the thick texture of the lived experience. The threads that hold the photographs together remind us of the fragility of all stories, but particularly that of Cuban stories, whose layered truths lie under the surface. The simple knot is an invitation to untie and unravel the thread, to reflect on the compelling need to understand the mystery of both personal and national histories (see Figure 5.15). Most of the images are, however, inaccessible to the spectator's gaze. The photos underneath the top one are "pure" photographic objects, in the sense that they are unrelated to any referential representation. Their presence *is* the meaning: Their material accumulation signifies the abstract notion of photographic representation.

In his book *Each Wild Idea*, Geoffrey Batchen agrees with Barthes that the truth of photography is not a "truth-to-appearance" or likeness, but about "truth-to-presence," a "matter of being" in space and time, "rather than resemblance" (2002, 125). In this way, Batchen speaks of photography as a message in itself, a message that is expressed even in the absence

Figure 5.14 José Manuel Fors. *Atados de memorias*. Mixed media. Toned gelatin silver print, 1999. Courtesy of the artist.

Figure 5.15 José Manuel Fors. *Atados de memorias*. Mixed media. Toned gelatin silver print, 1999. Detail image. Courtesy of the artist.

of a real photograph. In *Atados de memorias*, each one of those invisible photographs is the promise of a meaning, a sign without a specific referent. They are allusions to that which was never said, never understood, the *un*remembered. Critic Cristina Vives has noted about Fors that "his work plays crudely with one of the aphorisms of documentary photography (authenticity) and pays a subtle homage to [the photographer] Robert Frank . . . Frank understands that photographs do not have to be factually accurate to nevertheless present true feelings" (2002, n.p.). In Fors's work, however, the photograph is not only not accurate, it may not even be there. The mere presence of photographic paper suggests a photograph. The suggested photograph then becomes a metaphor of itself; it occupies the physical space of a document that only exists in a shared unspoken imaginary.

In language, the organization of words creates syntax. Likewise, the organization of photographs creates meaning. Photographic prints, arranged at times on the principle of accumulation and evocation rather than on an explicit curatorial intention, may allude to a private logic of the sort we find in a personal album rather than the public logic employed by museums. Perhaps it would be appropriate to say that the private and arbitrary organization of a photographic collection is analogous to *bricolage* as a strategy of signification. This becomes self-evident in those instances in which Fors adds objects to his "bundles." See, for instance, Figure 5.16, which shows a bundle in which a thimble appears sewed on to an old original print depicting a turn-of-the-century mother surrounded by two daughters. The halved thimble occupies the center of the mother's body, evoking femininity not only through the idea of sewing but also by suggesting a pregnant womb. That the thimble is a ready-made object helps emphasize the objectness of the adjacent photographs, in particular the faded photograph on top, itself an *objet trouvé*, and with a similar evocative power as the thimble itself (whereas this bundle uses an existing print, Fors usually makes his own prints out of old negatives seeking a similar aged effect). In addition to combining objects and photographs, the artwork also helps emphasize its objectness by virtue of holding a diminished representational power. For, whereas a century-old photograph is highly evocative, its direct connection to a referent is partly lost. A similar idea of *bricolage* provides the framework for my reading of the novel *Los palacios distantes* by Abilio Estévez, in which collected objects work as material signs. They become a form of saying—without actually speaking—a truth that, unadulterated by rhetoric, has become simultaneously self-evident and unimpeachable.

No Cuban novel of this period shows such a passion for the sheer beauty and symbolism of literary language as does *Los palacios distantes* by Abilio Estévez. Nor does any other novel, however, seek to expose the trap of metaphor more explicitly. From the opening paragraph describing "the old Royal Palm Hotel" and "the aged palace of a noble family" (2002, 3) in a profound state of decay, words appear as obsolete, openly precarious and useless to describe the surrounding reality truthfully. The fact that the two uninhabitable grand buildings are sustained by an intricate system of beams and props suggests the precariousness not only of the physical city, but also

Figure 5.16 José Manuel Fors. *Atados de memorias*. Mixed media. Toned gelatin silver print, 1999. Courtesy of the artist.

of a naming system that is about to collapse. This is why Estévez's narrator denounces that "to call them 'the palace' and 'the hotel' would be cynical, even perverse" (2002, 4). Victorio, the protagonist, is himself evidence of linguistic perversion. Victorio was named after the victorious attack on the Moncada barracks by his father, whom he calls "Papá Robespierre." Victorio, expected to embody the revolution's New Man, is a homeless homosexual looking for any type of pleasure that will bring happiness to a sad, austere life. By revolutionary standards, Victorio is a defeated man.

Estévez's language is self-consciously beautiful. This beauty is built on precision, repetition, and, particularly, on excess. His writing is both an act of creation and an act of unmasking the perversion of naming that is inherent to all language, and to post-Soviet political rhetoric in particular. Partly due to its hyperaestheticized stance, the novel can be read as a political commentary. By opening the novel with a statement on the nature of language, Estévez announces the main theme of his aesthetic project: the unveiling of the co-optation of words by the revolutionary state in its desire to perpetuate a social contract that has become obsolete (2002, 17–18). The act of naming, declared perverse in its inoperability, exposes the gap between official language and reality. Unlike literary language, which allows for fantasies such as getting "away from Havana without getting away from Havana" (138), the language of political slogans and official code words alludes to loyalty (that of the citizenry) and to victory (over the forces of imperialism) in a manner that no longer reflects reality. Every name in *Palacios* requires a certain degree of recognition but also of misrecognition. In *fin-de-siècle* Cuba, language has failed to adapt to the impossibility of Cuban reality. Language is self-deception. Estévez's Neo-Baroque aesthetics reminds us that beautiful, excessive, convoluted, creative language is beautiful as long as it produces, as Severo Sarduy suggests, an act of defenestration.[12]

I will focus on a scene of *Los palacios distantes* that dramatizes the co-optation of language. The protagonist, Victorio, leaves his decrepit home in an act of resignation or perhaps rebellion, and becomes homeless for some time. Eventually, he finds a home in the ruins of an abandoned theatre. As the narrator's initial observations on the Royal Palm hotel and the mansion suggest, Victorio also seeks solace against the precariousness of language by focusing on the eloquence of objects. The war between objects and words becomes particularly intense when Victorio returns to his old house after its demolition, and stands in the crowd behind the police tape. In this moment, Victorio falls pray to two intense, competing emotions: While he admires the beauty in the fragments of statues, window frames, and other broken objects piled up on the sidewalk, he detests the miserable presence of Mema Turné, the woman in charge of the CDR (Committee for the Defense of the Revolution, an organ for neighborhood vigilance), who, dressed in a conservative black dress, theatrically repeats monotonous instructions urging pedestrians to keep walking. In view of such authoritarian spectacle,

> Victorio can't resist the temptation: he picks up a smallish rock and tosses it at the old woman. He manages to hit her in the leg. The old woman jumps to her feet, flicks out her spotted tongue, and yells, "*Go ahead,* gusanos, *worms! Attack, cowards! The full weight of History will fall on you, the people united will never be defeated.*" The spectators applaud. (Estévez 2005, 227; emphasis added)

This well-staged scene, which shows the craft of an established playwright, eloquently illustrates the profound emptiness of official rhetoric. The words are as empty of signification as the partially destroyed objects piled up on the sidewalk. The mechanical repetition of political slogans by the spotted, contaminated tongue appears as a nonlinguistic ritual incapable of conjuring the truth, any truth, to anyone. In the alienating words of Mema Turné, the novel brings revolutionary rhetoric to an absurd degree. By contrast, the gesture of throwing stones is not just an act of aggression, but also an interpellation, a contestation carried out through objects against an impaired, useless language. The antagonism between mute words and signifying objects culminates when, at the end of the novel, Isabel/Salma defends herself against the tyrannical figure of Negro Piedad by hitting him with a bust of poet José Martí. The poet is used here not as an emblem of heroism and self-sacrifice but rather as a mere mass of bronze. This is, somewhat ironically, anticipated by Salma, when she claims earlier in the text that "Martí defends her wherever she might go and wherever there is danger, that trenches made of stone (or bronze) are better than trenches made of ideas" (2005, 153–154). While probably unbeknown to Salma, the altered maxim summarizes an ethical position in which Firstness becomes an effective form of antilanguage.

One could say that materiality as an ideological weapon in *Los palacios distantes* follows a similar curatorial logic in the hands of the redemptive figure of another character, the old clown Don Fuco. Don Fuco, Victorio's host in the abandoned theatre, is an authorial figure that manages the different narrative threads of the text (supporting this claim is the fact that puppets that look like the novel's characters are stored in the prop room). Don Fuco sees himself as the administrator of an alternative archive of "profane relics" of prerevolutionary Cuba. Metaphorically speaking, this collection of objects can be seen as an album of photographs. The combination of objects speaks of a romantic, artistic, and truly grand Cuba. As Don Fuco explains, it is in the theatre

> where the country's relics are kept, and kept well: the clothes of Rita Montaner, Barbarito Diez, Beny Moré, Celia Cruz, Alicia Alonso; here are the manuscripts of so many famous authors, the guitars of María Teresa Vera, Manuel Corona, Pablo Milanés, and Marta Valdés, the piano of Lecuona . . . the bloodstained shirt of Julio Antonio Mella, the likewise bloodstained tablecloth of the Lamadrid family on which Julián del Casal died, paintings by Portocarrero, Amelia [Peláez],

> Tomás Sánchez, Acosta León, Raúl Martínez . . . there are lots of relics here, my friend, and if I don't mention all of them it's because I don't want to overwhelm you. But I also know that some things are missing . . . I wish I could have the taste of sapodilla, the smell of rain, the morning dew from the Valle de Viñales; I wish I could store the tears of some of those who took to the sea in 1994 in those unstable rafts, I wish I could keep samples of the tragic farewells in airports, the echoing of horses' hooves at the Battle of Mal Tiempo. What I need is all the relics of our country—not the ones that are considered sacred, but the others, the real ones, the profane relics, the ones that aren't epic, that don't serve as weapons of war. (2005, 122)

Estévez confronts official language with the material logic of the photographic album: the enumeration and recontextualization of a selection of material objects organized according to the value attributed to them by the "collectionist" of images. Each object becomes an emblematic witness to glory, pain, or nostalgia, each with its own contestatory value, but capable in its accumulation of establishing the syntax of a countermanifesto.

What I have called "the material logic of the photographic album" in relation to both Fors's installation and Estévez's novel can be elaborated on the basis of two interrelated notions. The first one is *bricolage* and the second is what Geoffrey Batchen calls "post-photography." Claude Lévi-Strauss defines *bricolage* as an alternative, even magical, means to make sense of reality. Lévi-Strauss makes a contrast between science, which consists of handling concepts so as to elaborate structures to create events, and *bricolage*, which is defined as the creation of a new object on the basis of signs—not concepts—that privileges the material over the model. *Bricolage* incorporates events or, rather, residues of events to create structures. The strategy of using photographs as mere physical objects, as well as the inverse—to use objects as photographs—helps create a clandestine language. This is largely the operation at work in *Diglosia*, Ernesto Leal's video installation that I discussed at the beginning of this chapter. The apparently random redistribution of words (signs) as if they were mere objects is a strategy of voice on the basis of silence. In the context of this chapter, I understand that *bricolage* is an object-based art that is conceptual inasmuch as it lets the medium do its theoretical work.

To focus on the "objectness" of photography today responds to a specific epistemological situation. Concretely, as Geoffrey Batchen explains, photography as a medium has undergone an important evolution following the philosophical and technological developments of the last decades of the twentieth century, developments that have contributed to the erasure of the line traditionally separating the different media. Painting, sculpture, and performance have absorbed photography, turning it into a whole different thing. Furthermore, photography has lost its distinctive capacity to produce a "truth effect" in inverse proportion to technology's growing capacity of simulation, on the one hand, and to the philosophical suspicion of anything that calls itself "truth," on the other. Photography today has lost its status as a medium only to become a message in itself: "Photography is now a message rather than a medium, a message that can be conveyed and endlessly repeated even in the absence of any actual photograph" (Batchen 2002, 124).

Geoffrey Batchen calls "post-photography" today's altered status of photography, that is, the idea that photography has overcome its original function without truly abandoning its premises. Photography has now become an object: "What was once thought to be a window onto the world is transformed into an opaque, resistant surface volumetrically unfolding in space. We are forced to look at photography rather than through it" (2002, 110), but it is an object that speaks, ponders, and celebrates photography as pure concept. Batchen's conclusion is that

> Photography has become "photography," eternally framed by the quotation marks of historical distance and a certain awkward self-consciousness (that embarrassment one feels in the presence of the recently deceased). In short, for these artists, photography has taken on a memorial role, not of the subjects it depicts but of its own operation as a system of representation. (2002, 111)

We can say that photography in Fors is a *mise-en-scène* not only of the memory issues that plague a society like Cuba's, but also the staging of photography as post-photography. In *Atados de memorias*, the photographic medium is the message. This is in direct contrast to the materiality we find in Estévez's novel, where the theater itself functions as a museum, providing a context and an aura to a nationalistic statement built on the accumulation of material fragments. The objects selected, collected, and preserved in the theater create in their accumulation an elegiac installation. Let's reconsider this in the context of Sanders Pierce's theory. If Firstness refers to that which is perceived by the body spontaneously, as raw experience, Thirdness speaks of awareness and conceptualization. Fors's invisible photographs (pure Thirdness) and Estévez's materiality (pure Firstness) both represent an appropriation of the idea of photography that helps sublimate a nonrevolutionary past. By alluding to a shared, sublimated nostalgia, post-Soviet post-photography is an elegy for the dreams of modernity that includes, but is not limited to, the faith kept in the revolutionary enterprise.

SENSATION IN PEDRO JUAN GUTIÉRREZ

In *Regarding the Pain of Others*, Sontag suggests that the ethical value of a photographic image is inversely proportional to its aesthetic value. According to Sontag:

> Beautifying is one classic operation of the camera, and it tends to bleach out a moral response to what is shown. Uglifying, showing something at its worst, is a more modern function: didactic, it invites an active response. For photographs to accuse, and possibly to alter conduct, they must shock. (2003, 81)

Sontag's reasoning echoes the premise, advanced by Cuban film director and critic Julio García Espinosa, in favor an imperfect cinema. In his 1969 essay "For an Imperfect Cinema," García Espinosa argues that glossy, well-finished images numb our ethical judgment. For Sontag, like for García Espinosa, beauty is inherently conservative, whereas a production of ugliness has as its main aesthetic function the showcasing of moral value.

Notably, a distinctive process of uglifying is at work in the novel *Trilogía sucia de La Habana* by Pedro Juan Gutiérrez. *Trilogía*, written during the worst years of the Special Period and published in Spain in 1998, "offers sordid revelations of a society in despair," affirms Esther Whitfield (2003, 99). Indeed, in *Trilogía*, taking advantage of your neighbor for a few dollars, defecating out of the window to avoid the long lines for the collective bathroom, or trading sex for an antirabies vaccine speaks of living conditions that are opposed to a life of beauty, symmetry, and justice.[13] It is no doubt interesting that a text this ostensibly disagreeable has had the amount of international success that it has enjoyed: It was published in eighteen countries and Gutiérrez became a cause célèbre of *The New York Times Review of Books* and *Playboy Brazil*. As Esther Whitfield has observed, Gutiérrez accepted and manipulated the demands of the international market, forcing the foreign reader to assume the uncomfortable role of "voyeurs" (98–99). In my opinion, the "secret to the vitality" of *Trilogía sucia de La Habana*—what attracts both the bestseller readers in Spain and many academics in various countries—is the implacable aesthetic violence of the text. I suggest that Gutiérrez's appeal resides in the capacity of *Trilogía* to emulate the "idea" of photography inasmuch as the reality in the text imposes its presence on the reader directly. At some level, Gutiérrez's aesthetics is defined by a referentiality and an urgency that could be called photographic, and which projects the sensation of what Sontag has called the unique capacity of photography "to seize death in the making" (2003, 24). By this I am not referring to the fact that many literal deaths appear in Gutiérrez's text, even though several vignettes do in fact allude to suicide and murder in a straightforward way. Beyond the abundant references to death, what matters in *Trilogía* is that death appears as an extreme instance of the consistent dehumanization that takes place in the eyes of the reader, a process that writer Ena Lucía Portela, in her review of the novel, has called the moral mutilation of the average Cuban, assuming, she clarifies, that the average Cuban in Gutiérrez's work is low class (qtd. in Whitfield 2008, 10). At a rather basic level, which I will complicate below, one could say that Gutiérrez's text reveals vignette after vignette of the post-Soviet traumatic reality to the reader *as if* he were seeing it with his own eyes.

In both tone and architecture, *Trilogía* emulates the logic of the snapshot, that is, the photograph as an object. Indeed, *as if* it were a box of photographs with no organization whatsoever, the proliferation of images seems to respond to what Sontag calls in *On Photography* the "very insatiability of the photographing eye" (1973, 3). *Trilogía* consists of sixty short chapters or vignettes that seek to establish not so much a coherent narrative but rather to document the state of acute crisis as lived experience, that is, as a chaotic reality. The narrator, called Pedro Juan like the author, is unemployed and spends most of his time trying to commandeer ("resolver") food, rum, or pot, or just to survive. Within a social and economic infrastructure that is precarious and inhospitable, the bodies in the text, sexualized, racialized, at times almost animalized, offer counterpoints of unexpected beauty and dignity similar to the human landscape offered by Abigail González. Like in *Ojos desnudos*, the bodies in *Trilogía* are more dignified the more animalized they are. A sexuality that is decontextualized from any possible romanticism offers not only a space of control amid the disciplinary gaze of the state (as Abigail González states in "Sexual Healing"), but also offers a space of redemption, of a joy surplus that defeats the exhausting and often ineffectual fight for subsistence.

Like the photographic lens, Gutiérrez's writing does not pass judgment. The trademark of the narrator is to be a nonemotional, nonjudgmental, and unflappable observer capable of seeing the essential, human truth before his eyes. In a way, Gutiérrez's gaze reminds us of the "the camera's innate honesty" described by Edward Weston in "Seeing Photographically." According to Weston, the camera "provides the photographer with a means of looking deeply into the nature of things, and presenting his subjects in terms of their basic reality. It enables him to reveal the essence of what lies before his lens with such clear insight that the beholder may find the re-created image more real and comprehensible than the actual object" (1980, 174). Like Weston, Gutiérrez's text tries to achieve a camera-like effect by looking into the nature of things. However, unlike Weston, whose images are famous for their consummate clarity and beauty, Gutiérrez's realism depends on vulgar language and a rushed, clumsy manufacture. His writing avoids everything that one would have considered beautiful, thus shunning the inherent capacity of literature to produce metaphors. Furthermore, the lack of self-editing helps create the "grainy" texture of *Trilogía*. It constructs a synesthetic prose that "resonates" in the body of the spectator. In fact, it may be more appropriate to say that *Trilogía* is not so much *read* as it is *felt*.

As I have been suggesting, Pedro Juan Gutiérrez's work emulates the idea of photography in two different aspects. First, *Trilogía* showcases a factuality that is akin to photographic language as a way to speak truth to power.

Second, and most important, I suggest that *Trilogía* functions on the basis of its sensorial intensity. Indeed, it is through the violence of those senses that are the least "civilized," such as smell, that Gutiérrez's writing appeals to a private, precognitive ethics (i.e., an ethics that cannot be redeemed by the possibility of metaphor).[14] In Gutiérrez, the impact of photography assumes its greatest magnitude when understood as the immediacy that takes place through nonvisual senses like that of smell and produces an involuntary, prelinguistic reaction.

Exclusively from the formal point of view, the most obvious photographic characteristic of *Trilogía* is the illusion of describing things "as they are." It is possible to affirm that *Trilogía* participates or pretends to participate in the commerce between art and truth as if it were not "shady" at all, but rather, as a transparent, direct transaction. Such commerce appears as proposed by a narrator who demands a leap of faith from the reader, absolute trust becoming a precondition for the reading contract. The idea behind this aesthetic trend is that living conditions during the Special Period are so precarious that they cannot be grasped by the representational capacity of language. Conceptually, Gutiérrez seems to adopt Szarkowski's view that "the world itself is an artist of incomparable inventiveness, and that to recognize its best works and moments, to anticipate them, to clarify them and make them permanent, requires intelligence both acute and supple" (1966, n.p.). Szarkowski concludes that "the photographer's vision convinces us to the degree that the photographer hides his hand." Like Szarkowski, the narrator of *Trilogía* also explains his project in terms of the naïve illusion of authorial effacement. He proposes that one should write

> reality, just as it comes. You take it as it is out there in the streets. You grab it with both hands and, if you are strong enough, you pick it up and drop it on the white page. That's all. It's easy. No retouching. Sometimes reality is so hard that people don't believe you. They read your story and say: "No way, Pedro Juan. There are many things here that don't work. You went overboard making things up." But no. Nothing is made up. It is just that I gathered enough strength to grab the pile of reality and let it drop at once on the white page. (Gutiérrez 1998, 103–104)

When Gutiérrez's narrator defines himself as the one who "tells it as it is," we could say that he boasts about the indexicality, even the frontality, of his writing. Even though each vignette includes a micronarrative (an ex-lover becomes a *jinetera* and pays for his dinner; a neighbor who works at the morgue is arrested for selling human liver in the black market; and so on), it is the capacity of each vignette to create a durable, visceral impression that provokes a deep awareness of the Special Period as trauma.

According to Robert Capa, "if your pictures aren't good, you're not close enough" (qtd. in Szarkowski 1966, n.p.). In *Trilogía* the object represented is too close, too intimate. The most distinctive impression in the reader is not so much one of being inserted in a personal drama—in spite of the autobiographical emphasis underlined by some critics—as it is of submerging oneself in a world that is both dehumanizing and obscene. The vulgar language is, in fact, one of the elements that most resembles the capacity of photography to become too close to its subject, to pry into somebody else's life, and to allow the spectator a direct access to a horrible reality. Access to the private, insignificant detail is not only a distinctive capacity of the medium, but also one that largely determines its specific themes. While painting takes up the big topics, photography, being simpler and cheaper, focuses on the trivial and the irrelevant. For instance, critics have noted that while classical painting focuses on large battles, photography shows the cannonballs piled up on the road (Szarkowski 1966, n.p.). In the effort to describe the hardships of Centro Habana in the 1990s, photography no doubt provides a more appropriate visual language than painting. Only the factuality of photography, its ability to get too close for comfort, can truly show the inhospitable living conditions and the social and moral degradation of the "average" Cuban. The impact of the photographic detail in *Trilogía* takes place not in a simple, straightforward visual form, but rather through the somewhat counterintuitive notion of a "haptic" and an "olfactory view" as advanced by Laura Marks.

Conceptually speaking, when most people think of photography and literature, they think of ekphrasis. A linguistic rendition of the visual image is the most obvious and simplistic understanding of a "literary" photographic effect. However, what I call the photographic impulse of Cuban postmodern realism doesn't necessarily consist in the visuality of the image but, rather, in its Firstness. This corresponds roughly with what Barthes has described as the structural continuity between reality and signs and, above all, the inherent capacity of photography to produce an immediate impact in the spectator. Therefore, to discuss photography as an "idea" allows us to take the subject to a more complex speculative level, one in which we leave the visual image behind, at least temporarily, in order to think about photography as an ethics of representation. If, as Szarkowski points out, "a photograph evokes the tangible presence of reality" in a way that is "more convincing than any other kind of image" (1966, n.p.), one of the ways in which literature creates the effect of a tangible presence is through the fabrication of a sensorial stimulus of primary association, which imposes itself such that it leaves no room for argumentation. In other words, I am not considering visuality as carrying the burden of the sensorial impact, like photography usually does, but rather I am looking into the three main strategies that I have used to define hyperrealism as an ethics of representation: a blunt factuality, a sensorial overload, and an exaggerated materiality.

In my view, then, Cuban hyperrealism consists of the imposition of a sensorial experience on the spectator/reader in a way that predates not only aesthetic and moral judgments, but even predates the cognitive functions that allow us to comprehend a given perception according to cultural codes. This argument can be partly traced to Laura Marks, who argues that "smell is the most mimetic of the senses, because it acts on our bodies before we are conscious of it. Smell requires a bodily contact with the world, which in turn is mediated in the brain in an especially instinctual fashion" (2002, 115). As long as photography promotes a minimally mediated type of contact between object and spectator, photography as an idea works in a way that is analogous to the sense of smell or of touch, two senses that not only require the physical copresence between spectator and object, but also have the capacity to concretize an idea in an instantaneous, immediate, prediscursive manner. Understood this way, then, it is possible to extend the metaphor of "the photography as an idea" to include all representation with a sensorial dimension that promotes a directness of experience of the represented object within the prerogatives of the body in a way that is prior to the symbolic elaboration of language.

The most memorable lines of *Trilogía* make reference to smells—the smell of sweaty bodies that excites the narrator sexually: "it turns me on to smell myself" (2002, 6); "she liked my smell, my 'man smell,' she called it." (2002, 48); "the smell of her yearning wetness was driving me crazy" (2002, 51); "I like to smell my armpits while I masturbate" (2002, 140); "she is very dark, and her sex and her armpits have a strong smell to them. That turns me on so much that we must look like two lunatics rolling around" (2002, 223). But also the smell of excrement in the collective bathrooms, and many other smells that plague his writing: "Even I was revolted by the smell of rotting shit" (2002, 174); "I went down into a filthy basement, just like all the other basements in the neighborhood, full of rotting boards, puddles of stinking water, and a foul smell" (2002, 267). The sexual response is not surprising because, as Laura Marks notes, "sexuality is contained in . . . smell—something that most contemporary humans disdain, for our being is defined by our verbal, visual and intentional activity in the world" (2002, 133). The sense of smell speaks to both the cognitive and the precognitive areas of the brain in humans (134). Laura Marks also builds her theory of olfactory and haptic vision in the categories of Firstness and Thirdness by Charles Sanders Peirce. The category of Firstness refers to what the body perceives in a spontaneous manner, to experience in its raw state; by contrast, Thirdness refers to a state of awareness, to the leap to what Lacan would later call the symbolic (Marks 2002, 124). According to Marks, smell is characterized by Firstness, and immediately produces what Deleuze calls an "affect-image." The senses, particularly the sense of smell, have a unique capacity to establish an instantaneous connection between material bodies, or body and object, thus creating and more effectively sharing with the reader the affective field of disenchantment in a way that words may not. This is due to the fact that language in Gutiérrez appears as a damaged entity, a situation that is inherent to all trauma, but which is aggravated by the "wear-and-tear" of ideological language in five decades of revolutionary discourse. Such weaknesses in language amply justify, I believe, the insistence of sensorial immediacy in the literature, film, and art of the Special Period. In Pedro Juan Gutiérrez's work, for instance, the immediacy of photography as a concept (that is, *not* as ekphrasis) happens in the production of an elaborate olfactory network that implicates the reader affectively. This is similar to the way in which *Suite Habana* by Fernando Pérez emphasizes the haptic experience underlined by silence as a way to create an ethical moment.

The writing project that *Trilogía* represents, and which I am metaphorically describing as "photographic," is so partly because of the olfactory view advanced both explicitly and implicitly by the narrator. Even at the ethical level, Pedro Juan justifies his project with an olfactory metaphor: "I write in order to needle and to force others to smell the shit" (1998, 85). He claims that active censorship prevents journalism to speak—to use his right and obligation to voice—and the writer is left with little else than an animal corporeality that allows the writer to circumvent voice: In *Trilogía*, he claims, reality speaks for itself. Gutiérrez's metaphor of forcing others to "smell the shit" showcases the power that smell and postmodern realism have of producing knowledge beyond, or outside, ideology. Furthermore, the metaphor that encapsulates *Trilogía* as an aesthetic project is consistent with Sontag's suggested notion of uglifying. By creating disgust, smell is an intimate sense capable of producing an enduring ethical impact—more enduring than would beauty—and which can only take place when the reader is touched viscerally, beyond her own consciousness.

In an article entitled "Crap on the Map, or Postcolonial Waste," Warwick Anderson suggested that "postcolonial excrementalism"—an aesthetics of dirt—is a corrosive operation committed to "the 'de-fetishizing' of the notion of civic identity, with its fine play of ascetic and abject" (2010, 174). From Anderson's perspective, one could see dirty realism as an active process of destructiveness capable of divesting an idealized "civic identity" of the magical powers usually attributed to the conflation of man and citizen—of good man and good citizen—that is, of man as an active, productive, and disciplined participant in a political society. What is a citizen but someone who can rule and obey, who can willfully limit its own self to the well-being of the polis as a whole. Anderson underscores the corporeal dimension of citizenship by suggesting that, at the center of both excremental aesthetics and civic identity, is the subtle articulation between the abject, that which is disgusting, and *ascesis*, a practice of self-containment, a technology of the self, that which creates habits, and therefore ethics.

An aesthetics of disgust, I have suggested elsewhere, operates against the status quo (De Ferrari 2007a). It responds, in fact, to a desire to break away from modern notions of beauty that have been compromised by grand ideologies. Pedro Juan's hyperrealism derives its ethical power from a strategic rejection of beauty. By borrowing some of the representational principles of photography, literature becomes a moral witness while refusing to assume a political dimension: It turns indignity into spectacle, it combines the documentary with an assault on the senses that may metaphorically be called "pornographic," and it moralizes without a debate. Hence Sontag's elaboration on the superiority of ugliness that I discussed at the beginning of this section: As long as an image, be it photographic or literary, produces physical repulsion, an interpellation occurs that is both immediate and uncontestable. Perhaps more than any other work I discussed above, Gutiérrez's hyperrealism turns an "aesthetics of the senses" (in Kantian terms) into an "ethics of reflection," thus revealing the depleted moral reserves of the revolutionary enterprise, and therefore facilitating along the way the deconstruction of a certain prescription for civic identity mythified by revolutionary rhetoric.[15]

ETHICS IS THE NEW AESTHETICS

The transparency and materiality of contemporary Cuban realism operates either at the level of the sign (as an intellectual codification) or at the sensorial level (bodily stimulation) in such a way that matter "speaks for itself." Based on Eric Rosenberg's notion of photography as "the abdication of metaphor," I explored the idea of a hyperrealism not only as an intense sensorial aesthetics but also as a type of representation that, based on Firstness, interpellates the spectator as an ethical subject while rejecting the ineffectiveness of a desensitized ethical language. The different authorial figures I have discussed explore the way in which sensorial directness, and even repulsion, may help the reader/spectator make sense of a dehumanizing world.

Postmodern realism in Cuba is ethical precisely to the extent that it questions the relevance of two parallel social contracts that have a place in post-Soviet fiction and art. On the one hand, it questions the strict separation between reality and representation that is distinctive of the modern artistic social pact. This is justified by, though not limited to, the idea of trauma. A prerequisite of trauma is the recognition of a truth, however subjective and mediated, but which determines the conditions of representation of trauma: The trauma must have happened, must be a true experience, and must elicit empathy from fellow humans. On the other hand, it undermines the absolute commitment that the communist intellectual owes to cultural institutions, given that Cuban realism seeks to recover the use of voice by speaking the truth to power *as if* it weren't doing it. Structurally speaking, an artistic production based on silence, like the notion of a war without war, or a People without people, mirrors the notion of a revolution that has become pure simulation, as I argued in Chapter 4 of this book.

This brings me to the title of this chapter, as well as the larger context of ideology and ethics in Latin American art. Art critic Luis Camnitzer suggests in his book *Conceptualism in Latin American Art* that "ethics are the new aesthetics" (2007, 263). The phrase itself is not Camnitzer's. It was originally coined by José Mujica—who, as a Tupamaro, was part of the Uruguayan subversive forces of the 1970s that were directly inspired by the Cuban Revolution—at the time of his appointment as senator for the Frente Amplio in 2004 (he then became the president of Uruguay, and is famous for his personal austerity and pragmatism). Camnitzer uses Mujica's phrase in an effort to define the specifics of Latin American conceptual art. He claims that conceptual art in Latin America is, like in the US and Europe, an art of ideas, but, unlike in the US and Europe, it has refused to forgo political activism.

Let's stop for a moment and look at the elements surrounding Mujica's phrase, a phrase that largely attests to the political spirit in the continent that has evolved from the Cold War. The quote itself ("ethics is the new aesthetics"); the occasion (regular democratic elections); the speaker (José Mujica); his personal story (an ex-Tupamaro becoming an elected official); and Camnitzer's analysis (which covers artistic and political instances from the early nineteenth century to the end of the twentieth)—are all there to prove that, in Latin American art, ideas are inseparable from the political and moral search for the good life. Ostensibly, the historical arc traced by Camnitzer, with its emphasis in the 1960s and 1970s, seeks to confirm that the idealism of the Cuban revolution is not dead.

It is striking, however, that the commitment of Cuban artists today, which is both ethical (as I have argued in this chapter) and conceptual (as I will further discuss in the next one), is mostly inspired by the urgency to break away from the seduction and saturation of utopian politics. Indeed, the aesthetic trend I have called hyperrealism seeks to convey the revelation of trauma in a raw style, without metaphors, often without dignity, and ultimately, whether intended or not, it serves to make visible the broken promises of an aged socialist project. Under the rubric "ethics is the new aesthetics," post-Soviet Cuban art today is, contrary to Camnitzer's suggestion, moved by a lack of faith in political representation, in the political value of voice, and in the ethical claims of political ideologies. And this is how contemporary Cuban art can still be called political.

6 A Curated Culture

> There is nothing immoral here. Just as present-day art is beyond beautiful and ugly, the market, for its part, is beyond good and evil.
>
> —Jean Baudrillard (1993, 19)

Art is a social act. What it says largely depends on who is listening and how. Few critical texts approach the ethics of consuming post-Soviet Cuban art more suggestively than the short story "La guagua" (The Bus) by Alexis Díaz Pimienta (2000). The story recounts the seemingly banal experience of riding in a crowded bus in downtown Havana. It begins in a realistic tone: It is hot, it is hard to breathe, the rain outside prevents the passengers from opening the windows on the bus, and bodies keep piling in. Just when it seems as though no other person could possibly fit in the bus, the driver takes pity on a passerby, allows him to climb in, and closes the doors after him. The passengers suddenly realize that they are trapped, and "that at the next stop . . . there would be no room for [the doors] to open" (2000, 159). The bus reaches the end of its run and the driver, who has been kept cool thanks to a little fan, realizes what has happened, jumps out of his window and calls the fire department. The firefighters are unable to pry the doors open and are forced to cut the bus in half. When both sides fall off, there appears that:

> The mass of people was still compact. The bus had molded the group, which was now a block of faces, backs, profiles; a painting in 3-D of terribly open eyes and mouths. It looked like the somber work of an artist, carved in marble or ice.
>
> Some of the people, those on the periphery, appeared to be in one piece. Others were only an arm, or an ear, or a right shoe, just like me. From above, it was a collection of hair, bald spots, unfinished shoulders, shadows . . . Each side deserved to be signed by Velázquez, Rembrandt, Picasso: The faces! The chiaroscuros! The angular figures! (2000, 160)

So far, the story invites an allegorical reading of Cuba's recent history. As a closed space, the bus can be read as the blockaded island; the driver as a leader who is blind to the needs of his passengers; the bus's route as the journey of a revolution that has lost its capacity to serve the people. Yet, this reading is complicated by the meta-referential aspect of the story's denouement. The story resolves the ontological confusion of the bodily mass of passengers by placing the object, first in the gardens of the Department of Transportation (MITRANS), and finally at

> The Museum of Fine Arts, where the public can enjoy it Tuesday through Sunday, from 2 to 9. Some of the visitors, mostly foreigners, inquire after the author of such magnificent work, or they leave thinking that it is someone called Mitrans, because they confuse the author with the donor. (2000, 160)

"La guagua" has a metacritical dimension. In part, the story's end offers a parodic view of postmodern art, which is often based on questioning the very boundaries of what is art and what is not. At the local level, it amounts to a complaint. As the text suggests, the crisis in which Cuba is now immersed has become in itself a form of art. However, this view is not very popular in literary circles, where it has often been suggested that the novels that focus on contemporary living conditions only seek to feed the curiosity of a foreign readership.

The story, however, hides more than it actually tells. While "La guagua" proposes that new Cuban art is a combination of circumstance and error, the presence of the human mass in the museum obeys someone's active decision to place it there, a decision that helps determine the foreigners' "misreading" of the object. In this chapter, I argue that it is possible to consider that decision as a legitimate cultural act; that is, one that responds neither to market nor to political pressures, but instead to assumptions shared in the cultural world regarding the way in which objects are labeled, exposed, and circulated as art. Understanding how those decisions are made reveals more about the globalization of contemporary Cuban culture than the theories of artistic betrayal for hard currency suggested in many of the novels analyzed in the earlier chapters.

Behind the story is the international popularity of the art produced in Cuba during the economic crisis that became known as the "Special Period." This crisis, which was "a lot more than a mere crisis," in Kevin Power's words, reached unimaginable levels of intensity in the early 1990s (1999, 24). The hunger and indignity were such that Cuban reality often appeared more interesting than fiction. As I discussed in the previous chapter, it is not surprising that one of the most distinctive aesthetic projects to take place in Cuban culture since 1990 consists of presenting reality "as it is," presenting objects and telling stories in an exhibitionist, "unmediated" manner.

In literature, the following titles are self-explanatory: *Trilogía Sucia de La Habana* (Dirty Trilogy of Havana) and *Animal Tropical* (Tropical Animal) by Pedro Juan Gutiérrez, *El hombre, la hembra y el hambre* (Man, Woman, Hunger) by Daína Chaviano (1998), and *La nada cotidiana* (Yocandra in the Paradise of Nada) by Zoé Valdés (1995). These texts are devoted to the explicit portrayal of prostitution; of a lack of food, water and transportation;

and of an acute state of hopelessness. Other writers have produced more elaborate, less transparent narrations, but ultimately with a similar effect. Antonio José Ponte's story "Un arte de hacer ruinas" (An Art of Making Ruins), for example, elaborates a conspiracy theory about the overwhelming collapse of buildings in downtown Havana due to negligence and overcrowding. Ponte, who is an engineer by training, found inspiration in an article published in an urban studies journal that used the term "miraculous statics" as a way to explain the survival of many buildings in Centro Habana that should have already collapsed by all scientific calculations. The term of course lends itself to an allegorical interpretation when applied to the longevity of the revolutionary project in the post-Soviet era.

In film, it is quite common to come across hybrid examples that are aestheticized variations on the documentary genre, and which Cynthia Tompkins calls pseudodocumentaries (2013, 219). The most revealing ones are, perhaps, *Si me comprendieras* (If You Only Understood) by Rolando Díaz (1998) and *Suite Habana* by Fernando Pérez (2003), both of which use non-actors as their protagonists. These "actors" offer their own lives, their dilapidated houses, their complicated family stories, and their frustrated dreams to create the very texture of the film. *Si me comprendieras*, the less visibly mediated of the two, starts as metafiction but soon becomes completely absorbed by the real-life stories of the aspiring actresses, their families, and their houses. Interestingly, the director made a point of never interviewing the actresses off-camera so as to preserve their spontaneous, emotional reactions for the final film. In turn, *Suite Habana* can easily be dubbed a "visual poem" that intertwines (artificially, in fact) the daily lives of various families. As I discussed in the previous chapter, the unexpected silence (the film has neither dialogue nor voice-over), the slow camera, the extended repetition of familiar movements and domestic tasks, and, particularly, a very fine editing job help make this film intensely realistic and highly mediated at the same time. Like in the literary cases mentioned earlier, the appeal of both films seems largely to emanate from an exhibitionistic presentation of real life with apparently minimal authorial intervention.

GOING GLOBAL

As the short story "La guagua" suggests, international demand has been an important force behind this type of art production. With the insolvency of Cuban state publishing houses and the virtual collapse of the once booming local film industry, the dissemination of Cuban art and culture has passed on to foreign hands, mostly to Spanish publishers and film producers. The result has been the proliferation of Cuban art outside Cuba, allowing for a reinvigorated and redefined cultural production that has been the focus of much critical attention. *Suite Habana*, made with European funds, won several international awards including the Goya award for best foreign film in Spain 2004; Chaviano's novel *El hombre, la hembra y el hambre* won the Azorín award in Spain 1998; and Gutiérrez's *Animal tropical* obtained the Alfonso García Ramos award in 2000, also in Spain. The success of Cuban art in the international cultural circuits has led critics to discuss the existence of a cultural boom (J. Díaz 1998) that addresses the ethnographic curiosity of a foreign public (De Ferrari 2003), often serving as dictionaries of an attractive reality to the literary tourist (Whitfield 2002), and which is ruled by an international market that has effectively replaced state guidance about what Cuban art should be like, or even about (Buckwalter-Arias 2005). Indeed, as Sujatha Fernandes and others have noted, the marketing of Cuban culture in the 1990s cannot be separated from a new economy of export and exchange, one in which art is traded across nations in the absence of traditional export goods. I also agree with Fernandes, however, when she suggests that "the insertion of the Cuban culture industries into global markets . . . has opened up the site of culture to new contradictions," and, I may add, to unexpected redefinitions (2006, 10–11).

Not only does Cuban contemporary art offer an unprecedented combination of conceptualism, realism, and ethical activism, as I discussed in the previous chapter, but it does so in a highly mediated cultural world. I posited in the previous chapter that the aesthetic, social, and political relationship between art and truth that defines the voice of the intellectual can best be described with Susan Sontag's phrase "shady commerce." I have used the phrase "shady commerce" to describe the way in which the socialist social contract was reformulated following the demise of the Soviet bloc, as well as to allude to the obscure negotiations into which artists have had to enter in order to preserve their limited right to voice. In this chapter, I suggest that the notion of voice gets even more complex once all the players who have had significant roles in the production and dissemination of Cuban art have been factored in. To be sure, art, as Néstor García Canclini notes, "is not only an aesthetic question; we have to take into account how it responds at the intersection of what is done by journalists and critics, historians and museum writers, art dealers, collectors and speculators" (1995, 5).[1] However, it is fair to say that there are considerably more mediators in the management of post-Soviet Cuban culture than anywhere else. Bureaucrats, censors, publishers, art dealers, film producers, translators, academics, and international copyright lawyers have been called to negotiate the rules of what is art, whose art it is, and what it should be about. That these negotiations occur in a place where legal, artistic, and commercial rules are inflexible in theory yet constantly shifting in practice is, not surprisingly, a creative experiment. As Ariana Hernández-Reguant points out about the 1990s in her article "Copyrighting Che," "new social relations developed around the clash of socialist ethics and capitalist practices, along with new forms to imagine, mediate, and contest ideas of identification and community" (2004, 2). Furthermore, Hernández-Reguant understands globalized Cuba as a new form of "contact zone" (2004, 2). This is an unprecedented moment in the sociology of Cuban arts. Yet, I find it surprising that the complexities of this cultural phenomenon have been largely misunderstood among writers.

As the story "La guagua" seems to suggest, the literary boom based on the material reality of the Special Period, which has been named "literature of disenchantment," is seen as problematic within literary circles on the island.[2] This may be traced at least in part to the commercial success of this trend. Traditionally, a work with commercial appeal is deemed to be of lesser quality, equating the idea of "selling" with that of "selling out." Similar attitudes are held in the case of the political malleability of any given text (see Buckwalter-Arias 2005 and De Ferrari 2003). In fact, the association that was at first established between post-Soviet literature and a minor genre such as testimony, on the one hand, and the socialist realism of the early years of the revolution, on the other, clouded the reception of these works. In addition, art that traffics in the current state of affairs on the island—and thus depicts the far-from-beautiful reality of hunger, scarcity, and filth—does not categorically conform to the aesthetic notions that are upheld by, and indeed define, the artistic and intellectual class as a whole (a view that was discussed in Chapter 2 of this book). I have to admit that, although I do not share most of these assumptions, I would agree that a realist type of aesthetic in postmodern times seems somewhat suspicious. The apparent ingenuousness of these texts becomes all the more dubious when we consider the fact that they have been produced in Cuba, a country that takes pride in its sophisticated cultural tradition, and which has recently benefited from the generous cultural politics of the revolution.

Inspired, in part, by the story "La guagua," and convinced that art critics have had a much better grasp of the function, mechanisms, and, certainly, the aesthetics of cultural production in this period than literary critics, I would like to conclude this book by using the model of the visual arts to shed some light on the production, circulation, and reception of Cuban post-Soviet literature that I discussed in the earlier chapters. I would like to justify this comparison based on the higher visibility of the circulation of art than of literature—it is easier to know who exhibits a painting and who buys it than to know who buys a book, how it travels, and who reads it. Similarly, the institutional apparatus of biennials, international exhibitions, and mixed-capital foundations that disseminate Cuban art throughout the world render more visible the cultural mechanisms that I think also affect the literary world.

As post-Soviet Cuban art illustrates, to say that realism is the natural expression of the difficult living conditions is only half the truth. This trend has also been made possible by a series of agents who evaluate, select, and group these works according to both aesthetic and commercial criteria. Using the art world as a model, I suggest that Cuban culture since the 1990s can be thought of as a "curated culture." In using this term, I do not seek to minimize the intrusion of the marketplace in the socialist utopia, but to focus on the cultural processes, both in Cuba and abroad, that condition the management of art. In other words, I seek to view the Cuban trend as a complex process that, though inserted in an uneven international financial system, obeys laws and reasons that speak as much of Cuban politics as of First World cultural paradigms. I suggest two ideas: First, that the type of art I have been making reference to should be seen not so much as forms of testimony but as a cynical realism that amounts to an avant-garde, which I called hyperrealism in Chapter 5 of this book. Second, I propose to view the administration of Cuban contemporary culture as an imaginary space between center and periphery, art and market, self-exoticization and Neo-Avant-garde, which reflects Cuba's active participation in a postmodern world that is fascinated by difference.

AN ETHICS OF CONSUMPTION

In his essay "Report by Our Man in Havana," the eminent Cuban art critic Gerardo Mosquera alludes to a real story in order to explain the art production of the '90s. "No discourse speaks more eloquently to the contradictions in which Cuban art production is immersed today, than what happened in the recent V Biennial," during which elements such as toilet paper, soap, cigars, crucifixes, and toy guns were stolen from the installations. According to Mosquera, these unexpected social interventions lucidly comment on the acute state of necessity of the general population during these years (presumably of "violence, religion, pleasure and hygiene"). Mosquera concludes:

> The crisis is so deep, and simple survival so trying, that it is impossible for most Cubans to respect the line that separates aesthetics from reality—a reality dominated by scarcity and neglect. This situation affects how people react to the work of art when it contains objects that are badly needed, even when such work is located in an auratic space. (1995, 131)[3]

The anecdote mentioned by Mosquera took place in 1994—at the peak of the crisis—during a biennial that, under the title *Art, Society, Reflection*, has been considered a landmark in the history of Cuban art. Art critic Rachel Weiss describes the event as both an alternative aesthetic lab and a professional platform for the international market. In turn, a review that appeared in the Spanish newspaper *El país* celebrated the presence of renowned museum curators and prominent collectors from around the world (Vicent 1994).[4] The biennial, which took place between May and June of 1994 and included 171 works by artists from forty-one countries, promoted itself as a natural venue for Third-World art. However, it was Cuban art that met with the most enthusiastic acclaim. Considered to be simultaneously "daring and critical," "harsh and heart-breaking," these works focused on prostitution and the generalized desire for emigration that dominated Cuban society at this time (in fact about forty thousand people left the island in precarious boats that summer, although it is not clear how many survived). It is not surprising that the work that caused the most impact according to *El país* was the installation *La regata* (Regatta) by Alexis (Kcho) Leyva (1994) (see Figure 6.1). This piece, which re-creates the shape of a boat, is composed by objects found on shore, such as shoes and toys, but particularly by "testimonial objects" and materials (cork, wheels, chocolate wraps, and candles) that attest to the process by which Cubans make "an object that floats and allows them to leave the country" (Vicent 1994). A version of *La regata* was used as the cover of *ARTnews* in 2000.

Figure 6.1 Kcho Leyva. *La regata*. Wood, plastic, metal, ceramics, personal items, 1993–1994, as it appeared on the cover of *ARTnews* magazine. Photograph courtesy of *ARTnews*.

The international success of Cuban art in this biennial was mainly due to the originality of a type of art that, according to Mosquera, "brought the street into the gallery" (1999a, 37). In his anecdote, however, Mosquera seems to disapprove of the reaction such art had produced among the Cuban public, who had been unable or unwilling to respect the line separating art and life, even to the point of performing social interventions in the work of art (denying perhaps the fact that such interventions can become part of the works themselves). Although this realism derives from the fusion of the social and the aesthetic, such fusion must be conceptual, not accidental. This is why Mosquera seems worried that a literal reading of the work of art may negatively affect the aura of a piece whose very originality emanates precisely from its literality.

In spite of their stark differences, both Mosquera's anecdote and the short story "La guagua" promote the idea that there are incorrect ways to consume a given work of art. And both are partly right, because ultimately these works work precisely to the extent that they allow for a double reading that is not always easy to sustain. For instance, whereas "La guagua" promotes the need to read the material and to be suspicious of the aura, Mosquera's anecdote promotes the importance of trusting the aura of the piece, and to disengage from its materiality. In my view, the resistance to the double reading can be traced to a "structural" notion: Claude Lévi-Strauss made the distinction between primitive art, which stresses the material, and Western art, which stresses the model (1992, 27). According to this paradigm, the intense referentiality of the new Cuban art would help label it as primitive art and, therefore, minor. This would explain why critics have been more receptive to realist Cuban art and literary works when these establish an explicit dialogue with themes and tropes familiar to Western art history.

In the previous chapter, I framed the discussion on the referentiality of Cuban art in the context of the theory of photography. I suggested that, for the most part, new Cuban art is referential in the same way photography is referential, that is, by giving the impression of a direct sensorial connection between spectator and object. Although referentiality is an inevitable aspect in photography, no one referent is intrinsically preferable to any other. For instance, images by Carlos Garaicoa, like the novel by Abilio Estévez that I discussed in previous chapters, expressly combine a bleak view of Havana with Western traditional notions of beauty (see Figure 6.2). Garaicoa's two-panel installation *Acerca de esos incansables atlantes que sostienen cada día nuestro presente* (About These Untiring Atlantes that Sustain Our Present Day by Day) offers a photograph of downtown Havana in its current state of ruin. On top of the photograph is an architectural drawing of a similar landscape, in which the braces sustaining the decrepit buildings are replaced by figures of giant atlantes. The piece suggests that the fragile city is actually supported by mythological beings. In the photograph, the ruins aren't, in the words of Abilio Estévez in *Palacios distantes*, "like the Coliseum, which announces man's march through History; quite

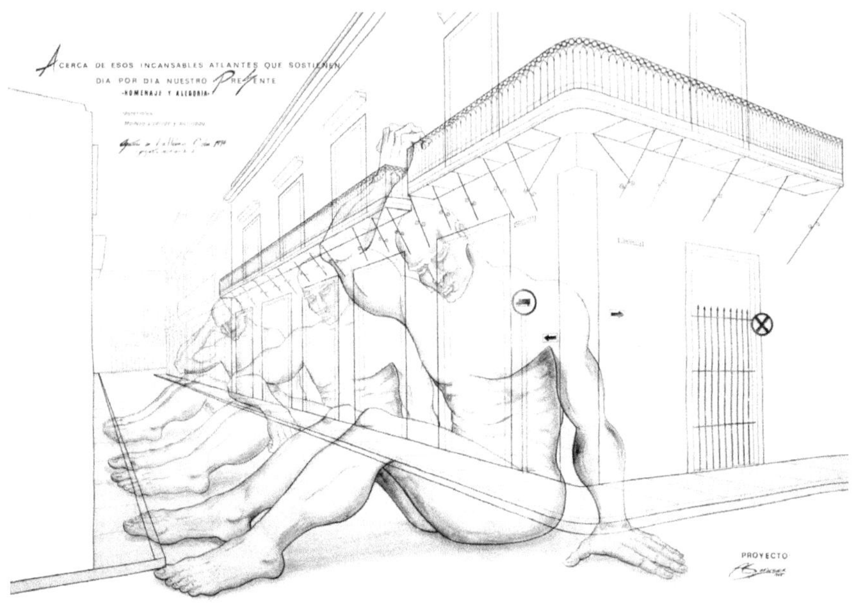

Figure 6.2 Carlos Garaicoa. *Acerca de esos incansables atlantes que sostienen cada día nuestro presente*. Ink drawing on vegetable fiber paper; color photograph, 1994–1995. Courtesy of the artist.

the contrary, these are ruins that announce History's march over men" (2002, 64). By contrast, the architectural drawing offers a "poetic intervention," to use the artist's words. It is a hallucinatory view of the ruins that is sustained by mythological figures. These figures speak of eternity, endurance, and civilization. The combination of these two images further reminds us of Estévez's protagonist, to whom "the city makes two impressions . . . at once: that of having been bombarded, of a city that is only waiting for the lightest thunderstorm, the slightest gust of wind, to tumble into a pile of stones; and that of a sumptuous and everlasting city, one that has just been built, erected as a concession to future immortality. Havana is never the same and is always the same" (2002, 7). The double structure of Garaoicoa's work has been seen as an attempt on the part of art to "cure" the city (see Torres del Sol and López Sabor 2006). Whereas the juxtaposition of ludic fantasy and harsh reality offers a humorous, medicinal take on Cuban reality, it still forms part of an "aesthetics of frustration," as it has been called in art, or of an "aesthetics of disenchantment," the term most commonly used in literature. Similarly, Estévez's novel casts the themes of ruins, hunger, and prostitution within an elaborate, highly poetic Neo-Baroque prose. The search for literary beauty in the text mirrors the search for worldly pleasures in characters that are exhausted by decades of forced heroism and austerity. Estévez's characters, much like Estévez himself, feel that only a good dose of beauty can redeem Cubans' exhausted souls.

I believe that the double aesthetic convention found in Garaicoa's work and in Estévez's writing produces two simultaneous effects. First, its commitment to a modernist idea of beauty clearly helps furnish the object with a recognizable "aura"—feeding, perhaps, what Laura Marks calls "analog nostalgia" (2002, 152). Second, the exhibitionism of some of these pieces amounts to an ethical statement, since they explicitly denounce the toll revolutionary heroism has taken on the Cuban people. However, duplication can be seen as duplicity when aesthetics turn into ethics without fully abandoning a traditional code of beauty that can be comforting to the spectator. By this I mean that the highly artistic elaboration that accompanies the testimonial aspects of the work softens its impact on the spectator's sensitivity. At a political level, then, this type of work is somewhat compromised. For, if we consider the Cuban revolution as a typically modern political event, we can say that the modernist notion of beauty present in the text expresses only partial disenchantment to the ideals and the utopias of modernity. At an aesthetic level, the explicit contrast between pure art and pure reality emphasizes the role played by the gaze—in this case, a second gaze offered by the artist himself—in lending the work its artistic status.

Another type of realism features prominently in this period, one that is much more violent to the spectator. This trend elaborates upon the same sort of problematic that we see in the works by Garaoicoa and Estévez mentioned above, but without appealing to the dignifying effect of the Western tradition. It is an austere rendering of a desolate society, one that shuns any expectation for originality, coherence, or beauty. Poorly constructed narrations, unclear plots, dirty streets, and cruel characters populate the novels by Pedro Juan Gutiérrez. This is also true about the photographic series *Ojos desnudos* by Abigail González. As I discussed in Chapter 5, both Gutiérrez and González cultivate, one through smell and the other through tactility, a sensorial directness that forces an intimate response from the reader/spectator.

Because of their sordid themes and raw manufacture, the art produced by Gutiérrez and González can be violent to the spectator. Often, the use of the human body becomes a privileged subject, which can in part be attributed to its availability—bodies are free. However, when the human body is cast in a way that it produces neither beauty nor desire, it usually forces the spectator to confront his or her own "animality." This type of artistic representation amounts to a political statement in that both the subject and the spectator are debased, humiliated. It makes the spectator, especially the liberal intellectual, question the real consequences of our idealism.

The exhaustion of ideology explains, in part, the intense referentiality of this type of art. As poet, critic, and curator Orlando Hernández states in his essay "The Pleasure of Reference":

> The tumultuous social and cultural atmosphere of the 1990s, in which the majority of these artists developed, has proved to be a more provocative and nourishing subject matter for their work than the usual wellsprings of the subconscious and the individual imagination. I am not sure if it constitutes a methodology, but the majority of these artists has explored the labyrinths of external reality to a much greater extent than their own inner depths and has preferred to take their ideas directly from everyday life rather than from the moldy archives of tradition, including the history of art. The focus is on the *here* and *now* rather than on historical legacies, which makes for a curious philosophy of the immediate—as though the natural distrust of promises for the future were united with disappointment and disillusionment with the past. (2001, 25; emphasis in the original)

Hernández proposes that referential art in the '90s in Cuba amounts to a Neo-Avant-garde defined in opposition to both the psychological incursions of past avant-gardes, as well as to the "moldy archives" of Western artistic traditions. Animated by a "philosophy of the immediate," this aesthetic reduces the ludic dimension of art to the minimum, which serves the purpose of communicating the artist's exhaustion vis-à-vis official rhetoric more aggressively. In other words, these hidden layers of conceptualization help build the aura of a realism that seems to purposely avoid the presence of any recognizable auratic elements in its structure.

There is no doubt that the most provoking case among these is that of Angel Delgado, who sculpted *San Lázaro*, a piece made from soap in 1991 (see Figure 6.3). The fact that Delgado re-created this religious icon using a nontraditional medium attests to the scarcity of objects and materials in Cuba in these years, but it also evokes prison art. From this perspective, the piece can be seen as a metaphor for the double siege that defined the situation on the island in the 1990s. In this case, however, it is not really a metaphor, as Delgado made this piece during the six-month sentence he served in 1990 for an artistic intervention with another type of nonconventional material. Notoriously, Delgado had defecated on a newspaper as part of an exhibit called *El objeto esculturado* (The Sculpted Object), which took place at the Centro de Desarrollo de las Artes Visuales in Havana in 1990. According to critics, Delgado sought to demonstrate that excrement was a human-sculpted object; naturally, "the police saw it differently" (Hernández 2001, 25). For the police it was key that the newspaper used for the occasion was *Granma*, the official daily publication of the Communist party. Delgado was accused of public indecency and sent to jail. While evoking the irreverent statements often made by the avant-garde artists of the early twentieth century, Delgado's gesture forcefully expresses the demoralization of an exhausted society.[5]

Figure 6.3 Ángel Delgado. *San Lázaro*. Soap, 1991. Photograph courtesy of the artist.

In fact, Delgado's performance anticipates the dirty narratives of collective bathrooms of Pedro Juan Gutiérrez's novels, whose protagonist shamelessly declares that "in the bathroom, there is shit up to the ceiling" (1998, 81). Not only do these provocations seek to "épater le communiste," as it were, but they also act as social criticism. Borrowing Joshua Esty's words, we can say that "even when understood according to the representation codes of realism . . . shit has a political vocation: it draws attention to the failures of development, to the unkept promises" of revolutionary dignity (Esty 1999, 32; see also Anderson 2010). The intervention by the police in Delgado's case underlines Mosquera's opinion that "new Cuban art has been able to play a unique function as a place for social discussion in a country where these places are nonexistent" (1999b, 49). In other words, these "artistic" gestures and works act as substitutes for the critical role usually expected from the press in non-authoritarian places—as Delgado seems to suggest in a none-too-subtle a way, and as the police seem to have understood quite well.

Like the short story "La guagua," Delgado's performance and its aftermath can also be seen as a story of readings and misreadings. On the one hand, there is the reading by the police, who have technically confused art with crime—thus reverting the irony in Díaz Pimienta's story, in which foreigners see art when facing "sculpted objects in non-conventional material." Again like "La guagua," Delgado's act underlines the determining role played by critical conceptualization in the process of labeling art as art. In Delgado's so-called artistic intervention, legitimacy is granted by his position as a known young artist, by the auratic space in which his act took place, and by the implicit dialogue established with the title of the exhibit. In turn, the exhibit of the mass of passengers in the Museum of Fine Arts that appears in the short story by Díaz Pimienta is in fact guaranteed by the mention of a donor and of spectators, as well as by the explicit comparison the story makes to the work of canonical painters and sculptors. Similarly, the legitimacy of the novels mentioned previously is granted by the fact that they are published by well-known publishing houses in Spain, and that are reviewed in *Babelia*, the cultural supplement to the newspaper *El país*. From a sociological point of view, we can say that Delgado's performance, the story "La guagua," and Mosquera's biennial anecdote effectively underline the particularly determining role of the "reader" in referential art. For while all three instances promote the idea that there are incorrect readings, they insist on the fact that such readings have consequences (be it fame, sales, jail, ostracism), and hence the importance of a professional reader with authority to grant "aura" to a given object. This person is, of course, the curator.

CURATING CUBA

A curator is usually defined as the person in charge of selecting the works that will be included in an exhibition of one or more artists, and of articulating the discourse that will lend identity to the exhibit. In Spanish, the word "curator" is very new—in fact, Mosquera defines himself as a "crítico, *curator* y narrador," using the word in English (1995, 140; emphasis added). Etymologically speaking, the Spanish word "curador" suggests a "curandero," a witch doctor. Although this connotation is partly in keeping with Garaicoa's idea of "curing" the city with humor, the practice itself is only tangentially related to medical discourse. The official translation of the word curator is "restaurador," a word that designates the person in a museum whose role is to preserve, or conserve, a given cultural patrimony, not to contest it or to initiate new discourses. By contrast, in Spain, the freelance curator is usually referred to as a "comisario," literally a sheriff, which doesn't suggest innovation either.[6] The word used in Latin America is "curador," an Anglicism, which, by virtue of being a new word, seems more attuned to the task of propitiating new discourses, thus becoming a true "author" in the sense given by Foucault (1977). What I find interesting about the freelance curator is that, by providing the work with its own metalanguage almost at the very moment of its production, the curator anticipates and even preempts the critics' work. At the same time, however, because his mission is to design a discourse capable of producing immediate meaning in a given society, the curator resembles the marketing agent. I don't want to imply here that the curator does not belong to the art world, but rather that his methods can place him in the hybrid role of being both the producer and the promoter of avant-garde art. What is more, because of the lack of an internal art market in today's Cuba, the curator is also, essentially, an exporter of avant-garde art.

The phrase "curated culture" appears in an essay by Kevin Power entitled "Cuba: One Story after Another." Power, an American professor at the Instituto Superior de Arte de La Habana, uses this term to refer to the determining role that the foreign public plays in Cuban art production. Power affirms that the "most dangerous corollary in the present situation is that curated cultures produce as a function of demands from the center," the center being galleries, museums, and publishers in some cities in the US and Europe, which tend to prefer works that comment on the ideological and social tensions in Cuba (1999, 44). However, Power also locates the referentiality of Cuban art in a complex dynamic:

> What, you might ask, has this [prostitution, hunger, black market] to do with art? Well, nothing and everything! Everything in the sense that much of the content of Cuban art is specifically concerned with sociocultural commentary and with ideological tensions. Indeed, should the artist turn away from certain *legitimized* themes (legitimized from the outside, although at the same time indisputably *natural* to the inside), he may well find himself outside the pale of interests of the international art world, debarred, as it were, through his own choosing, and

> isolated from the consequent economic benefits. It is clear in the present climate social criticism is like breathing in, i.e., literally, "in-spiration," even though the artist's attitude towards it may, in the harsh contradictions of the nineties, have acquired a hard-boiled, strategic, and cynical edge. (1999, 29; emphasis in the original)

Even though Power rejects the possibility that artists may be interested in making a political statement, he makes a welcome distinction between selling out and selling. It is true that an artist can get up to US$5,000 for one of his or her works, whereas a doctor usually makes US$20 dollars a month, which makes selling art a highly desirable activity. What is more important for Power is that the possibility to sell offers artists an opportunity to create, even if this relegates them to certain thematic expectations.

Power traces the international interest in Cuba to its situation as an ultra-periphery: "periphery functions best when it assumes its identity as periphery, and consequently, artists who leave for the center risk falling out of sight" (1999, 24). An artist who "emigrates" in themes and methods that are usually considered his or her "natural habitat" runs the risk of falling out of sight as much as an émigré artist. The main problem with catering to an international taste, however, is the simplification of the work of art: For a piece to travel well, it has to stick to themes that confirm their otherness and they must do so in a clear, reductive way so that the message doesn't get lost (29). When the consumer at the center wants difference, he or she usually wants such difference to be authentic. Hence the importance that the artist stays put (at least part of the time), and that the "curators/explorers" from the First World work with local curators (44). Such mixed processes or institutions help make the relationship between periphery and center more democratic, because they allow the periphery not just to own the work and the experience behind the work, but also its hermeneutic discourse as well, at least in part. In the end, however, they also help confirm the traditional roles that center and periphery usually play in cultural transactions given that their main objective is to certify the legitimacy of difference.

The titles chosen for Cuban exhibits around the world are clear indicators of the expectations of Cuban authenticity: "Made in Havana" (Australia 1989), "Nacido en Cuba" (Caracas 1991), and "Comment peut-on être cubain?" (Paris 1998). This situation is even re-created on the island itself, where a 1995 exhibit entitled *Inside Habana* was organized in "Espacio Aglutinador" (an alternative space created in artist Sandra Ceballos's private home). On the one hand, the English word "Inside," an invitation for the voyeuristic foreign spectator, contradicts the exceptionality and reveals, instead, the desire to not let the message get lost. On the other, the "b" in Habana acts as a certification of origin while suggesting the primitive charm of the native who is unable to translate himself.[7] Even the title of one of Mosquera's essay that I mentioned earlier, "Report by Our Man in Havana," re-creates a similar situation. Not only does it evoke

Graham Greene, but it also confirms that both exhibition and publisher are located outside Cuba, in this case in Barcelona, and that Mosquera lends the exhibition his stamp of authenticity. The fact that many Cuban critics mentioned in this article are quoted in English is probably the most curious piece of evidence. The words of many artists and critics quoted here appear in English as "originals in translation." This is due to the fact that these essays are usually requested, translated, compiled, and published for the first time by critics in the US and Europe. Even the catalogs and art criticism that are published in Spain often include an English translation at the end of the text. It would be wrong, in my view, to see this situation merely as an absolute indication of a colonizing pattern, as Cuban voices need these international mediators in order to be heard, although they are heard mostly by the mediators' public.[8] Ultimately, the international interest in this art helps ensure the survival of a cultural activity that surpasses the island's capacity to absorb it.[9]

At the local level, the control over the artist's voice gives rise to other mixed cultural processes. More concretely, a curious effect on Cuban art production is determined by censorship. Those in charge of censorship in Cuba are bureaucrats in the cultural sector who are themselves artists, and whose main role is to mediate between the artist and the state. Mosquera explains that during these years,

> Art has become more radical since it is ritually protected behind layers of metaphorical density and a cynical attitude. I say "ritually" because, ultimately, everyone knows what the works mean, but what matters is that they are not explicit. This gives cultural bureaucrats—the ones in charge of censorship—a way to protect themselves vis-à-vis those who control their work. (1995, 133)

In other words, in order to publish material that could be considered politically dangerous, the artist-bureaucrat needs to make sure that he or she can promote a nonpolitical reading. The artist-bureaucrat, then, is censor and curator at the same time, juggling labels and redefining aesthetics on the basis of its ambiguities. In contrast with the foreign curator, the censor needs that the message gets lost. After all, it is important for the artist to be on good terms with the state, given that official institutions manage the artists' right to travel—as traveling to foreign institutions and universities is one of the main sources of income in hard currency for artists and scholars.[10]

When we speak about money, we always imply a market. This point has not been missed by the Cuban government, which has founded and runs a number of stylish art galleries throughout Havana displaying contemporary Cuban art. They look, feel, and seem to function like independent art galleries anywhere else in the world. Galería Habana, the first to be founded, is the most autonomous one. It depends on the Consejo

Nacional de Artes Plásticas (CNAP), which appoints its director, and has the authority to sell and ship art directly. In practical terms, Galería Habana behaves more like a gallery in capitalist societies than a state-run art emporium, although in reality it cannot exhibit, promote, or sell anything without the approval of the CNAP. The government also created an enterprise called Génesis. As listed in its website, the explicit objective of Génesis is "to represent, promote, produce, and market contemporary Cuban art at national and international levels." Génesis views galleries as a link in a chain of command with the mission of implementing cultural and economic policies while ensuring "artistic quality and conceptual value."[11] None of the other galleries (Factoría Habana, Villamanuela, Servando, René Portocarrero) have a managing director, but instead depend on appointed specialists who assist in curatorial aspects exclusively. Through this complex marketing apparatus, the state promotes local artists and international tourism, while controlling in part the public circulation of voice. The socialist state profits financially and politically by exploiting the taste and economic laws of the global market. It may be true that, as critic Luis Camnitzer argues, Cuba uses capitalism without letting itself be totally used by it (1994, 150).[12]

MARKETING DIFFERENCE

What has determined this market and not any other is a state of mind in international intellectual circles that values alterity and is willing to pay its price. In her introduction to the book *Art Cuba*, Holly Block, director of Art in General in New York City, states that "remembering why Cuba is different remains important; in this global age, changing societies often undervalue what makes them distinctive" (2001, 11). What makes Cuba distinctive is a combination of characteristics that are both unique to the island and particularly attractive outside it. For starters, Cuba combines a racially and culturally Afro–Latin American makeup, with a political structure that is as heroic as it is anachronistic. For decades, it has defined itself as an anti-imperialist utopia, a claim that is now quite compromised in practice. What is more important, it produces exceptionally trained artists. Indeed, the cultural politics of the revolution created many art schools and institutions that form artists and promote art production. Thanks to the revolution, Cubans are highly educated and, since the early 1990s, their subsistence is mostly made possible by international sponsorship. That Cuban artists try to sell their art in international circles is hardly surprising. That international markets appreciate the affordable yet original Cuban art may be even less so.

Cuban curators such as Magaly Espinosa, Meira Marrero, Gerardo Mosquera, and Corina Matamoros considered the importance of the role of the curator in a symposium entitled *La curaduría, un laboratorio para el arte* (Curatorship: An Art Lab), which took place at the UNEAC (Unión Nacional de Escritores y Artistas Cubanos), and parts of which were published in a special dossier entitled "El oficio de curar" (The Art of Curatorship) in the journal *Artecubano* in 2001. The presentations show a certain anxiety to define the role of the curator, who is simultaneously seen as an activist (i.e., as an agent for change), and as the provider of a language with the capacity to make such change both possible and meaningful. In these texts, one notices a familiar anxiety over the meaning of multiculturalism. The curators in this symposium seem eager to better understand their working material in a world in which art, society, and culture are not only inseparable but are also analyzed in similar ways. In other words, Cuban curators seem to share the same preoccupations as other non-Cuban colleagues around the world.

The curators and critics in the UNEAC symposium seem to be somewhat concerned about the role that the international market plays in the production of art in Cuba. Some are proud of the prevalent notion that "the most innovating discourses in art" are produced in the periphery. It is not clear, however, if they are innovative because they are peripheral or if this situation helps redefine the traditional relationship between center and periphery. Divergent opinions on the connection between art and market are also apparent. For instance, Llilian Llanes Godoy, director of the legendary V Biennial, thinks biennials respond to the need to create alternative spaces for those who "have not yet had access to 'universality'" (1997, 18), whereas others undermine them as events designed for cultural tourism (Espinosa 2001, 7). I, in turn, can't help but wonder if it is productive, or even possible, to distinguish between spectator, consumer, and cultural tourist. At the same time, and somewhat paradoxically, Espinosa finds that "the boom of international exposure of our artistic production has increased the aesthetic quality of the pieces, and it has opened us to other forms of art such as installations, performance and *environments*" (Espinosa 2001, 7). We can conclude from the various comments included in the dossier "The Art of Curatorship" that the problems and questions faced by the local managers of Cuban art can be remarkably similar to those of other cultural critics and agents in the art world in general, and in peripheral societies in particular. I think, then, that these comments ultimately suggest that the Cuban boom may be less Cuban than it seems.

In a way, the relation between center and periphery that Cuba embodies is symptomatic of the place that Latin America occupies in the First World imaginary not just as primitive space, but more importantly as an "intelligible" primitive space. As Mosquera pointed out in an earlier essay, Latin America produces a hybrid alterity, one that allows the center to value difference without ever having to abandon Western sensitivity (qtd. in Power 1999, 44). Behind Mosquera's comment is a warning against the "paradoxical self-exoticization" of peripheral societies that wish to fulfill the "expectations of alterity dictated by Post-modern exotism" (2002, 626). Furthermore, Mosquera rightly condemns those

> so-called international cultural phenomena and institutions that not only consider themselves contemporary and universal, but also reserve themselves the right . . . to determine what should and should not be included in those categories. They constitute a conceptualizing system of power, one that legitimizes itself while failing to understand that "international" and "contemporary" are relative and relational terms. (2002, 626–627)

The situation described by Mosquera summarizes an international cultural practice whose methods need to be made evident. And this is, in my view, what new Cuban art does really well, at least when in the right hands.

A paradigmatic institution of the new era is the Fundación Ludwig de Cuba (FLC), in principle a nongovernment institution created in 1995 by German collectors Peter and Irene Ludwig as a result of their fascination with the V Biennial. The FLC is managed by a local president, Helmo Hernández, who has put his stamp on the art trends that have circulated during these years. The FLC "programming manager" Luisa Marisy, affirms that the foundation.

> is interested particularly in artists who are researching new expressive languages without abandoning their own identity . . . Because of the foundation's status as a non-governmental organization and its simple structure, the Foundation's work represents a new, experimental way of promoting and administering culture within Cuba. (1999, 48)

Not only does the foundation promote local artists through the organization of international exhibits and festivals, but it also organizes conferences, seminars, academic courses, and international exchanges. In other words, the FLC is an active (or rather, activist) agent in the international cultural exchange, promoting local art while educating its receivers. In this sense, the FLC works as a mediator between center and periphery from the periphery. It is not surprising, then, that the art promoted by the FLC reflects upon the very same themes the foundation redefines in its managing role.

In its early days, the FLC organized an exhibit entitled "Una de cada clase" ("One of Each Type"). In the video-catalog of the exhibit, new Cuban art is explained in these terms:

> One can today imagine a new realism centered precisely on the spectator, [on the quest] to make visible the relations that take place in the space of art between emitters and receivers, buyers and sellers, values, auras, prestige, groups and experiences.

Judging by this comment, then, one can understand Cuban hyperrealism as an art that not only describes the society of origin, but also the society in which it inserts itself, and whose mechanisms it keeps in function from its very intervention.

The complex critical spirit cited by the FLC exhibit is palpable in the two forms of hyperrealism that I mentioned above, even though they elaborate their critical position in different ways. The type of hyperrealism that is in explicit dialogue with Western artistic tradition, such as that of Garaicoa, Ponte, Estévez, Fernando Pérez, among others, offers an aesthetic project that is conscious of both their innovative and peripheral conditions. Making this paradox possible is the artists' cultivated, ludic spirit, which helps them evaluate the many aspects of their own historical and artistic situation. One of the effects resulting from the counterpoint between reality and sublimation in these cases is to render more evident the distressing living conditions of Cubans today. At the same time, however, because these works propose their own conceptualization more or less explicitly, we can describe them as "curated" art from their inception.

In contrast, the novels by Pedro Juan Gutiérrez and Zoé Valdés, as well as the film *Si me comprendieras* and the photography by Abigail González and René Peña, offer a raw type of hyperrealism. In these texts, both represented world and the representation itself appear as naturally chaotic. In a way, they act as open invitations for someone to organize, classify, and elevate them. A type of art that so overtly insists in its "curability" is understandably popular among curators. In spite of its appearance, however, this is not an innocent type of art. Its referentiality seeks more than to stress the material, as Lévi-Strauss had it, but to mimic the transparency of photography instead. As critic and curator Meira Marrero suggests, photography creates the illusion that reality imprints itself on paper. That is why photography is a naturalistic artistic medium, one in which reality appears written "by God himself" (2001, 12). We may conclude, then, that in its emulation of photography—that is, in its adoption of methods and expectations external to it—literature reinvents its own functions and mechanisms. Its realism, then, is highly conceptual. Paraphrasing Lévi-Strauss, we can say that Cuban hyperrealist art and literature are conceptual and primitive at the same time. We can go further and propose that hyperrealism is conceptual *because* it is primitive. By embodying its geographical and critical position in the world, new Cuban art forcefully unveils the pitfalls of both the global cultural spirit and the financial processes that condition Third World art production today. Hyperrealism, then, is a poetic intervention in post-utopian, postmodern societies. In this regard it is important to note that Latin American postmodernism is an acquired sensitivity. In the Cuban case, in particular, postmodernism is not a natural consequence of either of the two most common features associated with this trend. It neither founds itself on the exhaustion of grand narratives (Power 1999, 41), nor on a disengagement of art from history (48). The most interesting aspect of such complex cultural development may very well be that, by creating a postmodernism that is emptied of its sole historical justification, Cuban art has rendered postmodernism more genuinely postmodern.

Notes

NOTES TO CHAPTER 1

1. This and all translations are mine unless properly noted.
2. Ambrosio Fornet's "La crítica bicéfala" is a response to an article published by his son Jorge, entitled "La narrativa cubana entre la utopía y el desencanto" (Cuban Narrative between Utopia and Disenchantment). Jorge Fornet's essay later became the chapter "Cuba llegó tarde al desencanto" (Cuba Arrived Late to Disenchantment) in his book *Los nuevos paradigmas, Prólogo Narrativo al Siglo XXI* (*The New Paradigms: Narrative Prologue to the 21st Century*). I will discuss Jorge Fornet's essay in more detail later in this chapter.
3. Velia Cecilia Bobes studies the importance of ethics in the configuration of the socialist state from a sociological perspective. Here I paraphrase Bobes's statement "to insist in the symbolic aspects of power allows us to understand that, beyond coercion, there is a set of shared beliefs and values that, expressed in the form of practices (institutional or not), largely contribute to the creation of the political" (2000, 19). Similarly, Damián J. Fernández has written about the importance of "*lo informal* (the informal)" in the making of the political. According to Fernández, "the emotional impact of politics and the relevance of emotions for politics" have been absent in the studies of politics and even social Cuba. Like Fernández, I seek to bring to the fore the "informal social practices, the interactions among individuals in everyday life, and their political import," which "have been neglected or rendered invisible" in traditional Cuban studies (2000, vii–viii). Odette Casamayor-Cisneros also maps post-Soviet narrative from the point of view of ethics (2013). She understands that the ideas and affect characterizing a given time produces a particular cosmology that allows human beings to interpret their place in history in a given way (18). Whereas her book arrived too late for me to integrate it into my discussion, I hope their affinity will spur a productive dialogue.
4. It should be noted that, according to Cook, the contractual model does not equally represent certain sectors of the population, such as peasants or non-Slavic groups (1993, 4).
5. I will elaborate Hirschman's ideas in more detail in Chapter 2 of this book. Arcadio Díaz Quiñones also discusses the use of voice and exit in Cuba at the height of the Special Period (2000).
6. Restricted exit as a defining aspect of Cuban socialism didn't change until 2013. On October 16, 2012, the daily publication *Granma* published the news of a decree that would allow Cuban citizens to travel freely out of Cuba (i.e., without an exit permit) beginning January 14, 2013. However,

the decree defends the right to deny exit to some people "in order to preserve the human capital created by the Revolution." The first months of its implementation have seen dissident blogger Yoani Sánchez, who had repeatedly been denied exit visa requests, leave the country for a highly publicized world tour, and return without obvious penalties. See "Actualiza Cuba su política migratoria." See also Yoani Sánchez (2011).

7. Rousseau explains:

   > For a newly formed people to understand wise principles of politics and to follow the basic rules of statecraft, the effect would have to become the cause; the social spirit which must be the product of social institutions would have to preside over the setting up of those institutions; men would have to have already become before the advent of law that which they become as the result of the law. And as the lawgiver can for those reasons employ neither force nor argument, he must have recourse to an authority of another order, one which can compel without violence and persuade without convincing. (1968, 86–87)

   Also, see Routon (2010), in which he discusses "the magic of the Revolution" through the prism of Afro-Cuban deities.
8. During the speech for the fifty-fourth anniversary of the Moncada attack delivered in Camagüey on July 26, 2007, Raúl Castro said, "and this is how it's been during the 16 years or more of life in the Special Period; that is, 16 years of persistent efforts by the whole country to overcome difficulties so as to move forward. This is the way it has been and the way it has to be, given that we have not yet emerged from the Special Period." The speech was published in its entirety in the journal *Granma* and can be found at http://www.granma.cubaweb.cu/secciones/raul26/.
9. General Arnaldo Ochoa and three other officials were surprisingly charged with treason in obscure circumstances and executed in 1989.
10. In Alain Badiou's words:

    > I shall call "truth" (*a* truth) the real process of a fidelity to an event . . . Essentially, a truth is the material course traced, within the situation, by the evental supplementation. It is thus an *immanent break*. "Immanent" because a truth proceeds in the situation, and nowhere else . . . "Break" because what enables the truth-process—the event—meant nothing according to the prevailing language and established knowledge of the situation. (2001, 42–43)

    I will elaborate on this further in Chapter 4 of this volume.
11. Badiou here seems to be consistent with Rousseau's notion of "a newly formed people," which I discussed earlier in this chapter.
12. Originally published in March 1965 in *Marcha*, a Uruguayan newspaper, with the title "Desde Argel para *Marcha*: la Revolución cubana hoy."
13. See *Mauvaise conduite* (1984), particularly Juan Goytisolo's interview. See also Jean Franco (2002).
14. This entire section is based on Franco (2002, 90–93); Navarro (2002); *Mauvaise conduite* (1984). See also Epps (1995); Hernández-Reguant (2009); and Kapcia et al. (2012).
15. A good example of this trend is shown by "hyperrealist" texts, such as those written by Pedro Juan Gutiérrez and Zoé Valdés, in which the abject is usually celebrated. This kind of writing is often labeled as "bad" literature by the local intelligentsia because they see it as an example of the worst sort of opportunism, selling bad taste in order to make hard currency; that is, as a sort of intellectual prostitution (see De Ferrari 2003). The condemnation of this attitude may be justified not only aesthetically but also by the understanding that commerce, according to Harvey C. Mansfield, is an unmanly

practice (2006, 233). In art, however, this trajectory is somewhat different. I discuss this more extensively in Chapters 5 and 6 of this volume.

16. A portrayal of the underground book market can be found in Leonardo Padura's *La neblina del ayer* (*The Mist of the Past*) (2005).
17. A passionate discussion on male writers' detachment from material conditions is offered by Una in the novel *Las palabras perdidas* (*The Lost Words*) by Jesús Díaz.
18. See "Abjection and Aesthetic Violence in Pedro Juan Gutiérrez's *Trilogía sucia de La Habana*" in De Ferrari (2007a).
19. Rafael Rojas, 2008, "Pregunta a los socialistas cubanos," *Penúltimos días* (blog). This was first delivered as a talk in the conference "Cuba: New Research Directions" in Irvine, May 2008.
20. With the appointment of Mariela Castro Espín, sexologist and daughter of Raúl Castro, as director of the CENESEX (National Center for Sexual Education), significant attention has been drawn to LBGT equality issues. Among other achievements, Mariela Castro is a driving force behind the approval of sex reassignment surgeries at no cost. The record of the CENESEX is quite impressive for a country that had labor camps for homosexuals in the 1960s. However, there is considerable discussion about to what extent this space of sexual freedom is truly representative of larger social changes.
21. See Senel Paz's 1991 story "El lobo, el bosque y el Hombre Nuevo," the story that famously opened up the conversation about homosexuality and intellectual responsibility, and the basis of Tomás Gutiérrez Alea's 1994 film *Fresa y chocolate*. I agree with Jorge Fornet that Paz's story, which ends with the loaded image of a "pionerito" holding flowers, fails to express the disenchantment that transpires in the other stories I include here (2006, 64). I also agree with José Quiroga (2005) and Emilio Bejel (2001), among others, that, in spite of flirting with the idea of homosexuality, the story (and the film) offer too little, too late in favor of the redemption of the homosexual revolutionary subject. Sadly, for a text that seemed inaugural at first, when read today Paz's story falls short of the shock value it reportedly had at the time of its original publication.
22. See Blanchot (1988, 56). Notions of community and their relationship with communism are elaborated in Chapter 4 of this book.

NOTES TO CHAPTER 2

1. This summary best reflects Jesús Díaz's *Las palabras perdidas* (The Lost Words) and Padura's *La novela de mi vida* (The Novel of My Life). It also alludes to the Mario Conde series and Abel Prieto's *El vuelo del gato* (The Flight of the Cat), albeit more obliquely. Ena Lucía Portela offers an engaging counterpoint to this discussion in her novels *Cien botellas en una pared* (One Hundred Bottles; 2002) and, in an altogether different context, *Djuna and Daniel* (2007). I will discuss *One Hundred Bottles* in Chapter 3 of this volume.
2. For an in-depth analysis of Freemasonry in the Caribbean, see Arroyo (2013).
3. Braudy further quotes numerous philosophers, writers, and statesman that "supported the belief that the experience of war reveals the core of both individual and national character more truthfully and more naturally than does peace" (2003, 29).
4. In real life, a constant negotiation regarding both voice and exit can be followed in Sánchez's blog *Generación Y*. Sánchez was denied permission

to travel sixteen times in four years (see his blog entry, "En carne propia"). Sánchez was invited to participate in various cultural events and was granted the Ortega y Gasset award in journalism, which she could not receive in person. While being recognized as a journalist abroad, Sánchez was censured at home. Ten copies of her book *Cuba Libre*, published by Marea, were retained in customs. Sánchez received an official letter, which she posted on her blog, offering the following "ethical" reasons:

> The book *Cuba Libre* goes against the general interests of the nation. It argues for political and economic changes in Cuba that would improve the material welfare of its citizens, and that would ensure higher levels of personal and professional satisfaction. These extreme values are contrary to the principles of our society.

See "Bienestar y realización" in her blog, http://lageneraciony.com/bienestar-y-realizacion-%e2%80%9ccontrarios-a-los-principios-de-nuestra-sociedad%e2%80%9d/.

5. For more on the sociology of friendship, see Eisenstadt and Roniger (1984); see also Gutiérrez Coto (2010) in the Cuban case.
6. The novel *Todos se van* (Everyone Leaves) by Wendy Guerra presents a compelling portrait of friendship as resistance through the protagonist's mother.
7. The inclusion of Dalton is relevant to the theme of betrayal. In real life, the Salvadoran poet would be accused of being a spy for the CIA and killed by his own comrades.
8. This view of art, which is quite widespread among Cuban intellectual circles, shows a strong persistence of Kantian bourgeois aesthetic ideology. I discussed the implications of this attitude more in detail in the chapter "The Abject Body and the Neo-Colonial Imagination: The Dirty Realism of Pedro Juan Gutiérrez's *Trilogía sucia de La Habana*" in *Vulnerable States* (2007a).
9. The tetralogy spills over its original plan. Two novellas and one additional full-length novel were produced at later dates so far. Two changes become apparent in the afterlife of the Mario Conde series: Conde leaves the police force to become a clandestine bookseller, and he fails to follow through the Cervantine gesture of becoming an author of his own books. In contrast, this self-begetting gesture is not only suggested but also fulfilled in other novels, like Jesús Díaz's *Las palabras perdidas* or Pedro Juan Gutiérrez's *Animal tropical* (2000).
10. Ana Serra argues that Morín's murder indicates the death of the New Man (2006, 162). She later concludes that Morín's character suggests it never existed (167). Although I agree with Serra's overall reading, I would go further and argue that, although Conde and his friends (especially Andrés) appear critical to what I call "the post-Soviet social contract," the gender culture informing Padura's writing suggests an inherently co-optable intellectual class.
11. Girard adds "the mediator becomes an obstacle. His secondary function [that of an obstacle] conceals his original function of a model scrupulously imitated" (1976, 11).
12. In turn, René Girard states that

> The triangle is no *Gestalt*. The real structures are intersubjective. They cannot be localized anywhere; the triangle has no reality whatever; it is a systematic metaphor, systematically pursued. . . . The triangle is a model of sorts, or rather a whole family of models. But these models are not "mechanical" like those of Claude Lévi-Strauss. They always allude to the mystery, transparent yet opaque, of human relations. All types of structural thinking assume that human reality is intelligible; it

is a *logos* and, as such, it is an incipient *logic*, or it degrades itself into a logic. (1976, 2–3)

13. For a detailed discussion of Nancy, see Chapter 4 of this volume.
14. Nancy states

    Still, one cannot make a world of simple atoms. There has to be a *clinamen*. There has to be an inclination or an inclining from one toward the other, of one by the other, or from one to the other. Community is at least the *clinamen* of the "individual." Yet there is not theory, ethics, politics, or metaphysics of the individual that is capable of envisaging this *clinamen*, this declination or decline of the individual within community. (Nancy 1991, 3–4)

15. I see honor as explained by Leo Braudy, who states that,

    in order for honor to be truly satisfied, the opponent must be equally honorable, equally respected. Then, even though the enemy might be defeated and his body destroyed, his honor remains intact, as does that of the victor . . . But to defeat someone who is not your equal, or to do it from ambush, is dishonorable because honor must be risked in order to be validated. (2003, 53–54)

16. For more on the Robles story, see Ignacio Martínez de Pisón's *Enterrar a los muertos* (To Bury the Dead; 2005). Padura's use of a real-life betrayal echoes the presence of Roque Dalton in Jesús Díaz's novel. Padura's reference to Robles also bears resonances with a contemporary Cuban case, that of General Arnaldo Ochoa, who was surprisingly charged with treason in obscure circumstances and executed in 1989.
17. El gato copulando con la marta / no pare un gato / de piel shakesperiana y estrellada, / ni una marta de ojos fosforescentes. / Engendran el gato volante. (Lezama Lima n.d., 207)
18. In an unrelated article, Emilio Ichikawa suggests that both Epicureanism and Stoicism, along with skepticism, can be read as escape tactics vis-à-vis the ethical deterioration of the polis in postrevolutionary societies (2001, 66–67). There is no doubt that Prieto's novel is more aware of its political and ethical conditions of production than other texts studied in this chapter.
19. The matrix of genetical combinations suggested by Lezama Lima and Prieto are in essence similar to the one used by Fernando Ortiz to explain his seminal concept of transculturation (1963).

NOTES TO CHAPTER 3

1. While I have been discussing narrative queerness as part of a larger ethical disidentification in the Cuban context, performance critic José Esteban Muñoz has extensively theorized sexual disidentificationin the context of gay US Latino theater. Similarly, Muñoz follows the lead of Judith Butler and Slavoj Žižek and defines sexual disidentification as a double process that entails unmasking the workings of an open dominant cultural code as well as the refashioning of the code so as to empower disenfranchised gender, racial, and political positionalities. Both ethical and gender disidentifications seem to be revisionist by nature (see Muñoz 1999, 31).
2. Žižek bases the notion of "magical inversion" on the seminar *Les Psychoses*, in which Lacan discusses the transformation of all fears into courage in light of "the fear of God." A kind of "transubstantiation" takes place by "presenting their very opposite—God—as a thing more frightening than all earthly fears. And—that is the 'miracle' of *le point de capiton*—this supplemental fear, fear of God, retroactively changes the character of all other fears" (1991, 17). Žižek uses this notion to illustrate Hitler's "Jewish plot," according to which "the Jew" is *le point de capiton*, an "organizational device" that can

be called to bring clarity and a sense of orientation to "the misfortunes of the epoch, economic crisis, social disintegration, moral 'decadence'" (1991, 16).

3. Bourdieu also notes that "manliness, it can be seen, is an eminently *relational* notion, constructed in front of and for other men and against femininity, in a kind of *fear* of the female, firstly in oneself" (2001, 53). For more on the "unveiling of machismo" and its role in the formation of Cuban nationalism, see Bejel (2001).
4. Pierre Bourdieu defines "negative honour" as feminine honor:

   > Unlike a woman, whose essentially negative honour can only be defended or lost, since her virtue is successively virginity and fidelity, a "real" man is someone who feels the need to rise to the challenge of the opportunities available to him to increase his honour by pursuing glory and distinction in the public sphere. Exaltation of masculine values has its dark negative side in the fears and anxiety aroused by femininity. Women, weak in themselves and sources of weakness, being the embodiments of the *vulnerability* of honour, . . . are also strong, armed with the weapons of weakness, such as devilish cunning . . . and magic. (2001, 51; emphasis in the original)

5. Žižek explains "it is only in the 1970s, however, in the last years of his teachings, that Lacan provides the ground for this resistance of the superego to being integrated in the Symbolic: the ultimate trauma that resists symbolization is that of *enjoyment*, so the superego remains a foreign body that cannot be integrated into the subject's horizon of meaning precisely in so far as it commands enjoyment" (1991, 274 n12).
6. Blanchot claims that "by opening spaces of freedom, [the present time] makes us responsible for new relationships, always threatened, always hoped for, between what we call work, *oeuvre*, and what we call unworking, *désoeuvrement*" (1988, 56).
7. My use of "as if it were" echoes Rojas's title (2001). I also allude to Jonathan Glover, who states that

   > a person's character, as Aristotle saw, comes partly from individual decisions and actions. Repeated, these become the habits which set into character. The ways we respond to things that happen and to things people do also play a part. These responses may have no reference to ourselves. We may respect loyalty or detest cruelty when we see them in others. They leave a residue of personal commitment, perhaps to being a loyal friend, being a good Catholic, or being someone to speak out in an unpopular cause. Few people could easily give a list of what their own commitments are. We may only recognize them when they are challenged. But these commitments, even if hardly conscious, are the core of moral identity. (2000, 26)

8. See Raymond (1986, 16). Raymond clarifies that she envisions a type of friendship that may or not be expressed sexually (226). I also allude here to Carole Pateman's notion of the fraternal social contract elaborated in more detail in Chapter 1 of this volume.
9. Lacking Portela's usual hermeticism, *Cien botellas* is a reader-friendly text with coherent characters and an understandable plot set in a recognizable social world. Due to its formal and ethical clarity, *Cien botellas* does not belong in the chapter "The Poetics of Evil," in which I include other works by Portela. For, while evil destroys the social world, perversion *merely* establishes an ironic distance from the present so as to "discern signs of the New"—to borrow Žižek's injunction.
10. An earlier, longer version of this reading of *Palacios distantes* appears in De Ferrari (2009).

11. Sierra Madero's original phrase is "war understood as a permanent social relationship" (2006, 16).
12. Some critics underline the sociable aspect of *jineterismo*. For instance, Jorge F. Pérez-López defines the *jinetero* as "an individual whose strength is an ability to develop social relationships that will lead to being able to obtain goods and services in short supply" (qtd. in Fernández 2000, 115). Antonio José Ponte describes *jineterismo* on the basis of its social/sexual ambiguity:

    They simulated feeling pleasure in order to give it, as is required in the profession since the days of Babylon. But they went even further. They simulated affection and a relative disinterest in questions of money. They surprised their customers with their way of understanding their fare. They stayed longer than necessary, when the meter was no longer running (there was no electricity at home; the house was crowded; there was no home to go to . . .). And then, whenever a basic need was elevated to the rank of whim, it would become very hard to distinguish between courtship and prostitution. (2007, 73)
13. See "Self-Interest as Restraint" in Glover (2000, 18–19).
14. I quote this scene from David Frye's translation (2005, 61–62). See Estévez (2002, 73–74) for the Spanish original.
15. I should note that this idea is limited to social class both in Bersani and in Estévez. While this mechanism is true in relation to external social attributes such as wealth or political prestige, as I discuss above, it is not at all true in the case of beauty. In an earlier essay, Bersani describes bathhouses as "laboratories of ethical liberalism" (1988, 222) due to the lack of social markers, but also as a strict hierarchical society. There is a direct correlation between physical attractiveness and the happiness of the individual, and when rejection happens, it is brutal because it lacks the hypocrisy usually used in equivalent situations in the real world (206). In turn, Salma advances a similar idea in her criticism of communism: "Don't you think that beauty is one of the greatest forms of injustice? How can we demand the equality of men from other men, from the government, from American imperialism, from the United Nations, from the European Community, when the first one to disregard equality was God?" (2002, 53).

NOTES TO CHAPTER 4

1. This view echoes Hillis Miller's understanding of rhetorical figures as reprogrammed cells that I explored in the previous chapter.
2. Although a number of economic measures have been taken since the late 1980s, including the development of the tourism industry and of several kinds of private enterprises, these measures are not meant to undermine, but rather to ensure, the survival of socialist politics. At a political level, the biggest change was the possibility for Cubans to travel without an exit visa as of January 2013, however that is beyond the scope of this book. For more on the strategic separation of socialist politics from socialist economics, see Hernández-Reguant (2009).
3. See also Duanel Díaz 2009.
4. Rafael Rojas argues that this position is intentionally promoted by official discourse in his books *Isla sin fin* (Endless Island; 1998), *Tumbas sin sosiego* (Restless Tombs; 2006), and *El estante vacío* (The Empty Shelf; 2009).
5. This idea is partly an attack on utilitarianism; that is, on "the happiness of the greatest number" (Nietzsche 2000, 347).

6. Bataille explains

 > Good is given first as the good of the individual. Evil seems to be a bias that obviously acts against this or that given individual. Possibly, good is respect for individuals and evil their violation. If these judgments make sense, I can derive them from my feelings.
 >
 > On the contrary, good relates to having contempt for the interest of beings in themselves. According to this secondary conception (secondary, though remaining part of the totality of emotions) evil would be the existence of individuals—insofar as this implies their separation. Reconciliation between these conflicting forms seems simple, good would be the interest of *others*. (1992, 15; emphasis in the original)

7. English quotes are mine, although I have occasionally consulted Achy Obejas's translation (Guerra 2012). Page numbers refer to the Spanish original.
8. This novel by Gutiérrez has not yet been translated into English, a fact that Gutiérrez attributes to the fact that *El Rey* is too harsh. Neither has Portela's *La sombra del caminante*, which I will discuss next. In light of my discussion in the next chapter, I would suggest that evil literature resists being "curated."
9. Putridity is also a political stance. Following Warwick Anderson, for instance, one may see the abject in *El Rey de La Habana* as a "corrosive postcolonial critique." Given that "crap . . . remains unrepresentable if not unimaginable," putridity can be seen as an instance of strategic silence, "thus operating as the most corrosive postcolonial critique of all—as the postcolonial limit-experience" (Anderson 2010, 176). I will pursue this line of interpretation further in the next chapter of this book. See also De Ferrari 2007a.
10. For another reading of evil in Portela's *La sombra del caminante*, see Di Dío (2008).
11. This quote appears in Spanish in the epigraph of Portela's short story. For the English version of this passage, see Mann (2005, 71).
12. Like in Guerra's novel, the need for voice is played out in the bathroom. Allegorically speaking, the clogged toilet in the boarding home of Guillermo Rosales's novel doesn't allude to the incapacity of certain political projects to deliver the modernity they promised (like Pedro Juan Gutiérrez's infamous bathrooms), but rather to the desire of certain subjects to be heard. A Deleuzian machine of bodily secretions and excretions replaces that which can never truly be contained: the need for voice. Exit, however, is achieved through madness.
13. Rosales was a contemporary of (and friends with) Reinaldo Arenas. I believe that Rosales is an antecedent to the poetics of evil in the same way Arenas was an antecedent to perversion as discussed in the previous chapter.
14. Rojas states that "to talk about revolution after 1976 is possible . . . if one confuses revolution with the State, government with its leaders, and the leaders with the nation itself" (2013, n.p.).
15. The importance of the Overman in this discussion should not be underestimated. In *La sombra del caminante*, Portela speaks of the New Man as an absurd. In *Cien botellas*, Moisés is a prophet-like figure and anti-Christ, a Zarathustra. The female protagonist of Portela's *Pájaro, pincel y tinta china* (1998) complains after a miscarriage that Zarathustra will never be born. In Gutiérrez, the denial of a future as a seduction, as a form of living for the others, is a Nietzschean stance that we also see in Rosales, in which hope is stated as the worst of dangers (Rosales 2009, 88).

NOTES TO CHAPTER 5

1. An approximately twenty-minute looped sequence of video performances by Cuban artists, the *Video cubano* exhibit at the Bronx Museum of Arts is a

more concise version of the original *Video cubano*, which was an initiative started in 2010 as a response to an international initiative by the Guggenheim museum and YouTube entitled *YouTube Play: A Biennial of Creative Video*, in which artists from US-sanctioned countries—including Cuba—were barred from participating. The original *Video cubano* was an exhibit of thirty-one works by twenty-two Cuban video artists around the world that took place at the Eighth Floor Gallery in New York City in 2010. It was curated by Corina Matamoros, Curator of Contemporary Cuban Art at the Museo de Bellas Artes, Havana; Noel Smith, IRA Curator of Latin American and Caribbean Art at the University of South Florida; Alberto Magnan, Co-Director of Magnan Metz Gallery in New York; Ben Rodriguez-Cubeñas, Program Director of the Cuban Artists Fund at the Rockefeller Brothers Fund; and Rachel Weingeist, Curator of the Shelley and Donald Rubin Private Collection. For more information, visit http://www.cubanartnews.org/can/post/video_cubano_cuban_video_goes_global/.

2. http://www.cubanartnews.org/can/post/video_cubano_cuban_video_goes_global/.
3. By paraphrasing W. J. T. Mitchell's words, I am trying to overcome the overcoming of the "naturalistic fallacy" by exploring the ways in which photography is unlike language (Mitchell 2005, 344–345).
4. In her blog entry of March 20, 2009, "La trituradora" (The Meat Mincer), Yoani Sánchez calls the bureaucracy that manages an exit visa a "machine that profits from generating ideological fidelities." The occasion for the blog entry was the denial of her third request for permission to travel in order to receive international awards and to participate in her own book presentations abroad. Eventually, Yoani Sánchez was able to travel in 2013, once an exit visa was no longer required.
5. Says Szarkowski in a section entitled "The Thing Itself":

   > But [the photographer] learned also that the factuality of his pictures, no matter how convincing and unarguable, was a different thing than the reality itself . . . The subject and the picture were not the same thing, although they would afterward seem so. It was the photographer's problem to see not simply the reality before him, but the still invisible picture, and to make his choices in terms of the latter. This was an artistic problem, not a scientific one, but the public believed that the photograph could not lie, and it was easier for the photographer if he believed it too, or pretended to. Thus he was likely to claim that what our eyes saw was an illusion, and what the camera saw was the truth. (1966, n.p.)

6. See Hernández-Reguant (2004) for a fascinating account of Korda's famous photograph of Che Guevara in the context of changing copyright laws in post-Soviet Cuba.
7. See "Sexual Healing: The Mysticism of the Flesh," a piece written by Abilio Estévez with photographs and a brief commentary by Abigail González (2003, 27). See also the quote by Iván de la Nuez that I used as an epigraph to Chapter 3 of this volume.
8. See also Dopico (2002).
9. See Ponte's interview in Florian Borchmeyer's documentary "Havana: The New Art of Making Ruins" (2006).
10. This sensation is pushed further by certain theatrical gestures, like when the so-called actors greeted spectators like myself outside the Chaplin Theater the first day the film was shown there. After some hesitation on the part of the authorities, the film was shown to the public at the Chaplin in June 2003 for what promised to be only a few times. In the end, the film was on for several months. For more on the reception of this film

in Havana and Miami, see Salazar Navarro (2008), and Armas Fonseca (2003).

11. For an excellent reading of the ethics of work in *Suite Habana*, see Unruh (2009).
12. For a more elaborated comment on language and objects in *Los palacios distantes*, see De Ferrari 2005.
13. These words recall Elaine Scarry, who argues on the basis of John Rawls's theory of justice that, by the fact of being associated with notions of symmetry, beauty inspires a desire for justice (1999). My reading of hyperrealism contradicts Scarry's view.
14. As Sontag suggests, beauty fulfills a protective function against the moral impact of a given image. I agree with Laura Marks's suggestion that "works that simply offer the right configurations of politics ready for consumption are boring, safe, and ultimately conservative" (2002, 65). See also my chapter on Gutiérrez's aesthetics in De Ferrari 2007a.
15. I discussed Pedro Juan Gutiérrez's *Trilogía sucia de La Habana* in light of Kantian aesthetics and Bourdieu's sociology of taste in De Ferrari 2007a.

NOTES TO CHAPTER 6

1. The discussion that follows shares some of García Canclini's preoccupations regarding the national and global management of Latin American art. However, the historical context of this article could not have been envisioned by García Canclini when he wrote *Culturas híbridas*, which was first published in 1989.
2. See J. Fornet 2001. See also the essays by Odette Casamayor Cisneros, Waldo Pérez Cino, Margarita Mateo Palmer, and Jorge Fornet included in the November/December 2002 issue of *La Gaceta de Cuba*, which was devoted to the literary production of Cuba in the 1990s.
3. I have translated Mosquera's phrase "espacios auráticos" as "auratic space." This phrase, which refers to places that produce or attest to the artistic "aura" of an object (in the sense attributed to it by Walter Benjamin), can be seen in terms of what Rosalind Krauss calls "discursive spaces." I elaborated on Krauss's notion in the previous chapter.
4. The newspaper article lists notable figures such as "Nelson Aguilar, the curator of the São Paulo Biennial; Milton Esterow, the director of the art magazine *Art News*; María Corral, the director of the Museo Nacional Reina Sofía; [and] the American Alex Rosenberg, who has represented artists such as Dalí and Henry Moore."
5. Delgado's gesture is slightly more daring than Marchel Duchamp presenting a urinal to be exhibited under the title "Fountain" at the Society of Independent Artists in 1917. Although Duchamp's urinal was rejected for not being art, it soon became canonized as an example of Ready-Made Art, Neo-Dadaism, Surrealism, pop art, and even New Realism. Recently, one of its replicas sold for 3 million euros.
6. In 2006, when consulted on this matter through its website "Spanish Today," the *Real Academia Española* categorically denied the existence of the word "curador" in Spanish. This response is oblivious of the fact that the word appears frequently in both oral and written expression throughout Latin America, as well as in the articles published in the Spanish daily *El país* that I quote here.
7. Conflicting views regarding curators become apparent in two related exhibits. In 2008, Sandra Ceballos invited a number of artists for a noncurated

exhibit in Espacio Aglutinador called "Curadores, go home!," a show in which artists "curated" themselves. In contrast, in 2013, Ceballos organized another exhibit called "Curadores, come home!" For this, she invited five curators to organize successive exhibits on the walls of her home. Famously, Ceballos also organized an art contest in 2009 on the topic "Introspection" for which awards were granted by a lottery system. This was meant to undermine the authority of award juries by suggesting that there isn't such a thing as pure aesthetic judgment.

8. Theoretically, the use of the Internet by Cuban artists and critics should help them disseminate their work in a more direct manner. Virtual spaces should allow the dissemination of material through channels that are less intensely controlled by either the state or by foreign agents. However, the fact that individual use of the Internet is legally forbidden and that technology is difficult to access turns such practice into a direct challenge to the state. This also makes its real impact hard to measure.
9. International fame can also ensure the social survival of a certain artist or intellectual. Mosquera, for instance, has stated "if it weren't for the demand that my work has abroad, the regime would have made me a *desaparecido cultural* (cultural disappeared)" (1999b, 49).
10. In his comments on the V Biennial, Luis Camnitzer lists examples of state interventions on the exhibits that forcefully illustrate the impossibility of distinguishing between censorship, aesthetic judgment, and "curation" (1994).
11. "Génesis Galerías de Arte," Ministerio de Cultura de la República de Cuba, accessed May 28, 2013, http://www.min.cult.cu/loader.php?sec=instituciones&cont=genesisgalerias.
12. A notable (or notorious) exception is offered by *Buena Vista Social Club* (the film, the CDs, the phenomenon). José Luis "El Tosco" Cortés, a musician and creator of *timba*, echoes a generalized opinion when he refers to Ry Cooder as a Columbus-like figure:

    > I believe in reincarnation. Christopher Columbus was reincarnated as Ry Cooder. Ry Cooder arrived and said, "I am Christopher Columbus." He came to discover Cuba . . . He discovered [Compay Segundo and Elíades Ochoa] and he made a record and sold it to the world. That's all good and I am really happy, because in the end they are Cuban and their music is real Cuban music. [People think] there has been no new music in Cuba for forty years. That's not the music of Cuba. That's the old music of Cuba. That is the music of the Republic. (Cortés 2003, 128)

    I think it is a mistake to see Cooder's and Wenders's promotion of Cuban "flea market" aesthetic as emblematic of the overall process of cultural exchange that has taken place between 1991 and 2008. They were not only unable to negotiate Cuban tradition, but also Cuban artists' capacity of innovation. Ultimately, they failed to create a new discourse. I would argue that theirs is an extreme example of the inequalities of this type of cultural exchange.

References

"Actualiza Cuba su política migratoria." *Granma Digital Internacional.* Accessed October 16, 2012. http://www.granma.cu/espanol/cuba/16-octubre-migracion.html.

Adorno, Theodor W. 2000. *Problems of Moral Philosophy.* Edited by Thomas Schröder. Translated by Rodney Livinstone. Stanford, CA: Stanford University Press.

Aja Díaz, Antonio. 2000. "La emigración cubana hacia Estados Unidos a la luz de su política migratoria." La Habana: CEMI, Centro de Estudios de Migraciones Internacionales. http://bibliotecavirtual.clacso.org.ar/Cuba/cemi-uh/20120821035541/laemig.pdf

Alberto, Eliseo. 1997. *Informe contra mi mismo.* México, DF: Alfaguara.

Allan, Graham. 1989. *Friendship: Developing a Sociological Perspective.* New York and London: Harvester Wheatsheaf.

Anderson, Warwick. 2010. "Crap on the Map, or Postcolonial Waste." *Postcolonial Studies* 13.2: 169–178.

Arango, Arturo. 1997. "To Write in Cuba, Today." *The South Atlantic Quarterly* 96.1 (Winter): 117–128.

Armas Fonseca, Paquita. 2003. "Un suceso cultural." http://www.lajiribilla.cu/2003/n121_08/121_24.html.

Arroyo, Jossianna. 2013. *Writing Secrecy in Caribbean Freemasonry.* New York: Palgrave Macmillan.

Badiou, Alan. 2001. *Ethics: An Essay on the Understanding of Evil.* Translated and introduced by Peter Hallward. London and New York: Verso.

———. 2007. *The Century.* Cambridge: Polity Press.

Bal, Mieke. 2005. "The Commitment to Look." *Journal of Visual Culture* 4.2: 145–162.

Barthes, Roland. 1977. *Image-Music-Text.* Essays selected and translated by Stephen Heath. New York: Hill and Wang.

———. 1981. *Camera Lucida: Reflections on Photography.* Translated by Richard Howard. New York: Hill and Wang.

Bataille, Georges. 1992. *On Nietzsche.* Translated by Bruce Boone. Introduction by Silvère Lotringer. New York: Paragon House.

Batchen, Geoffrey. 1999. *Burning with Desire: The Conception of Photography.* Boston: The MIT Press.

———. 2002. *Each Wild Idea: Writing, Photography, History.* Boston: The MIT Press.

Baudrillard, Jean. 1993. *The Transparency of Evil: Essays on Extreme Phenomena.* Translated by James Benedict. London and New York: Verso.

Bauman, Zygmunt. 1993. *Postmodern Ethics.* Oxford: Blackwell Publishing.

———. 1995. *Life in Fragments: Essays in Postmodern Morality*. Oxford: Blackwell Publishing.

Benda, Julien. 2007. *The Treason of the Intellectuals*. Translated by Richard Aldington. New Brunswick, NJ: Transaction Publishers.

Bejel, Emilio. 2001. *Gay Cuban Nation*. Chicago and London: Chicago University Press.

Berger, John. 1980. "Understanding a Photograph." In *Classic Essays in Photography*. Edited by Allan Trachtenberg. Stony Creek, CT: Leete's Island Books, 291–294.

Bersani, Leo. 1988. "Is the Rectum a Grave?" In *AIDS: Cultural Analysis, Cultural Activism*. Edited by Douglas Crimp. Boston: MIT University Press.

———. 1995. *Homos*. Cambridge, MA, and London: Harvard University Press.

———. 2002. "Sociability and Cruising." *Umbr(a)*: 9–23.

Bersani, Leo, and Adam Phillips. 2008. *Intimacies*: Chicago: Chicago University Press.

Blanchot, Maurice.1988. *The Unavowable Community*. Translated by Pierre Joris. Barritown, NY: Station Hill Press.

Block, Holly. 2001. "Remembering Why." In *Art Cuba: The New Generation*. Edited by Holly Block. Translated by Cola Frantzen and Marguerite Feitlowitz. New York: Harry N. Abrams, 7–12.

Bobes, Velia Cecilia. 2000. *Los laberintos de la imaginación: Repertorio simbólico, identidades y actores del cambio social en Cuba*. México, DF: El Colegio de México.

Bourdieu, Pierre. 1984. *Distinction: A Social Critique of the Judgement of Taste*. Translated by Richard Nice. Cambridge, MA: Harvard University Press.

———. 1995. *The Rules of Art: Genesis and Structure of the Literary Field*. Translated by Susan Emanuel. Stanford, CA: Stanford University Press.

———. 2001. *Masculine Domination*. Translated by Richard Nice. Stanford, CA: Stanford University Press.

Braudy, Leo. 2003. *From Chivalry to Terrorism: War and the Changing Nature of Masculinity*. New York and Toronto: Random House.

Brooks, Peter. 1984. *Reading for the Plot: Design and Intention in Narrative*. New York: A. A. Knoff.

———. 2000. *Troubling Confessions: Speaking Guilt in Law and Literature*. Chicago: Chicago UP.

Buckwalter-Arias, James. 2005. "Reinscribing the Aesthetic: Cuban Narrative and Post-Soviet Cultural Politics." *PMLA* 120.2 (March): 362–374.

———. 2010. *Cuba and the New* Origenismo. Woodbridge, Suffolk, UK and Rochester, NY: Tamesis.

Butler, Judith. 2005. *Giving an Account of Oneself*. New York: Fordham.

Caballero, Rufo. 2003. "Amargo Cariño." http://www.lajiribilla.cu/2003/n121_08/121_05.html.

Cadava, Eduardo. 1997. *Theses on the Photography of History*. Princeton, NJ: Princeton University Press.

Camnitzer, Luis. 1994. Review of The Fifth Biennial of Havana. *Third Text* (Autumn-Winter): 147–154.

———. 2007. *Conceptualism in Latin American Art: Didactics of Liberation*. Austin: University of Texas Press.

Card, Claudia. 1995. *Lesbian Choices*. New York: Columbia University Press.

———. 1996. *The Unnatural Lottery: Character and Moral Luck*. Philadelphia: Temple University Press.

Carpentier, Alejo. 1967. *El reino de este mundo*. Barcelona: Seix Barral.

Casamayor-Cisneros, Odette. 2002. "Cubanidades de fin de siglo o breve crónica de ciertos intentos narrativos por salvar u olvidar la cubanidad." *La Gaceta de Cuba* (November-December): 36–40.

———. 2007. "Gritos negros." Paper presented at the 2007 Latin American Studies Association XXVII International Congress, Montreal, Canada, September.

———. 2013. *Utopía, distopía e ingravidez: Reconfiguraciones cosmológicas en la narrativa postsoviética cubana.* Madrid and Frankfurt: Iberoaméricana-Vervuert.

Castellanos León, Israel. 2005. "René Peña," *Art Nexus* 3.55 (January–March): 146–148.

Castro Ruz, Fidel. 1961. *Palabras a los intelectuales.* Montevideo: Comité de Intelectuales y Artistas de Apoyo a la Revolución Cubana.

Castro Ruz, Raúl. 2007. "Speech delivered for the 54th Anniversary of the Moncada Attack." Camagüey, July 26. http://www.granma.cubaweb.cu/secciones/raul26/.

Cepero Amador, Iliana. 2008. "Myths and Realities: Cuban Photography of the 1960s and 1970s." In *Cuba: Art and History from 1868 to Today.* Montreal: The Montreal Museum of Fine Arts, 232–239.

Chaviano, Daína. 1998. *El hombre, la hembra y el hambre.* Barcelona: Planeta.

Close, Glen S. 2008. *Contemporary Hispanic Crime Fiction: A Transatlantic Discourse on Urban Violence.* New York: Palgrave Macmillan.

Cook, Linda J. 1993. *The Soviet Social Contract and Why It Failed: Welfare Policy and Workers' Politics from Brezhnev to Yeltsin.* Cambridge, MA: Harvard University Press.

Cooper, John M. 2005. "Political Animals and Civic Friendship." In *Aristotle's Politics: Critical Essays.* Edited by Richard Kraut and Steven Skultety. Lanham, MD: Rowman & Littlefield Publishers.

Cortés, José Luis "El tosco." 2003. Interview by Hugo Pérez "The Babalawos of Cuban Music." In *Cuba on the Verge: An Island in Transition.* Edited by Terry McCoy. Boston, New York, and London: Bulfinch Press, 126–139.

Coyula, Mario. 2011. "The Bitter Trinquennium and the Distopian City: Autopsy of a Utopia." In *Havana beyond the Ruins: Cultural Mappings after 1989.* Edited by Anke Birkenmaier and Esther Whitfield. Durham, NC, and London: Duke University Press, 31–53.

Critchley, Simon. 1999. *Ethics-Politics-Subjectivity: Essays on Derrida, Levinas and Contemporary French Thought.* London and New York: Verso.

Damisch, Hubert. 1980. "Notes for a Phenomenology of the Photographic Image." In *Classic Essays on Photography.* Edited by Alan Trachtenberg. Stony Creek, CT: Leete's Island Books, 287–290.

De Ferrari, Guillermina. 2003. "Aesthetics under Siege: Dirty Realism and Pedro Juan Gutiérrez's *Trilogía sucia de La Habana.*" *Arizona Journal of Hispanic Cultural Studies* 7: 23–43.

———. 2005. "Las palabras y las cosas: El lenguaje de la revolución en *El siglo de las luces* de Alejo Carpentier y *Los palacios distantes* de Abilio Estévez." In *Alejo Carpentier ante la crítica.* Edited by Alexis Márquez Rodríguez. Caracas: Monte Ávila Editores, 307–350.

———. 2007a. *Vulnerable States: Bodies of Memory in Contemporary Caribbean Fiction.* Charlottesville: The University of Virginia Press.

———. 2007b. "Embargoed Masculinities: Friendship and the Role of the Intellectual in the Post-Soviet Cuban novel." *Latin American Literary Review* 69 (Spring): 91–115.

———. 2007c. "Cuba: A Curated Culture." *Journal of Latin American Cultural Studies* 16.2 (August): 219–240.

———. 2009. "La sociabilidad de los cuerpos en *Los palacios distantes.*" *La Habana Elegante* 46 (Otoño-Invierno).

de la Nuez, Iván. 1988. *La balsa perpetua: Soledad y conexiones de la cultura cubana.* Barcelona: Editorial Casiopea.

———. 2001. "El Hombre Nuevo ante el futuro." In *Cuba y el día después.* Edited by Iván de la Nuez. Almanaque, otoño 2001. Barcelona: Mondador, 9–22.

———. 2002. "El intelectual, el corazón y la piel." "Homenaje a Jesús Díaz." *Encuentro* 25 (Verano): 39–41.

Derrida, Jacques. 2005. *The Politics of Friendship*. Translated by George Collins. London and New York: Verso.

Di Dío, Paula. 2008. "'Menuda faena': *La sombra del caminante* de Ena Lucía Portela y sus representaciones del mal." *Revista de Estudios Hispánicos* 42.3, (October): 415–431.

Díaz, Duanel. 2009. *Palabras del trasfondo: Intelectuales, literatura e ideología en la Revolución Cubana*. Madrid: Editorial Colibrí.

Díaz, Jesús. 1992. *Las palabras perdidas*. Barcelona: Anagrama.

———. 1998. "De fiesta." *Encuentro de la cultura cubana* 8–9: 3–4.

Díaz Pimienta, Alexis. 2000. "La guagua." In *Nuevos narradores cubanos*. Edited by Michi Strausfeld. Madrid: Siruela, 157–161.

Díaz Quiñones, Arcadio. 2000. *El arte de bregar*. San Juan, PR: Ediciones Callejón.

Dopico, Ana María. 2002. "Picturing Havana: History, Vision and the Scramble of Cuba." *Nepantla: Views from South* 3.3: 451–493.

Eastman, Max. 1934. *Artists in Uniform: A Study of Literature and Bureaucratism*. London: George Allen and Unwin.

Eisenstadt, S. N., and L. Roniger. 1984. *Patrons, Clients and Friends: Interpersonal Relations and the Structure of Trust in Society*. London and New York: Cambridge University Press.

Epps, Brad. 1995. "Proper Conduct: Reinaldo Arenas, Fidel Castro, and the Politics of Homosexuality." *Journal of the History of Sexuality* 6.2, (October): 231–283.

Espinosa, Magaly. 2001. "Curaduría por qué y para qué." Dossier "El oficio de curar." *Artecubano* 1: 2–9.

Estévez, Abilio. 2002. *Los palacios distantes*. Barcelona: Tusquets.

———. 2005. *Distant Palaces*. Translated by David Frye. London: Vintage.

Estévez, Abilio, and Abigail González. 2003. "Sexual Healing: The Mysticism of the Flesh." In *Cuba on the Verge: An Island in Transition*. Edited by Terry McCoy. Introduced by William Kennedy. Epilogue by Arthur Miller. Boston, New York, and London: Bulfinch Press, 24–33.

Esty, Joshua. 1999. "Excremental Postcolonialism." *Contemporary Literature* 40.1: 23–57.

Fernandes, Sujatha. 2006. *Cuba Represent! Cuban Arts, State Power, and the Making of New Revolutionary Cultures*. Durham, NC, and London: Duke University Press.

Fernández, Damián J. 2000. *Cuba and the Politics of Passion*. Austin: Texas University Press.

Fornet, Ambrosio. 2002. "La crítica bicéfala: Un nuevo desafío." *La Gaceta de Cuba* (enero-febrero), 20–25.

———. 2008. "The Incredible Decade: A Personal Reminiscence." In *Cuba: Art and History from 1868 to Today*. Montreal: The Montreal Museum of Fine Arts, 252–257.

Fornet, Jorge. 2001. "La narrativa cubana entre la utopía y el desencanto." *La Gaceta de Cuba* (September–October): 38–45.

———. 2006. *Los nuevos paradigmas: Prólogo Narrativo al Siglo XXI*. Havana: Letras Cubanas.

Foucault, Michel. 1977. "What Is an Author?" In *Language, Countermemory, Practice: Selected Essays and Interviews*. Edited by Donald F. Bouchard. Translated by Donald F. Bouchard and Sherry Simon. Ithaca, NY: Cornell University Press, 113–138.

———. 1981. "De l'Amitié comme mode de vie: Un entretien avec un lecteur quinquagénaire." Interview with R. de Ceccaty, J. Danet, and J. Le Bitoux. *Gai Pied* (April).

———. 1990. *The Use of Pleasure*. New York: Random House.
Franco, Jean. 2002. *The Decline and Fall of the Lettered City: Latin America in the Cold War*. Cambridge, MA, and London: Harvard University Press.
Fromm, Erich. 1973. *The Anatomy of Human Destructiveness*. New York, Chicago, San Francisco: Holt, Rinehart and Winston.
García Canclini, Néstor. 1989. *Culturas híbridas: Estrategias para entrar y salir de la modernidad*. Mexico, D.F.: Grijalbo. Consejo Nacional para la Cultural y las Artes.
———. 1995. *Hybrid Cultures: Strategies for Entering and Leaving Modernity*. Translated by Christopher L. Chiappari and Silvia L. López. Minneapolis and London: University of Minnesota Press.
García Espinosa, Julio. 1992. "Por un cine imperfecto." *Cine Cubano* 140: 55–60.
García Vázquez, Jorge Luis. 2007. "El MININT y la Seguridad del Estado Contra el 'Diversionismo Ideológico.'" *Misceláneas de Cuba*. January 31. http://www.miscelaneasdecuba.net/web/Article/Index/518101bb3a682e0f88c4bb9b#.Uchmiz6DQXw.
Girard, René. 1976. *Deceit, Desire and the Novel: Self and Other in Literary Structure*. Baltimore, MD: Johns Hopkins University Press.
Glover, Jonathan. 2000. *Humanity: A Moral History of the Twentieth Century*. New Haven, CT: Yale University Press.
Guerra, Wendy. 2006. *Todos se van*. Madrid: Bruguera.
———. 2012. *Everyone leaves*. Translated by Achy Obejas. Las Vegas, NV: AmazonCrossing.
Guevara, Ernesto "Che". 2007. *El socialismo y el hombre en Cuba*. Melbourne, Australia: Ocean Press.
Gutiérrez, Pedro Juan. 1998. *Trilogía sucia de La Habana*. Barcelona: Anagrama.
———. 1999. *El Rey de La Habana*. Barcelona: Anagrama.
———. 2000. *Animal Tropical*. Barcelona: Anagrama.
———. 2002. *Dirty Havana Trilogy*. Translated by Natasha Wimmer. New York: Farrar, Straus and Giroux.
Gutiérrez Coto, Amauri. 2010. "La amistad en el arte como salvación de la política." In *Orígenes y el paraiso de la eticidad*. Santiago de Cuba: Ediciones Caserón.
Havana: The New Art of Making Ruins. 2006. Directed by Florian Borchmeyer. Raros Media.
Havel, Vaclav. 2000. "Politics, Morality, and Civility." In *The Essential Civil Society Reader: Classic Essays in the American Civil Society Debate*. Edited by Don E. Eberly. Lanham, MD: Rowman & Littlefield.
Hernández, Orlando. 2001. "The Pleasures of Reference." In *Art Cuba: The New Generation*. Edited by Holly Block. Translated by Cola Frantzen and Marguerite Feitlowitz. New York: Harry N. Abrams, 25–29.
Hernández-Reguant, Ariana. 2004. "Copyrighting Che: Art and Authorship under Cuban Late Socialism." *Public Culture* 16.1: 1–29.
———. 2009. "Writing the Special Period: An Introduction." In *Cuba in the Special Period: Culture and Ideology in the 1990s*. Edited by Ariana Hernández-Reguant. New York: Palgrave Macmillan.
Hirschman, Albert O. 1970. *Exit, Voice, and Loyalty: Responses to Decline in Firms, Organizations, and States*. Cambridge, MA: Harvard University Press.
Hoagland, Sarah Lucia. 1988. *Lesbian Ethics: Toward New Value*. Palo Alto, CA: Institute of Lesbian Studies.
Hobsbawm, Eric. 1994. *Age of Extremes: The Short Twentieth Century 1914–1991*. London: Penguin.
Hutter, Horst. 1978. *Politics as Friendship: The Origins of Classical Notions of Politics in the Theory and Practice of Friendship*. Waterloo, Ontario: Wilfrid Laurier University Press.

Ichikawa, Emilio. 2001. "Cuba helenística: Las fuentes de una reconfiguración moral. Hacia un egoísmo entendido como *self-love*." *Revista Encuentro de la Cultura Cubana* 21/22 (Verano/otoño): 65–69.

Juan de los muertos. 2010. Directed by Alejandro Brugués. La zanfoña producciones/Producciones de la 5ta avenida.

Kapcia, Antoni, Par Kumaraswami, and Meesha Nehru. 2012. *Literary Culture in Cuba: Revolution, Nation-Building and the Book*. Manchester and New York: Manchester University Press.

King, John. 1990. *Magical Reels: A History of Cinema in Latin America*. London and New York: Verso.

Krauss, Rosalind. 1989. "Photography's Discursive Spaces." In *The Contest of Meaning: Critical Histories of Photography*. Edited by Richard Bolton. Boston: MIT Press.

Kriebel, Sabine T. 2007. "Theories of Photography: A Short History." In *Photography Theory*. Edited by James Elkins. New York: Routledge, 3–51.

Lévi-Strauss, Claude. 1992. *The Savage Mind*. Chicago: University of Chicago Press.

Leyva, Kcho. *La regata*. 1994. *ARTnews*. June 2000, cover.

Lezama Lima, José. n.d. *Antología para un sistema poético del mundo de José Lezama Lima. Tomo I*. Edited, introduced, and annotated by Iván González Cruz. Valencia: Editorial Universitaria Politécnica.

Lipovetsky, Gilles. 1992. *Le crépuscule du devoir: L'éthique indolore des nouveaux temps démocratiques*. Paris: Gallimard.

Llanes Godoy, Llilian. 1997. "Presentación." *El individuo y su memoria: Sexta Bienal de La Habana*. Paris: Association Française d'Action Artistique, 18–23.

López, Iraida H. 2010. "Introduction." *Cien botellas en una pared*. Doral, FL: Stock Cero.

MacIntyre, Alasdair. 2007. *After Virtue: A Study in Moral Philosophy*. Notre Dame, IN: Notre Dame University Press.

Mann, Thomas. 2005. *The Magic Mountain*. Translated by John E. Woods. New York: Alfred Knopf.

Mansfield, Harvey C. 2006. *Manliness*. New Haven, CT, and London: Yale University Press.

Marisy, Luisa. 1999. "Luisa Marisy: Programming Manager, Ludwig Foundation of Cuba." *Flash Art* (January–February): 48.

Marks, Laura U. 2000. *The Skin of the Film: Intercultural Cinema, Embodiment, and the Senses*. Durham, NC, and London: Duke University Press.

———. 2002. *Touch: Sensuous and Multisensory Media*. Minneapolis and London: Minnesota University Press.

Marrero, Meira. 2001. "Se hace camino al andar." Dossier "El oficio de curar." *Artecubano* 1: 10–13.

Martínez de Pisón, Ignacio. 2005. *Enterrar a los muertos*. Barcelona: Seix Barral.

Matamoros, Corina. 2001. *"Dinámica curatorial en el Museo Nacional."* Dossier "El oficio de curar." *Artecubano* 1: 16–23.

Mateo Palmer, Margarita. 2002. "A las puertas del siglo XXI." *La Gaceta de Cuba* (November–December): 48–52.

Mauvaise conduite. 1984. Directed by Néstor Almendros and Orlando Jiménez-Leal. Playor.

McCauley, Anne. 2007. "The Trouble with Photography." In *Photography Theory*. Edited by James Elkins. New York: Routledge, 403–430.

Memorias del subdesarrollo. 1968. Directed by Tomás Gutiérrez Alea. ICAIC.

Merewhether, Charles. 1997. "Traces of Loss." In *Irresistible Decay: Ruins Reclaimed*. Edited by Michael S. Roth with Claire Lyons and Charles Merewhether. Los Angeles: Getty Research Institute for the History of Art and the Humanities, 25–40.

Miller, J. Hillis. 1987. *The Ethics of Reading: Kant, de Man, Eliot, Trollope, James and Benjamin*. New York: Columbia University Press.

Misztal, Barbara A. 1996. *Trust in Modern Societies*. Cambridge: Polity Press.

Mitchell, W. J. T. 2005. *What Do Pictures Want? The Lives and Loves of Images*. Chicago: The University of Chicago Press.

Moreno, José A. et al. 1998. *Cuba: Período Especial. Perspectivas*. La Habana: Editorial de Ciencias Sociales.

Mosquera, Gerardo. 1995. "Reporte del hombre en La Habana." In *Cuba: La isla posible*. Centro de Cultura Contemporánea de Barcelona. Barcelona: Ediciones destino, 131–141.

———. 1999a. "La isla infinita: Introducción al nuevo arte cubano." In *Contemporary Art from Cuba: Irony and Survival on the Utopian Island = Arte contemporáneo de Cuba: Ironía y sobrevivencia en la isla utópica*. Edited by Marilyn A. Zeitlin. Arizona State University Art Museum. New York: Delano Greenidge Editions, 31–37.

———. 1999b. "Gerardo Mosquera: Independent Curator and Critic." *Flash Art* (January–February): 49.

———. 2001. "New Cuban Art Y2K." In *Art Cuba: The New Generation*. Edited by Holly Block. Translated by Cola Frantzen and Marguerite Feitlowitz. New York: Harry N. Abrams, 13–16.

———. 2002. "Sobre arte, globalización y culturas." In *Ensayo cubano del siglo XX*. Edited by Rafael Hernández and Rafael Rojas. México, DF: Fondo de Cultura Económica, 620–637.

Muñoz, José Esteban. 1999. *Disidentifications: Queer of Color and the Performance of Politics*. Minneapolis: University of Minnesota Press.

Nancy, Jean-Luc. 1991. *The Inoperative Community*. Translated by Peter Connor, Lisa Garbus, Michel Holland, and Simona Sawhney. Minneapolis and Oxford: University of Minnesota Press.

Navarro, Desiderio. 2002. "*In medias res publicas*: Sobre los intelectuales y la crítica social en la esfera pública cubana." In *Ensayo cubano del siglo XX*. Edited by Rafael Hernández and Rafael Rojas. Mexico, DF: Fondo de Cultura Economica, 689–707.

Nietzsche, Friedrich. 1995. *Thus Spoke Zarathustra: A Book for All and None*. Translated and prefaced by Walter Kaufmann. New York: The Modern Library.

———. 1996. *On the Genealogy of Morals*. Translated by Douglass Smith. Oxford: Oxford University Press.

———. 2000. *Beyond Good and Evil*. In *Basic Writings of Nietzsche*. Introduction by Peter Gay. Translated and edited by Walter Kaufmann. New York: Modern Library.

———. 2009. "Part II." *Human, All-Too-Human (Parts I and II): A Book for Free Spirits*. Translated by Paul V. Cohn, B.A. DigiReads.

Ortiz, Fernando. 1963. *Contrapunteo cubano del tabaco y el azúcar*. La Habana: Consejo nacional de cultura.

———. 1973. *Historia de una pelea cubana contra los demonios*. Madrid: Ediciones ERRE.

Padura, Leonardo. 1995. *Pasado perfecto*. La Habana: Ediciones Unión.

———. 2001. *Adiós, Hemingway & La cola de la serpiente*. La Habana: Ediciones Unión.

———. 2001. *La novela de mi vida*. Santo Domingo: Casa de Teatro.

———. 2005. *La neblina del ayer*. Barcelona: Tusquets.

———. 2009. *El hombre que amaba a los perros*. México: Tusquets.

Pateman, Carole. 2002. "The Fraternal Social Contract." In *The Masculinity Studies Reader*. Edited by Rachel Adams and David Savran. Malden, MA: Blackwell Publishing, 119–134.

Paz, Senel. 1991. *El lobo, el bosque y el Hombre Nuevo*. Mexico City: Ediciones Era.

Pérez Cino, Waldo. 2002. "Sentido y paráfrasis." *La Gaceta de Cuba* (November–December): 22–29.

Ponte, Antonio José. 2000. "Un arte de hacer ruinas." In *Nuevos narradores cubanos*. Edited by Michi Strausfeld. Madrid: Siruela, 123–139.

———. 2002. *Contrabando de sombras*. Barcelona: Mondadori.

———. 2007. "Caja negra de la fiesta." In *La fiesta vigilada*. Barcelona: Anagrama, 69–140.

———. 2011. "Lezama en los archivos de la Stasi." *Diario de Cuba*. June 10. http://www.diariodecuba.com/cultura/1307701546_1423.html.

Portela, Ena Lucía. 1998. *Pájaro, pincel y tinta china*. Havana: Ediciones Unión.

———. 2000. "El Viejo, el asesino y yo." In *Nuevos narradores cubanos*. Edited by Michi Strausfeld. Madrid: Siruela, 309–330.

———. 2001a. *La sombra del caminante*. La Habana: Ediciones Unión.

———. 2001b. "Tan oscuro como muy oscuro." In *Cuba y el día después: Doce ensayistas nacidos con la revolución imaginan el futuro*. Edited by Iván de la Nuez. Barcelona: Mondadori, 183–195.

———. 2002. *Cien botellas en una pared*. Barcelona: Random House Mondadori.

———. 2007. *Djunia y Daniel*. La Habana: Ediciones Unión.

Power, Kevin. 1999. "Cuba: One Story after Another." In *While Cuba Waits: Arts from the Nineties*. Edited by Kevin Power. New York: Smart Art Press, 23–65.

Prieto, Abel. 2000. *El vuelo del gato*. Barcelona: Ediciones B.

Prieto, José Manuel. 2009. "Introduction." *The Halfway House*. Translated by Anna Kushner. Preface by José Manuel Prieto. New York: New Directions.

Quiroga, José. 2005. *Cuban Palimpsests*. Minneapolis: University of Minnesota Press.

Raymond, Janice G. 1986. *A Passion for Friends: Toward a Philosophy of Female Affection*. Boston: Beacon Press.

Rojas, Rafael. 1998. *Isla sin fin: Contribución a la crítica del nacionalismo cubano*. Miami: Ediciones Universal.

———. 2001. "La filosofía del 'como si.' *El Nuevo Herald*, April 2.

———. 2006. *Tumbas sin sosiego: Revolución, disidencia y exilio del intelectual cubano*. Barcelona: Anagrama.

———. 2008. "Pregunta a los socialistas cubanos." May 6. http://penultimosdias.com/2008/05/06/pregunta-a-los-socialistas-cubanos/#more-7291.

———. 2009. *El estante vacío*. Barcelona: Anagrama.

———. 2013. "Por una democracia soberana en Cuba," April 2. http://www.librosdelcrepusculo.net/2013/04/por-una-democracia-soberana-en-cuba.html?spref=fb.

Rosales, Guillermo. 2009. *The Halfway House*. Translated by Anna Kushner. Preface by José Manuel Prieto. New York: New Directions.

Rosenberg, Eric. 2006. "Walker Evan's Depression and the Trauma of Photography." In *Trauma and Visuality in Modernity*. Edited and with an Introduction by Lisa Saltzman and Eric Rosenberg. Hanover and London: University Press of New England.

Rothenberg, Molly Anne, and Dennis Forster. 2003. "Introduction. Beneath the Skin: Perversion and Social Analysis." In *Perversion and the Social Relation*. Edited by Molly Anne Rothenberg, Dennis Foster, and Slavoj Žižek. Durham, NC, and London: Duke University Press, 1–14.

Rousseau, Jean-Jacques. 1968. *The Social Contract*. Translated and introduced by Maurice Cranston. London: Penguin Books.

Routon, Kenneth. 2010. *Hidden Powers of State in the Cuban Imagination*. Gainesville: University Press of Florida.

Rubin, Gayle. 1975. "The Traffic in Women: Notes on the 'Political Economy' of Sex." In *Toward an Anthropology of Women*. Edited by Rayna R. Reiter. New York and London: Monthly Review Press, 157–210.

Said, Edward. 1994. *Representations of the Intellectual*. New York: Pantheon Books.

Salazar Navarro, Salvador. 2008. "*Suite Habana*: La ciudad de Fernando Pérez." *Caribbean Studies* 36.2 (July–December): 281–285.

Sánchez, Yoani. 2009. "La trituradora." *Generación Y*. March 20. http://lageneraciony.com/la-trituradora/.

———. 2010. "Bienestar y realización 'contrarios a los principios de nuestra sociedad'." *Generación Y*. November 25. http://lageneraciony.com/bienestar-y-realizacion-%e2%80%9ccontrarios-a-los-principios-de-nuestra-sociedad%e2%80%9d/.

———. 2011. "En carne propia." *Generación Y*. August 2. http://lageneraciony.com/en-carne-propia/.

Sandel, Michael J. 2009. *Justice: What Is the Right Thing to Do?* New York: Farrar, Straus and Giroux.

Scarry, Elaine. 1999. *On Beauty and Being Just*. Princeton, NJ: Princeton University Press.

Schachter, Stanley. 1974. "The Psychology of Affiliation." *Doing Unto Others: Joining, Molding, Conforming, Helping, Loving*. Edited by Zick Rubin. Englewood Cliffs, NJ: Prentice Hall, 7–16.

Sedgwick, Eve Kosofsky. 1985. *Between Men: English Literature and Male Homosocial Desire*. New York: Columbia University Press.

Serra, Ana. 2006. "La Habana cotidiana: Espacio urbano en el cine de Fernando Pérez." *Chasqui*, 35.1 (May): 88–105.

———. 2007. *The 'New Man' in Cuba*. Miami: University Press of Florida.

Shore, Stephen. 2007. *The Nature of Photographs*. New York: Phaidon Press.

Short, T. L. 2007. *Peirce's Theory of Signs*. Cambridge University Press.

Si me comprendieras. 1998. Directed by Rolando Díaz. Luna Llena Producciones.

Sierra Madero, Abel. 2006. *Del otro lado del espejo: La sexualidad en la construcción de la nación cubana*. La Habana: Fondo Editorial Casa de las Américas.

Simmel, Georg. 1971. "Sociability." In *On Individuality and Social Forms: Selected Writings*. Edited and with an introduction by Donald N. Levine. Chicago: The University of Chicago Press.

Sontag, Susan. 1973. *On Photography*. New York: Farrar, Straus and Giroux.

———. 2003. *Regarding the Pain of Others*. New York: Farrar, Straus and Giroux.

Suite Habana. 2003. Directed by Fernando Pérez. Wanda e ICAIC.

Szarkowski, John. 1966. *The Photographer's Eye*. New York: The Museum of Modern Art.

Todorov, Tzvetan. 1977. "The Typology of Detective Fiction." In *The Poetics of Prose*. Translated by Richard Howard. Ithaca, NY: Cornell University Press.

Toirac, José A. 2005. *Opus*.

Tompkins, Cynthia. 2013. *Experimental Latin American Cinema: History and Aesthetics*. Austin, TX: University of Austin Press.

Torres del Sol, Ludmila, and Yusleydy López Sabor. 2006. "Construir entre la realidad y la utopía. El proyecto visto desde la plástica: Un acercamiento al tema de la ciudad." *Arteamerica*. July 28. http://www.arteamerica.cu/5/dossier/ludmila.htm.

Una de cada clase: Arte joven cubano. 1995. La Habana: Fundación Ludwig de Cuba.

Unruh, Vicky. 2009. "All in a Day's Work: Ruins Dwellers in Havana." In *Telling Ruins in Latin America*. Edited by Michael J. Lazzara and Vicky Unruh. New York: Palgrave Macmillan, 197–210.

Valdés, Zoé. 1995. *La nada cotidiana*. Barcelona: Emecé.

Vicent, Mauricio. 1994. "Una gran balsa llamada Cuba: Artistas cubanos exponen obras críticas y denuncian el drama migratorio de su país en la V Bienal de La Habana." *El país*. May 15, Cultural Section.

Vives, Cristina. 2001. "Cuban Photography: A Personal History." In *Shifting Tides: Cuban Photography after the Revolution*. Edited by Tim B. Wride. Los Angeles: Los Angeles County Museum of Art, 82–129.

———. 2002. "Any Resemblance Is Not Purely Coincidental." In *Jose M. Fors: Fallen Leaves*. Los Angeles: Coutourier Gallery.

Warner, Michael. 1999. *The Trouble with Normal: Sex, Politics and the Ethics of Queer Life*. New York: Free Press.

Weiss, Rachel. 1995. Review of Quinta Bienal de La Habana. *Review: Latin American Literature and Arts* 50: 95–98.

Weiss, Robert S. 1974. "The Provisions of Social Relationships." In *Doing unto Others: Joining, Molding, Conforming, Helping, Loving*. Edited by Rubin Zick. Englewood Cliffs, NJ: Prentice Hall, 17–26.

Weston, Edward. 1980. "Seeing Photographically." In *Classic Essays on Photography*. Edited by Alan Trachtenberg. Stony Creek, CT: Leete's Island Books, 169–178.

Whitfield, Esther. 2002. "Autobiografía Sucia: The Body Impolitic of *Trilogía sucia de La Habana*." *Revista de Estudios Hispánicos* 36.2 (Mayo): 329–351.

———. 2003. "The Novel as Cuban Lexicon: Bargaining Bilinguals in Daína Chaviano's *El hombre, la hembra y el hambre*." In *Bilingual Games: Some Literary Investigations*. Edited by Doris Sommer. New York: Palgrave Macmillan, 193–201.

———. 2008. *Cuban Currency: The Dollar and the Special Period*. Minneapolis and London: Minnesota University Press.

Wittig, Monique. 1969. *Les Guérillères*. Paris: Éditions de Minuit.

———. 1992. "On the Social Contract." In *The Straight Mind and Other Essays*. Boston: Beacon Press.

Wride, Tim B. 2001. "Three Generations: Photography in Fidel's Cuba." In *Shifting Tides: Cuban Photography after the Revolution*. Edited by Tim B. Wride. Los Angeles: Los Angeles County Museum of Art, 20–81.

Žižek, Slavoj. 1989. *The Sublime Object of Ideology*. London: Phronesis.

———. 1991. *For They Know Not What They Do: Enjoyment and a Political Factor*. London: Verso.

———. 2003. "The Ambiguity of the Masochist Social Link." In *Perversion and the Social Relation*. Edited by Molly Anne Rothenberg, Dennis Foster, and Slavoj Žižek. Durham, NC, and London: Duke University Press, 112–125.

———. 2007. *Robespierre: Virtue and Terror*. Translated by John Howe. London and New York: Verso.

Index

For Product Safety Concerns and Information please contact our EU representative GPSR@taylorandfrancis.com
Taylor & Francis Verlag GmbH, Kaufingerstraße 24, 80331 München, Germany

www.ingramcontent.com/pod-product-compliance
Lightning Source LLC
Chambersburg PA
CBHW071524110726
47908CB00003B/943

* 9 7 8 1 1 3 8 9 3 4 3 8 2 *